Praise for

The
Cult
of
Trump

"[Hassan] is an authority on breaking away from cults . . . an argument that . . . bears consideration as the next election cycle heats up."

—*Kirkus Reviews*

"A brilliant analysis of a unique modern phenomenon. Readers will nod their head in recognition as Hassan expertly takes them through a fascinating, engaging exploration of the coercive control techniques that President Donald Trump uses daily to influence his followers."

—Dr. Philip Zimbardo, author of
The Lucifer Effect and professor emeritus
of psychology, Stanford University

"There is a growing recognition of an important cult-like element in Donald Trump's many-sided destructiveness. Steve Hassan confronts this element and takes us to the far reaches of possible cultic influence."

—Robert Jay Lifton, author of *Losing Reality*

"[This] book should become part of the compendium of essential reading on the Trump phenomenon."

—Bandy X. Lee, MD, MDiv,
editor of the *New York Times* bestseller
The Dangerous Case of Donald Trump

"Hassan has been studying cult mind control for decades and his work is illuminating. This book explains how mind control stops people from thinking critically, thinking beyond what they are told."

—Professor Yaneer Bar-Yam, president of the
New England Complex Systems Institute

"[A] must for anyone who wants to understand the current political climate."

—Judy Stevens-Long, PhD, and coauthor of
Living Well, Dying Well

"Drawing on both his experiences as cult expert and ex–cult member, Hassan opens a wide-ranging, thoughtful, and well-researched analysis of some of the most puzzling aspects of the current presidency, including the remarkable passivity of fellow Republicans, the gross pandering of many members of the press, the curious avoidance of clear labels that could and should be applied by the media. . . . Highly recommended."

—Thomas G. Gutheil, MD, professor of psychiatry,
Harvard Medical School

"*The Cult of Trump*, in step-by-step detail, examines the inner-workings of our current presidential administration. The picture is much darker than mere buffoonery."
    —Robin Boyle Laisure, JD, advisory council member
of the International Cultic Studies Association
and author of "Employing Trafficking Laws
to Capture Elusive Leaders of Destructive Cults"

"A brilliant book."
    —Anthony Scaramucci, former White House
Director of Communications

A Leading

Cult Expert

Explains How the

President Uses

Mind Control

THE
CULT
OF
TRUMP

Steven Hassan

FREE PRESS
New York London Toronto Sydney New Delhi

_f_P

Free Press
An Imprint of Simon & Schuster, Inc.
1230 Avenue of the Americas
New York, NY 10020

First Free Press trade paperback September 2020

FREE PRESS and colophon are trademarks of Simon & Schuster, Inc.

For information about special discounts for bulk purchases,
please contact Simon & Schuster Special Sales at 1-866-506-1949
or business@simonandschuster.com.

The Simon & Schuster Speakers Bureau can bring authors
to your live event. For more information or to book an event,
contact the Simon & Schuster Speakers Bureau at 1-866-248-3049
or visit our website at www.simonspeakers.com.

Interior design by Lewelin Polanco

Manufactured in the United States of America

5   7   9   10   8   6

Library of Congress Cataloging-in-Publication Data is available.

ISBN 978-1-9821-2733-6
ISBN 978-1-9821-2734-3 (pbk)
ISBN 978-1-9821-2735-0 (ebook)

I dedicate this book to all those who have suffered from abusive mind control in the hope that it helps them heal. Freedom of mind—which includes critical thinking, pursuing facts, listening to one's conscience, and acting with integrity—is the foundation of all our other freedoms, including freedom of religion.

CONTENTS

AUTHOR'S NOTE

I was nineteen and attending Queens College when I was recruited—tricked—into joining a dangerous mind-controlling cult: Sun Myung Moon's Unification Church. During my time in the group, I experienced a radical personality change, fervently believing and spreading the cult's doctrine. I felt totally in control of my mind and thoughts—something I can now confidently say was not the case. It was only through luck, and some clever maneuvering on my family's part, that I was able to free myself. I was a cult member for only two and a half years. I'm one of the fortunate ones. Since then, I've become a mental health professional and have devoted my life to helping people break free from destructive cults, passing on the lessons learned through my own deprogramming. Over the past forty years, I've gotten a close look at hundreds of dangerous groups—as well as individual relationships—and know what, exactly, makes them destructive and cultish. I have spoken out publicly about cults and have faced a lot of backlash from some pretty scary and powerful organizations. I've faced lawsuits, death threats, and slander upon my character. Still, I feel privileged to do the work that I do.

I talk to a lot of people, some of whom disagree with me, and it's important for me—both personally and professionally—to be as

unbiased and trustworthy as possible. The people whom I help—along
with their families—need to trust that I am telling the truth. I have always sought to be nonpartisan and keep politics out of my work. But
Donald Trump's authoritarian tendencies, and the cultlike aspects of
his presidency, have become too obvious to ignore. I realize that the
title of this book, *The Cult of Trump,* and its central argument—that
the president of the United States may be viewed as the leader of a
cult—may be off-putting, if not outrageous, to some. I hope that my
expertise, which I have gained through decades of work, will persuade
you to continue with an open mind. My goal is not to write a political
book about Trump—many have already been written—but instead to
look at the Trump presidency through the lens of psychology, and in
particular the psychology of mind manipulation and influence. I believe that the ultimate weapon against mind control is knowledge and
awareness. That is what I try to provide in this book.

I have done my best to ensure that the material in this book is as
accurate and verifiable as possible. Of course, when writing about
another person, there is always a certain amount of subjectivity, and
many opportunities for bias to creep in. I have no doubt that some
will take issue with what I have written. I ask you to take the wider
view. I also invite you to differ with me. My goal is to empower people to think for themselves, which may mean moving outside of our
ideological bubbles.

This is a book about an area of human behavior that I liken to a
dark forest. As a former cult member, I personally have seen the trees,
as have millions of people who have escaped destructive groups and
found their way to freedom. As a mental health professional, I've also
spent decades mapping the contours of the cult mind control phenomenon. My hope is that this book may help point a way out of the
dark forest of authoritarianism.

Steven Hassan
April 2019

and social techniques for their own ends. It became clear to me that Trump was exploiting those methods to great effect. He certainly was not playing by traditional political rules. He was a master media manipulator, calling media outlets like Fox News to insult his opponents and brag about his own accomplishments, attracting the attention of other cable networks like CNN and MSNBC with his circuslike behavior—and gaining an estimated $2 billion worth of free publicity.[1] He was an entertaining, if blustery, speaker who used simplistic, almost hypnotically repetitious, terms. He gave insulting but catchy nicknames to his opponents—"Crooked Hillary," "Lying Ted," "Low Energy Jeb"—and used slogans that became rousing anthems at his rallies—"Lock her up" and "Build the Wall."

I had a bizarre kind of déjà vu. It struck me that Trump was exhibiting many of the same behaviors that I had seen in the late Korean cult leader Sun Myung Moon, whom I had worshipped as the messiah in the mid-seventies. Moon had promised to make America—indeed the entire world—great. He promised a re-creation of the Garden of Eden. No wars, poverty, crime. Everyone would live in harmony together in God's paradise on earth. Moon, of course, was not a messiah, nor were his aims beneficent. That is the case with many cult leaders—they promise something that people want to believe in but that they can never actually deliver. They do so by utilizing a set of influence techniques that can be likened to a cult leader's playbook.

I now believe—and it is the argument of this book—that Trump has gotten where he is today in large part because he has exploited that same playbook. Trump's air of absolute confidence, his grandiosity—"Only I can fix this"—his practice of sowing fear and confusion, his demand for absolute loyalty, his tendency to lie and create alternative "facts" and realities, his shunning and belittling critics and ex-believers—these are the same methods used by Moon and other cult leaders such as L. Ron Hubbard, David Koresh, Lyndon LaRouche, and Jim Jones, to name just a few high-profile ones. Moon thought American democracy was satanic, and sought to install in its place a worldwide theocracy with himself at the head. His family and designates were 100 percent loyal and obedient. They promised to do whatever they were told, including, as I found out in my top leadership meetings, amending the Constitution to make it legal to execute those who were not faithful to Moon's policies. As I watched Trump, especially as he has revealed his infatuation with authoritarian leaders like Vladimir Putin, Recip Tayyip Erdogan, and Kim Jong-un, I grew worried that he might have similar aspirations or, at the very least, that he might try to push American democracy toward authoritarianism. When a leader gains psychological sway over his followers and also over other politicians—members of Congress, the cabinet, and even the judiciary—the checks and balances of healthy democracy can be stripped away.

Once I noticed the connections between Trump and Moon, I could not stop seeing them. My colleagues who have studied cults, especially those who are former members, agreed with my assessment when I started blogging about Trump in 2015. One of the most effective and insidious of Moon's techniques, and of many cult leaders, is the way he manipulated his followers' emotions. He would begin by making them feel special, part of an "inside" group in opposition to unenlightened, unbelieving dangerous "outsiders." Playing on ancient human tribal tendencies, cult leaders encourage a kind of dualistic "us versus them" mindset. Trump uses this trope constantly, and to great effect. During his campaign rallies, he would single out members of the audience whom he perceived as hostile and eject them, often to deafening cheers from his supporters. He was demonstrating who counts as "us," and what needs to be done about "them."

Like Moon, Trump commands, and even demands, devotion and adoration from his audiences, but I also saw telling differences. Trump's over 500 rallies are far more choreographed and stage-managed than Moon's mass assemblies ever were. Rousing patriotic music heralds his appearance onstage, while enthusiastic supporters stand behind him cheering. Trump rallies are also, strangely, more intimate. Part of Trump's effectiveness is the way he talks to his audience, taking them into his confidence with personal asides, talking about how misunderstood and maligned he is by the media. He further earns his followers'

sympathy and allegiance by telling them how great they are to be followers of his, and how much he loves them.

Moon always set himself apart, which was appropriate for someone who was, as he was fond of saying, "ten times greater than Jesus."
But just beneath the surface of Trump's woe-is-me facade is a messianic streak. He may not come out and say that he believes he is a
messiah, but he has done nothing to dispel the notion, popular among
some Christian followers, that God has chosen him to be their leader.
Certainly he makes no bones about the fact that he is the only one who
can restore America to an imagined past glory—and save them from
a terrible future. One of Trump's earliest campaign moves was to establish the image of a great shining Wall in the minds of his followers.
The Wall was a key piece of Trump propaganda to insulate, isolate,
and elevate America from the rest of the dangerous world. The idea
was actually suggested by political consultants Roger Stone and Sam
Nunberg, who were looking for a mnemonic device that would keep
Trump on message.[2] Trump didn't love the idea at first, but he tried it
out at a rally and the crowds went crazy.[3] It turned out to be a stroke
of marketing genius. Not only did it play on the us versus them trope,
but it also allowed Trump to conjure images of murderers and rapists
amassing at the southern border. It allowed him to instill fear in the
hearts and minds of his followers, far beyond what is the norm at
campaign rallies and yet straight out of the cult leader playbook. The
Muslim ban, which Trump tried to implement early in his presidency,
was a variation on this theme as many of the Christian right fear that
Islam wants to rule the world and impose sharia law on Americans.

Trump uses all kinds of cult tactics—lying, insulting opponents,
projecting his weaknesses onto others, deflecting, distracting, presenting alternative facts and competing versions of reality—to confuse,
disorient, and ultimately coerce his followers. Repetition programs
the beliefs into the unconscious. But fearmongering tops the list.
In my experience, phobia indoctrination—the creation of fearful
thoughts to promote and reinforce a desired set of beliefs or behaviors
in followers—is one of the most powerful and universal techniques
in the cult leader's arsenal. This is why Trump spends so much air

and Twitter time painting a frightening picture of the danger posed by immigrants—Mexicans, Muslims, the migrant caravan. The more vivid the thought or image installed in people's minds, the greater a hold it has, and the less susceptible it is to rational or critical thought. There are other enemies in Trump's world—globalists, radical left-wing Democrats, socialists, Hollywood actors, the liberal media—all of whom want to destroy America. Inspiring fear of real or imagined threats overrides people's sense of agency. It makes them susceptible to a confident authority figure who promises to keep them safe, and can make them more compliant and obedient.

Fear defines Trump's philosophy, his personality, and his presidency. It is also his definition of power, according to Bob Woodward's aptly titled book, *Fear*. In it, Woodward reported that Trump told him: "Real power is, I don't even want to use the word: fear." Trump, like cult leaders and dictators throughout history, seizes upon people's needs and fears and amplifies them. Like these authoritarian leaders, he may manufacture problems that do not exist, and then say "trust me" or "believe me" and promise that only he can fix it.

Given the right circumstances, sane, rational, well-adjusted people can be made to consider and ultimately believe the most outrageous leaders and propositions. There is a method to the madness. Cult leaders may look and behave differently, but even the craziest, most chaotic ones follow a similar pattern. While they usually have no academic training, they are masters of human psychology, especially social psychology. They understand that human beings are social creatures who, at some level, are wired to follow leaders and powerful members of their group. They know that they can confuse people with false information and lies, and then sow doubt by claiming that they never said what they said in the first place. People like to think they are rational and in control, but the lessons of history and social psychology demonstrate, time and again, that simply isn't so. We go about our days, and our lives, using unconscious mental models. When cult leaders manipulate those models, in subtle and overt ways, we can be persuaded to believe and do things we might never have considered without such systematic psychological influence.

Ultimately, their goal is to make people dependent and obedient. Before the 24/7 world of smartphones and the internet, cult leaders would physically isolate members in order to control all aspects of their lives—their behavior, information, thoughts, and emotions, or what I call the BITE model of indoctrination. But physical isolation is not always necessary for indoctrination to occur. Through the media and the internet, people can be indoctrinated—and even recruited— on their smartphones or in their own homes. Some cult leaders, including pimps and human traffickers, use smartphones and digital technology to monitor and control their followers.

Taken to an extreme, the indoctrination process can break down a person's fundamental identity to such an extent that they could be said to have a new pseudo-identity, cast in the image of the group's leader or ideology. In her documentary, *The Brainwashing of My Dad*, Jen Senko shows how her once loving and liberal father, Frank, came to espouse hate-filled racist views after listening to Rush Limbaugh and other right-wing radio hosts for many hours a day while commuting to work. He was essentially radicalized by these shows and also by Fox News television. I have met and heard about followers of Trump who have undergone radical personality changes, adopting viewpoints that would have been abhorrent to their former selves. Perhaps most confounding is how so many devout Christians have come to believe that a man who cheated on his pregnant wife was handpicked by God to be president.

Of course, Trump is not carrying out this indoctrination single-handedly through his Twitter account. In the case of Frank Senko and many others, Trump was aided by a vast and mutually supportive right-wing media machine—notably news programming like Fox, Breitbart, Sinclair, Nexstar, Trinity Broadcasting Network, and many others. He has also been helped by internet trolls, social media manipulators, and even—as has been shown by numerous federal investigations—by agents of the Russian government.

Some may reject the characterization of Trump and his followers, including members of his administration, as a cult. The cult of Trump does not fit the stereotype of religious devotees dressed in special garb—Hare Krishnas in their saffron robes or followers of the late cult leader Rajneesh (also known as Osho) clothed in red. It turns out, these cults are the exceptions. Most people involved in destructive cults dress like you or me, and many work regular jobs. Nor are they necessarily religious—there are political cults as well as psychotherapy and commercial cults as well as personality cults. As we will see, it's not their beliefs that define these groups as cults but the way they deceptively recruit, indoctrinate, and ultimately control the lives of their members. It may be hard to view an elected figure, much less the president of the United States, in this light. But having worked with victims of cult leaders for more than four decades, the warning signs are hiding in plain sight.

I am not alone in seeing them. On June 7, 2018, the *New York Times* ran an editorial, "The Cult of Trump," describing how the Republican Party was obediently, almost blindly, rallying around the president in a cult of personality.[4] Former Tennessee Republican senator Bob Corker was quoted in the *Washington Post* as saying, "It's becoming a cultish thing, isn't it?" In 2019, Maryland Democratic representative Jamie Raskin said, "The Republican party is almost like a religious cult surrounding an organized crime family. That's the mentality."[5] Former White House staffer and *Apprentice* contestant Omarosa Manigault Newman ends her book, *Unhinged*, with these memorable words: "I've escaped from the cult of Trumpworld. I'm free."

Prominent psychiatrists and psychologists detailed their concerns in *The Dangerous Case of Donald Trump: 37 Psychiatrists and Mental Health Experts Assess a President*, edited by Yale forensic psychiatrist Bandy X. Lee. The book is filled with descriptions and also dire warnings about Trump's mental health and his fitness to serve. "In Donald Trump," one of the authors in the book declares, "we have a frightening Venn diagram consisting of three circles: the first is extreme present hedonism; the second, narcissism; and the third, bullying behavior. These three circles overlap in the middle to create an impulsive, immature, incompetent person who, when in the position of ultimate power, easily slides into the role of tyrant, complete with family members sitting at his proverbial 'ruling table.' Like a fledgling dictator, he plants psychological seeds of treachery in sections of our population that reinforce already negative attitudes."

Perhaps most pertinent are my many colleagues in the field of cult studies—researchers, academics, and practitioners such as Robert Jay Lifton, Philip Zimbardo, Jon Atack, Stephen Kent, Steve Eichel, Janja Lalich, Alan Scheflin, Dennis Tourish, Alexandra Stein, Dan Shaw, and others—who see, all too clearly, the cultlike aspects of the Trump presidency.

In this book, I will show how Trump employs many of the same techniques as prominent cult leaders, and displays many of the same personality traits. He has persuaded millions of people to support, believe, and even adore him by exerting control in four overlapping areas: Behavior, Information, Thought, and Emotion (BITE). I will describe how cult leaders exert control in each of these areas and then show how Trump and his adherents have exploited them to their own ends.

They may not approach people on street corners like members of the Moon cult (often referred to as Moonies) did, but Trump and his supporters are using social and mainstream media to gain access to followers in ways Moon never could. Through his barrage of daily tweets, Trump sows confusion and distorts reality, and has ultimately called into question the foundations of national institutions. Questioning government, politicians, and the media are all signs of a healthy democracy, one that values free and critical thinking. Trump's exhortations do the opposite. By promoting the idea of "fake news" and calling journalists who disagree with him "enemies of the people," he is closing his followers' minds to disconfirming evidence and arguments. He sounds to me like notorious cult leader Jim Jones, who, as he was taking his last breaths, told his followers at Jonestown that it was all "the media's fault—don't believe them."

Over the years, I've received thousands of calls, emails, and letters from people who have lost loved ones to a destructive group or relationship. Many describe how their loved one has undergone a radical personality change. They are not the loving son, daughter, parent, or friend they once knew. They hold beliefs that are diametrically opposed to the values they once held and are not willing to discuss issues and look at facts. A similar thing appears to be happening to the nation and to individual families and relationships, many of which have been broken by the recent presidential election. I have known critics as well as supporters of Trump who are rigidly closed-minded to any opposing evidence or information. I encourage them to think analytically and consciously and not on "automatic pilot."

What I've learned in working with such people is that attacking a person's beliefs is doomed to fail. When I first began confronting this reality, I realized I had to develop a process to help people recover their individual faculties and, ultimately, their true, or authentic, selves. I found that to reach that authentic self, I needed to encourage a positive, warm relationship between cult members and families—essentially, to build trust and rapport—while raising essential questions for cult members to consider. My goal in this book is to educate and inspire people to regain their capacity for critical thinking and to free their own minds. By presenting this approach, and showing how it applies to the current situation, my hope is that it might be used to heal fractured families, fractured relationships, and a fractured nation.

CHAPTER ONE

What Is a Cult?

F ew political scenes have been as strange and unsettling as Donald Trump's first cabinet meeting, which took place six months
into his tenure. It was televised, though there seemed to be no
real agenda. The camera panned around the room as members of the
president's cabinet, one by one, praised Trump.

"We thank you for the opportunity and the blessing to serve your
agenda," said then chief of staff Reince Priebus. Agriculture secretary Sonny Perdue, just back from a trip to Mississippi, said, "They
love you there, Mr. President." Outdoing the previous devotional,
Steve Mnuchin, the Treasury secretary, told Trump that it was a "great
honor traveling with you around the country for the last year, and an
even greater honor to be here serving on your cabinet." Labor secretary Alexander Acosta also claimed to be "privileged and honored,"
echoing words used earlier by Vice President Mike Pence, who set the
tone for what amounted to a spectacle of love and flattery.

It was stunning. The country had already witnessed the almost
daily onslaught of bizarre and contradictory statements and behavior
coming from the Trump White House, but this should have been different. Wasn't the cabinet supposed to give the president unadulter-
ated, honest advice for running the country, not praise him or stroke

his ego? It seemed that the video cameras had been allowed into the room for the sole purpose of publicizing the fawning display. As the members carried on their praise, Trump smiled, almost gleefully, nodding vigorously. He interrupted the adulation just long enough to offer his own somewhat contradictory self-praise.

"I will say that never has there been a president, with a few exceptions—in the case of FDR, he had a major depression to handle—who's passed more legislation, who's done more things than what we've done."

Some forty years earlier, I was seated in a closed room with another narcissistic leader, Sun Myung Moon—the self-ordained reverend and leader of the Unification Church, popularly known as the Moonies—along with a number of his most devoted followers. I was only twenty years old but was being groomed for a leadership role. All of us in the room understood how blessed we were to be in Moon's presence. We adored him as the greatest man who ever lived. If we had doubts or criticisms, we were taught to block, or "thought stop," them. If we dared disagree or point out inconsistencies, we would be kicked out. It seemed the only difference was that the Moon meetings always began with us bowing and even kneeling with our heads to the floor. (Trump would narrow the grandiosity gap when he accused Democrats of treason for not clapping during his first State of the Union address.)

Did Trump's cabinet members believe what they were saying? Did they know what they were getting into when they agreed to serve? I did not knowingly join the Moon cult. I was nineteen, newly split from my girlfriend, and was sitting in the Queens College student union cafeteria when I was approached by three attractive women—students, or so they said. The women turned out to be members of a front group for Moon's Unification Church. They invited me to dinner that evening, and over the following weeks, I experienced the full arsenal of influence techniques. I cut off connection with my family and friends—and my previous life and self—and was thrown into recruiting and indoctrinating others. Before I knew it, I was rising rapidly through the Moonie ranks. I was already a fanatical follower of Moon when I was invited into his inner sanctum, though the proximity to power was a heady incentive to do even more for him.

Trump's appointees may not have been passionate followers when they had that first televised meeting with Trump, but simply being invited to join the cabinet, where they might exercise real power, already tied them to Trump. To my eyes, a huge amount of social and psychological manipulation was happening inside that meeting room. Not all of it came from Trump. Some of it came from the cabinet members themselves who felt compelled to outdo one another in their praise—and it is often true that cult members compete with and indoctrinate one another.

But most of the pressure did come from Trump. How could it be otherwise when the president equates power with fear? Mnuchin, Acosta, and the others had already seen, as had the world, what happens to those who "betray" Trump—the shunning, bullying, baiting, and outright expulsion. They had seen Trump unleash the full fury of his anger on one of his earliest and most devoted followers, then attorney general Jeff Sessions, for recusing himself from the FBI investigation into possible collusion with Russia during Trump's presidential campaign. They had seen Trump fire the head of the FBI, James Comey, for reportedly refusing to stop that same investigation.

The parallels between Trump and Moon—and also other cult leaders—extend far beyond that cabinet meeting, as we will see. But simply using the word "cult" conjures up all kinds of images in people's minds, which raises the central question: what is a cult?

Say the word and most people usually think of a religious group. Merriam-Webster dictionary defines it as "a religion regarded as unorthodox or spurious." According to Google, it is "a relatively small group of people having religious beliefs or practices regarded by others as strange or sinister." Some expand the definition beyond religion to a "small or narrow circle of persons united by devotion or allegiance to some artistic or intellectual program, tendency, or figure." In fact, most cults do tend to revolve around a central figure—the leader. Cult leaders often appear to be devoted to, and even embody, the religion or ideology practiced by their group. In my experience, cult leaders are often motivated by three things: power, money, and sex—in that order. It is estimated that there are now more than five thousand destructive cults operating in the United States, of varying size, directly—and unduly—influencing millions of people.

THE STUDY OF BRAINWASHING

Though cults have been around for centuries, it was during the second half of the twentieth century that they were approached in a systematic fashion. The former air force and Yale psychiatrist Robert Jay Lifton was one of the first to study how authoritarian leaders and regimes, such as those experienced in a cult, exert their power. Lifton spent much of the 1950s studying the experiences of political prisoners in China and American soldiers held as prisoners during the Korean War. He came to understand that under conditions of totalitarianism, the human mind can be systematically broken down and remade to believe the exact opposite of what it once did. In his seminal 1961 work, *Thought Reform and the Psychology of Totalism*, Lifton identified eight criteria of what he called "thought reform," popularly known as "brainwashing" (a term coined in the early 1950s by the intelligence agent and writer Edward Hunter to describe how the Chinese communist army was turning people into followers). The Trump parallels are striking:

1. *Milieu control.* The leader, or inner circle, has complete control of information—how and where it is communicated, disseminated, and consumed, resulting in nearly complete isolation from the outside world. People learn to trust only the publications and news that come from the group itself. (The rest is "fake," in Trump parlance.) Eventually, people internalize the group mindset, becoming their own "mental police."

2. *Mystical manipulation.* Group and individual experiences are contrived, engineered, and even staged in a way

that makes them seem spontaneous and even supernatural or divine. A leader may be told something about a new member and then present that knowledge to the new recruit as if they had somehow divined it. Witnessing such things, the member believes that there are mystical forces at work.

3. *Demand for purity.* Viewing the world in simple binary terms, as "black versus white," "good versus evil," members are told that they must strive for perfection—no messy gray zones. They are set impossible standards of performance, resulting in feelings of guilt and shame. No matter how hard a person tries, they always fall short, feel bad, and work even harder. (Out of twenty-four cabinet posts, at least forty-six appointees have been fired or resigned since Trump's inauguration, a record for the presidency.[1])

4. *Confession.* Personal boundaries are broken down and destroyed. Every thought, feeling, or action—past or present—that does not conform to the group's rules should be shared or confessed, either publicly or to a personal monitor. Nor is the information forgiven or forgotten. Rather, it can be used by the leader or group to control members whenever the person needs to be put in line. (Trump appears to have an elephant's memory for perceived betrayals.)

5. *Sacred science.* Group ideology or doctrine is considered to be absolutely, scientifically, and morally true—no room for questions or alternative viewpoints. The leader, often seen as a spokesperson for God, is above any criticism. (Trump, who denies the scientific evidence of climate change and regularly ignores and even denigrates science, could be said to put his own spin on this, promoting a kind of "sacred anti-science.")

6. *Loading the language.* Members learn a new vocabulary that is designed to constrict their thinking into absolute, black-and-white, thought-stopping clichés that conform to group ideology. ("Lock her up" and "Build the Wall" are Trumpian examples. Even his put-downs and nicknames—Crooked

Hillary, Pocahontas for Elizabeth Warren—function to block other thoughts. Terms like "deep state" and "globalist" also act as triggers. They rouse emotion and direct attention.)

7. *Doctrine over person.* Group ideology is privileged far above a member's experience, conscience, and integrity. If a member doubts or has critical thoughts about those beliefs, it is due to their own shortcomings.

8. *Dispensing of existence.* Only those who belong to the group have the right to exist. All ex-members and critics or dissidents do not. This is perhaps the most defining and potentially the most dangerous of all of Lifton's criteria. Taken to an extreme, which it has been by some cult groups, it can lead to murderous and even genocidal actions. Trump doesn't go that far, but some have argued that his racist tweets—against Muslims, Mexicans, and immigrants—may have fueled hate crimes, such as the killing of Heather Heyer in Charlottesville and eleven people at the Tree of Life synagogue in Pittsburgh, to name just a few. The FBI has reported that hate crimes went up 17 percent in 2017 alone, continuing a three-year rise.[2]

THE MYSTERY OF MIND CONTROL

In addition to Lifton, researchers such as army psychologist Margaret Singer, psychologist Edgar Schein, and military psychiatrist Louis Jolyon West had been studying American POWs held captive by Korean and Chinese communists and were making contributions to understanding coercive persuasion and cults. Singer would later write a book, *Cults in Our Midst*, with cult expert Janja Lalich, identifying six conditions for exerting undue influence on a person.

- Keep them unaware of what is happening and how they are being changed one step at a time.
- Control their social and/or physical environment, especially time.

- Systematically create a sense of personal powerlessness.
- Implement a system of rewards, punishments, and experiences that inhibits behavior that might reflect the person's former social identity.
- Implement a system of rewards, punishments, and experiences that promotes learning the group's ideology or belief system and group-approved behaviors.
- Put forth a closed system of logic and an authoritarian structure that permits no feedback and cannot be modified except by the leaders.

Whatever term you wish to use—mind control, thought reform, brainwashing—it is ultimately a process that disrupts an individual's ability to make independent decisions from within their own identity.

After World War II, American intelligence agencies began to aggressively engage in mind control research. The CIA performed drug, electroshock, and hypnosis experiments on human subjects in order to develop new ways of extracting information and confessions from Soviet spies and other captives, largely, they claimed, in response to the alleged use of mind control techniques on U.S. prisoners during the Korean War. This program, code-named MK-ULTRA, began in 1953 and continued for nearly twenty years, during which time fear of communism was reaching new heights.

Meanwhile, branches of the military—including the newly formed Defense Advanced Research Projects Agency (DARPA), which was created in 1958 in response to the Soviet launching of Sputnik 1—began funding the work of social psychologists at major universities, as well as in branches of the armed forces. Two of these military-funded projects came to fruition in the early 1970s, each showing in a different way how easily people can be influenced by authoritarian settings. Stanley Milgram, working at Yale University, conducted experiments showing that subjects could be induced to administer ever more powerful and painful electric shocks to what they thought were innocent subjects when directed by an authority figure. Meanwhile, Philip Zimbardo, in his famous Stanford Prison

Experiment, showed how easily and rapidly subjects—in this case, college students who were randomly assigned to play the part of either prisoner or guard—would take on social roles, exhibiting either submissive or authoritarian behaviors, sometimes in quite extreme fashion. After six days, Zimbardo had to stop what was to be a two-week experiment.

Spurred in part by this and other new research, destructive groups were developing ever more sophisticated techniques. During the late 1960s, the Human Potential Movement in psychology began to experiment with approaches that might enhance people's lives. One of these was a form of group therapy known as sensitivity training. It started with good intentions—to help people out of debilitating mental ruts. People were encouraged to publicly speak about their most intimate experiences. One technique widely popular at the time was the "hot seat," which was first used by the drug rehabilitation cult of Charles Dederich, called Synanon. Someone would sit in the center of a circle while other members confronted the person with what they considered to be his or her shortcomings or problems. Without the supervision of an experienced therapist—and sometimes even with it—such a technique opened up considerable possibilities for abuse. Today the hot seat is used by some destructive cults to demean and control their members.

Another development was the popularization of hypnosis. Originally this set of approaches for reaching the subconscious mind was used only on willing participants, many of whom reported positive experiences. Eventually hypnotic techniques percolated out into the general culture, where they became available for anyone to use and abuse. Unscrupulous con artists began using them to make money off unsuspecting subjects while would-be cult leaders used them to gain power by manipulating a coterie of unwitting followers.

Due in part to these new understandings and methods for controlling people's minds, cults began to proliferate in the late 1960s and 1970s. Some of them, like Charles Manson's group, which committed a series of murders in four different locations over two days in 1969, made front page headlines. One of the biggest cult stories of the time was of Patty Hearst, the daughter of one of the country's most powerful newspaper publishers, William Randolph Hearst III. On February 4, 1974, she was violently abducted from her Berkeley, California, apartment, locked in a closet, raped, and systematically indoctrinated. She emerged to the world two months later, during a dramatic bank robbery, as Tania, a member of a left-wing terrorist cult, the Symbionese Liberation Army. Hearst was captured, jailed, and ultimately freed and would later talk about her experiences as a form of brainwashing.

Perhaps the biggest and most devastating story, one that turned "cult" into a household word, was the 1978 massacre in Jonestown, Guyana. More than nine hundred followers of Jim Jones, about a third of them under the age of sixteen, drank cyanide-laced fruit punch and died, on the order of Jones. The idea of brainwashing had been in the culture but that it could be carried out in such a massive and devastating way stunned the world.

A MODERN PHENOMENON

The rise of cults can be attributed to a few other factors. Among the most fundamental is the breakdown of families and communities and the growing sense that our society is in disarray. Economic factors play a role. A large and growing segment of the world's population is poor, while a relatively small elite controls an ever-increasing share of the world's resources. More people have been uprooted, even in the United States. Whereas once they could expect to spend their entire life within a five-mile radius of their birthplace, today it's not unusual to relocate to faraway places. Such big transitions can create greater susceptibility and vulnerability in people. They feel disenchanted and separated from their culture, and seek answers in fringe groups of all types, from fanatical religious sects to militia groups.

Today, with so much access to information at our fingertips and a greater awareness of the dangers of persuasion and influence, you might think there would be a decline in cult activity. The opposite is true: computers and the internet have taken this phenomenon to the next level. Children, adolescents, and adults may become addicted to video games and deprive themselves of the social contact that people need to function in healthy ways. While apocalyptic visions are not new, the means by which they can be promulgated is changing at an unprecedented pace. We have television, social networks, and the internet to spread alarmist ideas. With the internet, it's easy to download information and training manuals and to use them to manipulate others into new beliefs, behaviors, and cult identities. The internet has been used to great advantage by terrorist groups like ISIS and Boko Haram, and human trafficking rings—all of which fit the definition of a cult.

THE INFLUENCE CONTINUUM

The cult mindset might be black-and-white but cults themselves exist on a kind of continuum. Groups with charismatic leaders and devoted followers are not always harmful. Unlike destructive cults, which have members who tend to lie and deceive to recruit people, and which control information to keep people from doubting or questioning, some groups are transparent in their recruiting. They allow members to freely read, talk, and even leave the group. Fans of a sports team, musician, or a popular game might fall into this category. Bruce Springsteen has legions of adoring followers who revere him and call him the Boss, but they are free to leave a concert, are permitted to not like a particular song or album, and are allowed to like other musicians. This is a fanciful example but it makes the point that groups exist along a continuum—from healthy ethical influence to destructive unethical influence. Distinct criteria can be used to discern harmless groups from destructive ones. Depending on which criteria are used, groups may fall at different points along this continuum. They may be more or less harmful with regard to certain aspects, and less so regarding others, though destructive behaviors do tend to cluster.

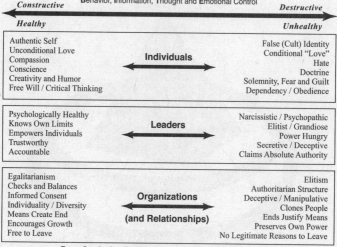

Influence Continuum

Using the **BITE** Model:
Behavior, Information, Thought and Emotional Control

Constructive ←→ *Destructive*

Healthy   *Unhealthy*

Individuals	
Authentic Self	False (Cult) Identity
Unconditional Love	Conditional "Love"
Compassion	Hate
Conscience	Doctrine
Creativity and Humor	Solemnity, Fear and Guilt
Free Will / Critical Thinking	Dependency / Obedience

Leaders	
Psychologically Healthy	Narcissistic / Psychopathic
Knows Own Limits	Elitist / Grandiose
Empowers Individuals	Power Hungry
Trustworthy	Secretive / Deceptive
Accountable	Claims Absolute Authority

Organizations (and Relationships)	
Egalitarianism	Elitism
Checks and Balances	Authoritarian Structure
Informed Consent	Deceptive / Manipulative
Individuality / Diversity	Clones People
Means Create End	Ends Justify Means
Encourages Growth	Preserves Own Power
Free to Leave	No Legitimate Reasons to Leave

From *Combating Cult Mind Control* (2015) by Steven Hassan

Ultimately, it's not a group's content or ideology but rather its pattern of behavior that generally defines it as a destructive cult. Cults can promote all kinds of beliefs in all kinds of areas—commercial, political, psychological, beliefs in UFOs, science fiction, as well as religious—but they typically possess a common structure.

Most destructive cults exhibit a pyramid structure, with a leader, or some kind of authority figure (or figures), at the top who uses deceptive recruitment and an arsenal of mind control techniques to render people dependent and obedient. Those closest to the top, the inner sanctum or circle, are deepest in the group and often most indoctrinated. Those at the bottom may have never even met the leader and may be more or less actively involved with the group.

If we apply the pyramid structure to Trump the businessman sitting in his gilded offices at the top of Trump Tower, his family would make up the first tier of trusted business advisors; associates like his former attorney Michael Cohen and others would be the second tier. Lower down would be various underlings, whom he rules with an iron hand, demanding absolute loyalty and obedience, rewarding good deeds and punishing or expelling those he deems disloyal.

Destructive Cult Structure

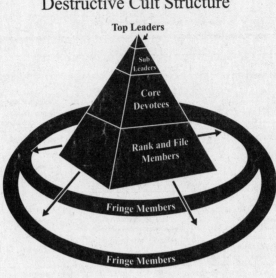

We can also apply a similar schema to Trump the president, sitting in the Oval Office, surrounded most closely by family members and then by aides, advisors, staffers, and the vice president. The next tier comprises his cabinet as well as Republican members of Congress, to the extent that they come into his personal orbit. Lower down, the structure widens to include state politicians, Republican donors, and then finally his fans and supporters, who may be more or less fervent—literally his base. (As we will see later, the Cult of Trump is much more complex. For example, Trump's power over his base and his use of Fox News and other right-wing media are what help to keep the middle tiers—members of Congress—obedient.)

Some of Trump's followers may have disliked, even hated, him at the start but have come to respect and even revere him, thanks to the policies he has implemented. Much of Trump's support, both in his base and in the upper echelons, comes from the Republican Party, the Christian right, libertarian groups, the National Rifle Association, the alt-right, and white supremacy groups. These movements and organizations, if not their individual members, may see in Trump a useful tool for enacting their own political agendas. Trump himself has no real ideology other than the one he had as businessman: winning. He has depended on advisors such as Steve Bannon, Kellyanne Conway, and Stephen Miller; a covey of wealthy donors such as the Mercers, the Koch brothers, and Sheldon Adelson; Rupert Murdoch, Roger Ailes, Bill Shine, and the right-wing media, especially commentators like Sean Hannity and Ann Coulter; factions on the Christian right; and certain extremist groups to set an agenda.

Initially, cults exert their control through other members—the power of community is huge. The social setting may be intimate—such as three women chatting you up in a cafeteria—and become progressively more expansive. People can also be recruited and indoctrinated online. Humans are intensely social and cults play upon this, often creating an instant sense of community through techniques such as love bombing; group prayer, singing, and chanting; and staged and dramatic group experiences, such as those that occur at political rallies.

THE BITE MODEL

Cult members may bring other people through the door but what ensnares them is a complex array of influence techniques, applied incrementally to control almost every aspect of a person—the way they act (behavior), what they read, watch, or listen to (information), the way they think (thoughts), and how they feel (emotions). Trump has gotten millions of people to believe, support, and even adore him by using techniques in each of these areas:

Behavior: Trump demands loyalty and obedience, and often gets it, using a variety of tried-and-true cult tactics such as shunning and publicly insulting those who disagree with him. He creates false enemies—Mexicans, Muslims, the media, to name just a few—to engender us versus them thinking, which renders people more fearful and obedient. He rewards those who support him and punishes those who don't. He holds mass rallies filled with people wearing Trump and Make America Great Again hats and T-shirts and chanting slogans, which promote identification with him and the group in opposition to outsiders, though this is a common feature of many political rallies.

Information: Cult leaders are masters of deception but they, like Trump, use other tactics: discouraging access to noncult or critical sources of information; compartmentalizing information into insider versus outsider doctrines. Clearly Trump's branding of the "liberal media" as "fake news" or "phony" hits these nails right on the head. On the flip side, cults flood their members with cult-generated information and propaganda—videos and podcasts distributed by YouTube and social media. They take "outsider" statements out of context or misquote them. Of course, Trump could not have done this without the propaganda machine of right-wing TV shows like Fox and Breitbart News, as well as right-wing talk radio.

Thought: In the Moonies, I was taught to suppress negative thoughts by using a technique called thought stopping. I repeated the phrase "Crush Satan" or "True Parents" (the term used to describe Moon and his wife, Hak Ja Han) whenever any doubt arose in my mind. Another way to control thoughts is through the use of loaded language, which, as Lifton pointed out, is purposely designed to invoke an emotional response. When I look at the list of thought-controlling techniques—reducing complex thoughts into clichés and platitudinous buzz words; forbidding critical questions about the leader, doctrine, or policy; labeling alternative belief systems as illegitimate or evil—it is astounding how many Trump exploits. As I have mentioned, one of the most effective techniques in the thought control arsenal is hypnosis. Scott Adams, the creator of the cartoon *Dilbert*, described Trump, with his oversimplifications, repetitions, insinuating tone of voice, and use of vivid imagery, as a Master Wizard in the art of hypnosis and persuasion.[3]

Emotion: Cults have many techniques for controlling their members' emotions, such as making them feel that they are special and chosen—true Americans, in Trump's parlance. But the most effective is by fanning fear and implanting phobias. Trump's Wall is most compelling because of what it will do—keep out murderers and rapists. Inspiring fear of real and imagined threats is what cult leaders do best.

It was by exaggerating the threat of foreigners that he gained his foothold in the political landscape. Trump's perverse genius, and he follows in the footsteps of cult leaders and dictators alike, is to convince his followers that the world is a dangerous place that only he can fix.

As *New York Times* columnist Charles Blow observed, "Trump's magical mixture is to make being afraid feel like fun. His rallies are a hybrid of concert revelry and combat prep. Trump tells his followers about all the things of which they should be afraid, or shouldn't trust or should hate, and then positions himself as the greatest defense against those things. His supporters roar their approval at their white knight."[4] The unfortunate thing is, all his fearmongering has made the country and the world a more divided and dangerous place.

AUTHENTIC SELF/CULT SELF

Ultimately the goal of the cult indoctrination process is to render a person dependent and obedient—to create a kind of "cult self" that suppresses the "authentic self" that a person is born with. Through my work, I've come to believe that people want to be free—they do not like being lied to, manipulated, or exploited. Reaching that authentic self, and helping to liberate it, is the goal of my work with cult members. It was striking how Trump's former personal lawyer Michael Cohen described himself in dichotomous terms during his February 2019 congressional testimony. He was the devoted husband, father, and son of a Holocaust survivor who "tried to live a life of loyalty, friendship, generosity, and compassion." He was also the man who ignored his conscience and was "so mesmerized by Donald Trump that I was willing to do things for him that I knew were absolutely wrong." He claimed that he was even prepared to take a bullet for Trump.

THE FIVE MAIN TYPES OF CULTS

As I mentioned, groups using mind control operate in many different areas of society, but they roughly fall into five categories: religious cults, political cults, psychotherapy/educational cults, commercial cults, and cults of personality. Their philosophical inclinations may vary, but their methods are strikingly similar.

Religious Cults

Religious cults, like the Moonies, Heaven's Gate, and more recently, the Islamic terrorist group ISIS, are the best known and most numerous. These groups use religious dogma to justify their ends. Some, like the Moonies or the World Mission Society Church of God, use their interpretation of the Bible. In the case of ISIS, it's of the Koran. Some, like Soka Gakkai, are based on their own version of Buddhism. Shoko Asahara, leader of the notorious Japanese sarin gas cult, Aum Shinrikyo, claimed to be Jesus and Buddha. Others draw on occult lore. Some are purely the inventions of their leaders, like Bonnie Nettles and Marshall Applewhite of Heaven's Gate. Although most claim to involve the spiritual realm, or to follow a strict code of religious principles, it is common for these cult leaders to enjoy a luxurious lifestyle, with the groups owning millions of dollars of real estate and running extensive business enterprises.

Political Cults

These groups are organized around a particular political dogma. The Aryan Nations believes in white supremacy and has ambitions to take over the U.S. government. Lyndon LaRouche, the apocalyptic and conspiracy-obsessed cult leader who ran for president of the United States eight times, once from prison, started on the far left and ended on the far right. The now-defunct Democratic Workers' Party of California, headed by Marlene Dixon, was for years an extreme left-wing cult, as was the Symbionese Liberation Army, the cult that kidnapped Patty Hearst. The Nazi Party, under Adolf Hitler, was an infamous political cult. This is true of many dictatorships. They are brutal, repressive regimes that imprison or kill critics and dissidents and, like Hitler, use propaganda to spread their message and keep people in line. Kim Jong-un's North Korea, Robert Mugabe's Zimbabwe, Vladimir Putin, the Saudi prince Mohammed Bin Salman—they control the press and prevent free assembly and elections that might check their power. Rarely do people hear about the deceptive recruitment and mind control practices that link these authoritarian regimes to political cults. But despots tend to play by similar rules. They use similar words, techniques, and political moves to acquire control and power. Dictators don't just install irrational fears—they actually have the power to imprison, torture, hunt down, and kill opponents.

Psychotherapy/Education Cults

These cults hold expensive workshops and seminars that provide participants with "insight" and "enlightenment," usually in a hotel conference room. They use basic mind control techniques to provide participants with peak experiences, which are usually hypnotically induced trances or states of euphoria. For many, that is all that happens, but others are manipulated to sign up for more expensive advanced courses. Graduates of the advanced courses may then become enmeshed in the group. Once committed, members are told to bring in friends, relatives, and coworkers, or to cut off contact with them if they disapprove. Some members have experienced nervous breakdowns, broken marriages, and business failures, as well as suicides and accidental deaths by reckless accidents as a result of their involvement. The people who run these groups sometimes have questionable personal backgrounds, and, often, few or no credentials.

Commercial Cults

Commercial cults prey on people's desire for wealth and power. Many are pyramid-shaped marketing organizations whose members deceptively recruit people who, in turn, recruit others, who then provide income for the recruiting member. Companies like Amway and Herbalife promise get-rich-quick schemes through selling goods, such as health and beauty products or supplements. These pyramid-scheme or multilevel marketing organizations promise big bucks, but in fact

99 percent of participants lose money.[5] Some of these companies have gotten into trouble with federal regulators for defrauding members. Yet members of these groups are indoctrinated to believe that the pyramid scheme works. If they lose money, it's their fault.

Some multilevel marketing organizations sell services, such as business and leadership programs and seminars. Major legitimate businesses unwittingly hire these pseudo-consultants to train their employees. Believers within the company pressure other employees to attend the programs. One of the most notorious groups is Keith Raniere's NXIVM, which in early 2018 came crashing down. Raniere was arrested, and later convicted, for sex trafficking, conspiracy to commit forced labor, and other charges. He had previously been shut down by no fewer than twenty attorneys general for his multilevel marketing, pyramid scheme, Consumers Buyline. He then created a coaching entity, Executive Success Programs, that employed many of the psychological techniques used in destructive cults. The 2018 arrest made headlines not only for the organization's lurid practices—using a cauterizing iron to forcibly brand women with Raniere's initials—but also because of its celebrity involvement. One of Raniere's main lieutenants was *Smallville* actress Allison Mack, who was also arrested. She would later plead guilty to racketeering and racketeering conspiracy.[6]

Perhaps the most pernicious of all commercial cults are pimps and human trafficking rings who deceptively recruit people with dreams of making money, and then buy and sell them for sex and labor. An estimated 4.8 million people are victims of sex trafficking worldwide, and more than 40 million are victims of labor trafficking. Organized crime, drug cartels, and gangs often make money from extortion, selling on the black market, and human trafficking.

Though cults generally fall into one or more of the above categories, there are numerous other variations, from computer to science fiction and UFO cults. Heaven's Gate falls into the last category but it was also a religious cult—and it is often true that cults fall into more than one category. NXIVM was a sex cult as well as a commercial cult. Political cults may use religion as a cloak, as do the Moonies and some Christian right groups. Cults can be huge and have many

THE CULT OF TRUMP

millions of people, like the Jehovah's Witnesses, a group that satisfies many of the main criteria of the BITE model. Others may be tiny, consisting of just two people.

Personality Cults

Sometimes the charisma, fame, money, and celebrity of a single person—often male—can form the basis for a high-demand relationship or group. These microcults may consist of a few members or even just an abuser and his or her victim. In such cases, a person controls or dominates another person to such an extreme that they cannot think for themselves, rendering them dependent and obedient. The abuser can be a spouse, a parent, a therapist, or someone completely unrelated. Many domestic abusers are adept in BITE model techniques, and use them to control their victims. Most abusers are male but there are a percentage of women who fit the profile. Personality cults can also exist on a massive scale, especially in political cults. Korean leader Kim Jong-un's face is plastered all over North Korea, where he is idolized and venerated as a deity, though that is partly due to the structure of his office. At some point, most cults do depend on the power and charisma of their leader.

Trump is an interesting and unique case. He ran the Trump Organization as a business that used his personality to sell products, especially real estate, but he has also branded product lines from casinos to steaks, vodka, and an airline—all failures. When he became a reality TV star, a persona of savvy businessman was constructed through careful editing and information management. I would describe his presidency as a personality cult that uses politics and religious right-wing ideology—anti-abortion, antiscience, antidiversity, white power, if not outright racism—to sell himself and, by association, the Republican Party. But the influence goes two ways. Organizations holding those right-wing ideologies use Trump to sell their own political and religious agendas. Former FBI director James Comey likened Trump to a mafia kingpin, another nod to the cult of personality surrounding him.

In their edited anthology, *The Dangerous Case of Donald Trump*, Bandy X. Lee and her colleagues describe what they perceive to be Trump's psychological makeup—the mental instability, extreme hedonism, grandiose omnipotence, and narcissistic tendencies. In fact, the list applies to many cult leaders—Sun Myung Moon, L. Ron Hubbard, David Koresh, Jim Jones, Keith Raniere, to name just a few. Most cult leaders were either born into a cult, later joined one, or had significant exposure to authoritarian figures. The question arises, how do these experiences contribute to the making of a cult leader?

In their 1991 book, *Age of Propaganda*, Anthony R. Pratkanis and Elliot Aronson provide, somewhat tongue in cheek, a formula. In a chapter titled "How to Become a Cult Leader,"[7] they describe seven "mundane but proven-effective tactics," which I summarize here:

1. Create your own social reality by eliminating all sources of information other than that provided by the cult (in Trump's words, fake news). Provide a picture of your world (a walled-in America) that members can use to interpret all events.

2. Create an in-group of followers (Trump supporters) in contrast to an evil out-group (Democrats, Mexicans, Muslims) to be hated and feared.

3. Create an escalating spiral of commitment, beginning with simple requests (small donations, rally attendance).

4. Establish your credibility and attractiveness through myths and stories that can be passed from member to member (that Trump made his own fortune and was chosen by God to lead the nation).

5. Send members out to proselytize the unredeemed (Campaign!).

6. Prevent members from thinking undesirable thoughts by continually distracting them (with outrageous tweets or by manufacturing your own fake news).

7. Dangle a notion of a promised land before the faithful (Make America Great Again, but only for true believers).

"When it comes to teaching your social reality," Aronson and Pratkanis advise, "there is one additional point to keep in mind: Repeat your message over and over and over again. Repetition makes the heart grow fonder and fiction, if heard frequently enough, can come to sound like fact." Trump appears to have taken this advice to heart, not just in the way he states and restates fabrications and falsehoods, but also in the way he tells, over and over again, self-serving, often inaccurate versions of his own life story—stories that blur the line between myth and reality.

CHAPTER TWO

The Making of a Cult Leader

In early 2019, a political brawl broke out between President Trump and Congress over Trump's plan to build a wall on the U.S. southern border. This led to the longest government shutdown in history. For Trump, it was all about making good on a campaign promise. He threatened to—and later did—declare a national emergency, using false information about a huge migrant caravan supposedly filled with drug dealers and rapists to drum up fear and to justify his actions.[1] His insistence on a wall put more than 800,000 government employees out of work (and pay) for thirty-five days. Meanwhile, thousands of people, many fleeing dangerous situations in embattled Central American countries, were unable to exercise their legal right to seek asylum because of the backlog at the border. Trump's actions, which appealed to his most loyal base, constituted an unprecedented act from a man who is used to having his way—and using any means to get it.

Trump loves to wield authority, though he often does so in a ham-fisted and frenetic fashion. Like all cult leaders, he came to his authoritarian tendencies through a long and varied life, filled with a variety of formative experiences. He has reinvented himself many times—president is his latest manifestation. To hear him tell it, his life story is that of a self-made man who has weathered many ups and downs by dint of his personal attributes, and most of all, a belief in his own abilities.

Trump has seized upon and created opportunities, yes, but he has also been helped, and even rescued, many times—by his father, his creditors, by the Hollywood producer Mark Burnett, and later by those who helped make him president. Like all of us, Trump has been shaped by people and events that reach back decades in time, to his early childhood, and even before that.

To understand how he has come by his particular constellation of traits requires looking at his personal narrative. What is interesting is that though Trump's story diverges in many respects from other cult leaders—he was born into wealth, while many had much scrappier beginnings—it is possible to discern a pattern: a cold or absent mother, an authoritarian father or other relative, a childhood filled with acting out and aggressive behavior, in some cases exposure to a military setting, spending time with a church or set of teachings, and falling in with other authoritarian figures, in some cases other cult leaders.

Of course, Trump's story is uniquely his own, but what is striking considering his views on the Wall and the migrant caravan is how closely it resembles a classic immigrant tale.

In 1885, a thin, blond-haired man named Friedrich Drumpf—later changed to Frederick Trump—left the Bavarian town of Kallstadt carrying only a small suitcase, and arrived by boat in New York City at just sixteen years of age.[2] He worked as a barber before moving to the Pacific Northwest, where he made a name for himself running restaurants, boardinghouses, and brothels in the booming mining towns. In 1901, he returned to Kallstadt a wealthy man, where he met his wife, Elizabeth, and planned to settle, but the Bavarian authorities, ruling that he had emigrated to avoid military service, revoked his citizenship. After appealing unsuccessfully, the couple moved to New York, where Frederick successfully continued his work managing hotels and restaurants and developing real estate.

In 1905, the couple had a son, Fred. When Frederick died thirteen years later, during the 1918 flu pandemic, Elizabeth, displaying remarkable business talent, hired a contractor to build houses on an empty piece of property left to her by her husband. She sold them and lived off the mortgages paid by the new owners. When Fred was a teenager, she folded him into the business, founding Elizabeth Trump & Son (later known as the Trump Organization). Fred took to the business quickly, displaying a flair for showmanship and salesmanship, eventually becoming one of New York's biggest real estate developers.

He would go on to marry Scottish immigrant Mary MacLeod and have five children. The fourth, born in 1946, was Donald J. Trump. In 1950, Fred built, and moved his family into, a huge twenty-three-room, nine-bathroom redbrick mansion, staffed with a cook and chauffeur and fully equipped with a color television, a luxury back then, and an intercom system.[3] Sophisticated and impeccably dressed, Mary played the "perfect housewife." As Trump remembers in *The Art of the Deal,* she was "enthralled by the pomp and circumstance," and seemed happy to take on the societal duties as the wife of a real estate mogul.

MARY, FRED, AND DONALD

Mary was apparently less enthusiastic about her maternal duties. Trump's childhood friends report that they rarely saw her. "His father would be around and watch him play. His mom didn't interact in that way."[4] Though Mary clearly played a role in young Trump's life, it is defined, in some ways, by her absence. To this day, Trump rarely mentions her. "You don't have to be Freud or Fellini to interpret this," said Mark Smaller, past president of the American Psychoanalytic Association (APA), speaking with Michael Kruse for his *Politico* article, "The Mystery of Mary Trump."[5] Kruse quotes other experts, including past APA president Prudence Gourguechon, who describes the all-important role that the mother plays in establishing the cognitive and emotional architecture of a person. "The capacity to trust.

A sense of security versus insecurity. Knowing what's real and what's not real. Your mother helps you identify your feelings and develop a cognitive structure so you don't have to act on them immediately. And I think it's fair to say that the capacity for empathy develops through your maternal relationship."[6]

A disruption in the bonding process, called "insecure parental attachment," during the first two years of life can predispose a person to developing a narcissistic personality disorder, which we will explore in the next chapter. It turns out that several cult leaders, including Charles Manson, Jim Jones, and David Koresh, had problematic relationships with their mothers, and in some cases no relationship at all. Manson's mother would go out drinking and actually went to prison for robbery, and would abandon him to relatives or neighbors. Koresh grew up believing his aunt was his mother and spent time shuffling between relatives' houses. Jones's mother was out working, leaving him to wander the neighborhood even as a toddler.

By Trump's own account, the most formative influence on him was his father. Tough, demanding, and a workaholic—he wore a tie and jacket even at home—Fred was not an affectionate parent, which was true of many men of his generation. He was hypercritical and did not offer praise. According to Harry Hurt III, author of *Lost Tycoon: The Many Lives of Donald J. Trump*, ever since he was a little boy, Trump's father had been "hammering the same lines into his head: You are a killer . . . You are a king . . . You are a killer . . . You are a king. Donald believes he can't be one without the other."[7] Fred would also point out repeatedly, "Most people are weaklings. Only the strong survive."[8] According to Leonard Cruz, author of *A Clear and Present Danger: Narcissism in the Era of President Trump*, children who have experienced a lack of warm parental affection can behave in inappropriate ways. "It might evoke ways of acting that are increasingly bombastic and attention-seeking. The child becomes almost exaggerated in the ways they try to court attention."[9]

By his own admission, Trump was a difficult child. As he confessed in *The Art of the Deal*, "I was a very assertive, aggressive kid. In the second grade, I actually gave a teacher a black eye—I punched my music teacher because I didn't think he knew anything about music and I almost got expelled. I'm not proud of that, but it's clear evidence that even early on I had a tendency to stand up and make my opinions known in a very forceful way. The difference now is that I like to use my brain instead of my fists."[10]

Jim Jones would get into shouting matches on the school grounds. In his book, *Raven: The Untold Story of the Rev. Jim Jones and His People*, Tim Reiterman quotes Jones as saying: "I was ready to kill by the end of the third grade. I was so fucking aggressive and hostile. . . . Nobody give [sic] me any love, any understanding." Future cult leader Charles Manson would get others to do his bidding. As a youth, he persuaded girls to beat up boys he didn't like, and would insist the girls had acted on their own—a foreshadowing of his later actions. Shoko Asahara, the leader of Aum Shinrikyo, was born sightless in one eye and attended a school for the blind. Though his partial sightedness elevated him to the role of protector, he occasionally acted as a bully, reportedly breaking a classmate's eardrum in a fight. When chastised, he threatened to burn down the dormitory.[11]

As a child, Trump misbehaved so often and was sent to detention so frequently that his initials, DT, became his friends' shorthand for "punishment."[12] One student, Steven Nachtigall, now a doctor, described Trump as a "loudmouth bully" who once jumped off his bike to "pummel" another boy.[13] Charles Walker, one of Trump's teachers, after learning of Trump's presidential run, reportedly described him in even less flattering terms: "Even then he was a little shit." Trump would later describe his approach: "When somebody tries to push me around, when they're after my ass, I push back a hell of a lot harder than I was pushed in the first place."

"GOD'S SALESMAN"

Trump's early and aggressive quest for attention and validation would find an outlet in the teachings of Norman Vincent Peale, who was the pastor of Marble Collegiate Church, located on West Twenty-Ninth Street in New York City. Fred was an avid follower and would travel with his family into Manhattan every Sunday to hear Peale's sermons. When Peale first began preaching at Marble Collegiate, he spoke to sparsely filled pews—only a few hundred attendees in a space designed for thousands. Peale would soon change that by offering his congregants a more dynamic and supposedly pragmatic view of Christianity.

"We have made the mistake of thinking that Christianity is a creed to be recited," he wrote. "On the contrary, it is a power to be tapped."[14] Peale's influence grew quickly. He would host a long-running weekly radio program, called *The Art of Living;* found the organization and magazine *Guideposts;* and write several books, including *You Can Win* and *The Power of Positive Thinking.* The latter became a huge bestseller, selling millions of copies and remaining on the *New York Times'* bestseller list for 186 weeks. With chapter titles like "Expect the Best and Get It," and "I Don't Believe in Defeat," Peale's book promised absolute self-confidence and practically made self-doubt the work of the devil.

"BELIEVE IN YOURSELF! Have faith in your abilities," the book begins, painting a bold, black-and-white ideology. "Without a humble but reasonable confidence in your own powers you cannot be successful or happy, but with sound self-confidence you can succeed. A sense of inferiority and inadequacy interferes with the attainment of your hopes, but self-confidence leads to self-realization and successful achievement."

Nicknamed "God's salesman," Peale taught a kind of forerunner to contemporary prosperity gospel—if you believe in yourself 100 percent and pray for financial success, God will grant you blessings. In a religious tradition where material wealth and success are the consequences of faith, poverty and failure are the wages of sin and doubt.

Peale taught his followers to control their thoughts by pushing aside self-doubt, a form of self-hypnosis akin to thought stopping. Such a practice banishes doubt but also leaves no room for skepticism, criticism, introspection, or any of the other tools necessary for free thought.[15] The flip side was a kind of positive magical thinking: if you think and will something strongly enough, you can make it happen—a

kind of early version of the new age "wishful thinking" philosophy offered in *The Secret, The Law of Attraction,* and other works. Charles
Manson learned a similar approach through a Dale Carnegie course
he took when he was a young man in prison, doing time for a car
theft. As Jeff Guinn observed in his biography, *Manson: The Life and
Times of Charles Manson,* later in life, people would say it was like he
could read their minds. " 'He came and talked to me and it was like he
was immediately the friend I'd wanted and had never had.' Every line
he used, almost word for word, comes from a Dale Carnegie textbook
called *How to Win Friends and Influence People.*"[16]

Theological critics accused Peale of making religion about the
person, and not about God.[17] Mental health experts denounced his
techniques as dangerous, possibly leading to delusions and harmful
behavior, despite Peale's inclusion of unnamed "scientific studies"
that supported his philosophy.[18]

Peale was enormously popular with the Trumps, and especially
young Donald. "I still remember [Peale's] sermons," Trump told the
Iowa Family Leadership Summit in July 2015. "You could listen to
him all day long. And when you left the church, you were disappointed it was over. He was the greatest guy." According to Trump,
the feeling was mutual: "He thought I was the greatest student of all
time."[19]

Peale remained connected to Trump for years. He would offici-
ate at Trump's first wedding, to Ivana, as well as the weddings of
Trump's two sisters, Maryanne and Elizabeth, and also at the funerals
of Fred and Mary.[20] Trump would often quote or thank Peale. In a
2009 interview, Trump credited Peale's teachings with helping him
survive his bankruptcies and other financial hard times. "I refused to
give in to the negative circumstances and never lost faith in myself. I
didn't believe I was finished even when the newspapers were saying
so," he said.[21] In August 2015 then-candidate Trump told reporters,
"I am a Presbyterian Protestant. I go to Marble Collegiate Church,"
adding that he tried to attend church as often as possible, even while
traveling. Soon after, Marble Collegiate Church—which is Reformed
Protestant rather than Presbyterian—published a statement saying

that though Trump has a "longstanding history" with the church, he was "not an active member of Marble."[22]

Whether or not he attended the church, Trump's debt to Peale is undeniable. Trump's extreme self-confidence, bordering on grandiosity; his refusal to negotiate or take no for an answer; his predator-versus-prey stance toward other people; his taste for winning—all were forged in part during those Sunday morning sermons. Years later, Trump would draw upon Peale's positive thinking ideology in his own "sermons"—his campaign speeches before thousands of cheering followers.

MILITARY SCHOOL

As Michael Kranish and Marc Fisher describe in their book, *Trump Revealed*, Trump was finishing seventh grade, and still getting into a fair amount of trouble, when Fred, furious over his discovery of a set of knives that his son had been collecting, decided to enroll him in the New York Military Academy, a boarding school miles away from his Queens home.[23] As Michael D'Antonio writes in his biography, *Never Enough: Donald Trump and the Pursuit of Success*, this was a "profound rejection of Donald,"[24] one that he apparently took quite personally.

At boarding school, Trump met a man who would become his new taskmaster. Colonel Theodore Dobias was a World War II vet who did not suffer fools gladly. Nor did he care about heritage or how much money a family had. As Trump describes in *The Art of the Deal*, "Like so many strong guys, Dobias had a tendency to go for the jugular if he smelled weakness. On the other hand, if he sensed strength but you didn't try to undermine him, he treated you like a man. From the time I figured that out—and it was more an instinct than a conscious thought—we got along great."[25]

Trump, the hypercompetitive boy, blossomed at the academy, even if he did keep up his reputation as a bully—he once tried to push a fellow cadet out of a second-floor window during a fight.[26] Even away from home, Trump was following the guidance of his disciplinarian dad—that in life, there were killers and prey, and to succeed you needed to be a killer. Tony Schwartz, Trump's ghostwriter for *The Art of the Deal*, stated in an interview: "You either created and exploited fear, or you succumbed to it, as he thought his older brother had. This narrow, defensive outlook took hold at a very early age, and it never evolved."[27] Trump's brother, Fred Jr., died of alcoholism at the age of forty-three, a reason that Trump says he does not drink or smoke.

Fascinated with Hollywood and moviemaking, Donald wanted to attend the University of Southern California but was rejected.[28] He enrolled instead at nearby Fordham University. After two years, he transferred to the University of Pennsylvania's Wharton School of Business, where he graduated without honors.[29]

EMULATING FRED

In 1968, Trump began working with his dad, snatching up middle- and low-income housing throughout the outer boroughs of New York City. Successful as Fred was, his business practices had come into question. There were whispers that he was a swindler with racist tendencies. In 1927, on Memorial Day, a thousand Ku Klux Klansmen clashed with police on the streets of Queens.[30] Fred, then twenty-one, was one of seven men arrested in connection with the riot.[31] This reputation followed him as his son Donald joined the family business. In 1973, Fred and Donald Trump were accused of "racially discriminatory conduct" and sued by the Civil Rights Division of the U.S. Justice Department for creating a "substantial impediment to the full enjoyment of equal opportunity" at Trump buildings.[32] The case would later be enshrined in pop culture. Woody Guthrie, who had lived in the Trump-owned Beach Haven apartments from 1950 to 1952, wrote a song called "Old Man Trump."[33]

> *I suppose that Old Man Trump knows just how much racial hate*
> *He stirred up in the blood pot of human hearts*
> *When he drawed that color line*
> *Here at his Beach Haven family project.*

Trump's early years in Queens may shed light on his later policies as president. In a *New York Times* opinion piece, Thomas B. Edsall quotes Harvard sociologist Robert Sampson as saying, "[I]t was no accident that *All in The Family* was set in Queens. The explosion of immigration and the racial change in the makeup of Queens might have left an especially deep imprint, because [Trump's] constant references to making America great again evoke an earlier time that was considerably less diverse. Indeed, building walls and stemming the tide of such change seems to be at the heart of Trump's appeals to a remembered national past, and in this case, of his childhood."[34]

ROY COHN'S INFLUENCE

After the Justice Department charges were made, the Trumps needed big legal guns to represent them. Enter Roy Cohn—a blustery, brutally coldhearted lawyer, famous for his harsh prosecution during the McCarthy anticommunist congressional hearings in the 1950s.[35] As the story goes, Trump met Cohn at Le Club, a hot midtown night spot, and asked him how they should counter the racial discrimination claim. "Tell them to go to hell and fight the thing in court and let them prove you discriminated," Cohn reportedly replied. The Trumps ultimately settled.[36]

That night a friendship was formed. Trump gained a confidant and mentor, one who would teach him how to maneuver his way, using tricky business practices and ruthless negotiating tactics that would make them both a lot of money. Cohn was an attack dog who went on the offense whenever threatened, a style Trump would take to heart. In a profile in *Esquire,* Ken Auletta described Cohn as "a legal executioner—the toughest, meanest, vilest, and one of the most brilliant lawyers in America. He is not a very nice man." Scientology leader L. Ron Hubbard would practice a similar style—"never defend, always attack," and would send his followers, and even hire agents, to harass, sue, or trick perceived enemies, a practice he called "fair game."

Trump was not Cohn's only client—he also represented mafia bosses, like Fat Tony Salerno and Carmine Gallante.[37] Most likely through Cohn, Trump made extensive use of mob-owned construction companies. Construction in New York was rife with mob ties—it was hard to be in real estate and *not* be in business with them. Yet we know from various reportage by journalists Wayne Barrett, David Cay Johnston, and others that the ties between Trump and the mob go back decades.[38] And we know through records of a federal investigation in 1986 that he hired mafia-owned firms to build Trump Tower and Trump Plaza, including a concrete company controlled by Salerno and the head of the Gambino family, Paul Castellano.[39] The New York construction industries were famously corrupt, but with Cohn presumably acting as an intermediary, Trump's projects were built on schedule. His involvement with the mob continued as he established his real estate career.

MOVING ON UP

The father-son team continued developing mostly low- and middle-income properties in Brooklyn and Queens. At some point, the younger Trump decided to make a name for himself. Using that now famous million-dollar "very small" loan from Dad—the *New York Times* recently estimated that Trump's father actually lent him more than $60 million—he set out to make his own flashy mark in New York City. His unconventional business practices helped him get the backing to branch out beyond the outer boroughs, over the bridge, and into Manhattan, where he took a big gamble and transformed the old Commodore Hotel into the sparkling Grand Hyatt. In 1979 he broke ground on what would become the opulent Trump Tower, which dripped with gold and marble.[40]

In 1985, he acquired the abandoned rail yards along a stretch of the west side of Manhattan. "No sooner had I announced my plans publicly than other bidders for the rail yards suddenly came out of the woodwork," Trump wrote in *The Art of the Deal*. "I'm the first to admit that I am very competitive and that I'll do nearly anything within legal bounds to win. Sometimes, part of making a deal is denigrating your competition."[41]

Having made his mark in New York City, Trump went on to place a bigger bet by buying up hotels and casinos, and also land from mob-owned sources, in Atlantic City, New Jersey. New Jersey had legalized gambling in 1977. Disappointed that New York hadn't opened up the state for gambling, Trump started looking south for new opportunities. Trump Plaza opened in 1984, and soon after, Trump Castle & Casino. Still wanting more, Trump poured nearly $500 million into the making of the glitzy Taj Mahal. Initially this buying spree gave him a big payday and made him a household name. Everything he touched seemed to turn to gold. He wrote his bestselling book, *The Art of the Deal*, with ghostwriter Tony Schwartz. In it they drew a vivid picture of a shrewd, rich, brash, and successful businessman, one who lived by an eat-or-be-eaten understanding of the world. Trump also made movie cameos and plastered his name on everything from steaks to airplanes. He married a model, Ivana Zelníčková, in 1977, with Reverend Peale presiding, and had three children: Donald Jr., Ivanka, and Eric. Ivana would become a vital part of the Trump Organization, leading the design of Trump Tower and overseeing the revamp of Trump Castle Hotel & Casino.

It was at the Jersey Shore in the late 1980s that Trump embraced the boxing world, hosting a number of matches promoted by silver-haired Don King. He also hosted two World Wrestling Entertainment (WWE) events—Wrestlemania IV and V. It had been the glory days for the sport, with the likes of Hulk Hogan and Randy Savage storming the ring for an outsize takedown that would be viewed by millions of fans. WWE's rough-and-tumble, ready-for TV antics seemed simpatico with Trump's larger than life personality. The audience knows the fights are all scripted but the old story line of good versus evil draws people in—a story that Trump the politician would use over and over.

Trump remained friends with WWE chairman and CEO Vince McMahon and his wife, Linda, over the years. The McMahons would donate generously to Trump's presidential campaign—it's been claimed that they were his biggest donors, at $4 million.[42] In 2016, Trump would appoint Linda to be administrator of the Small Business Administration.[43]

In 1989, when Trump hosted Wrestlemania V, the economy had tanked. The Taj Mahal's renovations had already cost more than $800 million. Trump was suddenly looking at two bankruptcies—the Taj Mahal in 1991 and Trump Plaza in 1992. His other casinos were drying up and the Trump Shuttle, his vanity airline brand, had been grounded. He had to sell his yacht. According to a *New York Times* report, Trump's losses between 1985 and 1994 totaled $1.17 billion.[44] On top of all this, his fourteen-year marriage to Ivana ended, following a scandalous affair with a former beauty queen, Marla Maples.[45]

Maples and Trump's relationship made for salacious headlines and gossip fodder for more than a year. As the story goes, Trump brought Marla to Aspen, Colorado, on a family vacation, where she confronted Ivana. In October 1993, Marla had a daughter, Tiffany, with Trump. The couple soon married, though they divorced six years later. In 2005, Trump married the Slovenian born model Melania Knauss, who bore him a son, Barron. A few months later, Trump would allegedly have a secret affair with the porn star and director Stormy Daniels. The hugely publicized affair with Maples had already earned Trump a reputation as a womanizer—one he did little to refute. In fact, he seemed to revel in it, often speaking with radio show host Howard Stern about his conquests and, on one occasion, with the *Access Hollywood* host Billy Bush. It was during this conversation that Trump made his infamous remarks about how being a star allowed him to grab women by the genitals. A recording of his conversation with Bush would surface during his 2016 campaign. In general, Trump's misogynistic views on women would make for controversy as he ran for president in 2016.

THE COMEBACK KID

Trump's various bankruptcies and scandals did not keep him down for long. He made his comeback on TV, finding a kindred spirit in Mark Burnett, the hugely successful producer of the reality show *Survivor.*[46] Burnett had the idea to make an urban jungle version of *Survivor*. Using his classic reality-competition formula, a powerful CEO would

pit corporate hopefuls against each other for a job. He needed someone bigger than life, someone who had a recognizable name, someone
with "feral charisma." When he saw Trump at an event, he knew he
had found his man.

Like his other reality shows, the drama was synthetically ratch-
eted up on the new show, *The Apprentice*. In her book, *Unhinged*,
Omarosa Manigault Newman describes the advice she was given from
a TV production friend before starting the show, "Reality TV is about
conflict and tension." Omarosa was told to be the one starting a fight,
stirring one up or breaking one up.

At the time, casting Trump as host was seen as a huge gamble.
He had been labeled a "D-lister"—someone who lost all his money, a
clownlike figure who couldn't be taken seriously. Supervising editor
of *The Apprentice* Jonathon Braun told the *New Yorker*, "We knew
Trump was a fake . . . but we made him out to be the most important
person in the world, making the court jester the king."[47] The smoke
and mirrors worked. Burnett and Trump agreed to be partners. The
show was a phenomenal success, making hundreds of millions of dollars and searing Trump's name into the public consciousness.

Some say the show launched Trump's presidential campaign by
rehabilitating his image into a "Master of the Universe," a self-made
man who typified the American dream. "Mark Burnett's show was the
single biggest factor in putting Trump in the national spotlight," said
ghostwriter Tony Schwartz.

The relationship with Burnett would continue beyond Trump's
stint on the show. They remain good friends and, outside of criticizing the way Trump ran his 2016 campaign, Burnett hasn't said or
done anything to criticize Trump's actions as president. In addition,
he has not yielded to calls to release the *Apprentice* tapes that are
purported to have captured damaging racist and sexist remarks from
Trump. Burnett, a devout evangelical Christian, along with his wife
the actress-producer Roma Downey, introduced Trump at the 2018
annual National Prayer Breakfast, held in Washington, D.C., an event
that was founded by the conservative Christian foundation the Fellowship, also known as the Family.

THE TRUMP BRAND

Trump took advantage of his newly burnished celebrity by promoting self-branded companies and aggressively seeking out licensing deals. He made dozens of deals over the years, including Trump hotels, Trump golf courses, Trump Steaks, *Trump Magazine,* Trump: The Game, and Trump Fragrance. In 2009, he licensed his name to the Trump Network for an undisclosed sum.[48]

The Trump Network was a rebranding of a pseudo-medical vitamin company called Ideal Health, founded in 1997 by three alumni of the multilevel marketing organization NuSkin—Lou DeCapri and brothers Todd and Scott Stanwood. In their sales materials, they promised that "Ideal Health is the only company in America that puts the power to regain nutritional balance and restore metabolic health back in your hands." They promised miracles in bottles. The company was actually another pyramid-style scheme that relied on recruiting a vast network of people to sell questionable products using questionable practices. They promised great wealth to its network of salespeople but it was typically only those at the very top of the pyramid who made money.[49] The founders were thrilled to have Trump as the public face promoting their products. In a sales video, they proclaim "It's a no brainer. That brings so much to the [network marketing] industry, it brings credibility, it brings us to a new level. Because everyone recognizes and trusts that Trump brand name."[50]

Though Trump had no role in the development or manufacturing of the products, he began speaking at conferences in Miami and Las Vegas, allowing his name and family crest to be used in promotional materials, and appearing in at least one online video to promote the business.[51] The Trump name was gold to people who worked for Ideal. "Oh, my god, people cried when they heard it was him," says Jenna Knudsen, a former salesperson for Ideal Health. "They cried and looked at each other and said, 'We're going to be millionaires!'"[52]

The partnership initially paid off. Between 2009 and 2010, the Trump Network grew more than 300 percent.[53] Trump received millions from his name and endorsement. There was little effort to determine whether the products actually worked, or whether the organization was sound. In their *Daily Beast* article, "Trump Vitamins were Fortified with B.S.," Abby Haglage and Tim Mak quote Pieter Cohen, a Harvard doctor specializing in supplements, as saying that there was "zero evidence" to back up the company's claims about their products. "This is a scam, it's a bogus program to make profit for the people who are selling it. It's fantasy," Cohen said.[54]

Eventually the company struggled, receiving repeated Federal Trade Commission complaints and lawsuits alleging everything from defrauding its salespeople to making bogus medical claims. In 2012 its remaining assets were sold.

Then there was Trump University, which ran from 2005 until 2010. Millions of dollars were spent on marketing the eponymous university as a place where one could learn Trump's real estate investment secrets. Students would shell out thousands of dollars for expensive seminars and retreats but were not taught any investment secrets. A 2013 lawsuit alleged aggressive, even illegal, sales tactics including deception, outright lies, and other undue influence maneuvers. Trump tried to fight it but a judge decided to let the case go to trial as a class-action lawsuit.[55] The trial was set for late November 2016. On November 18, ten days before the trial date, Trump decided to settle the case for $25 million. By then he had been elected president.

EYES ON THE PRIZE

It turns out, Trump was considering the presidency as early as 1980. In an interview that year, TV personality Rona Barrett asked Trump: "Would you like to be the president of the United States?"

"I really don't believe I would, Rona," Trump answered. "Because I think it's a very mean life. I would love, and I would dedicate my life to this country, but I see it as being a mean life, and I also see [that] somebody with strong views, and somebody with the kind of views that are maybe a little bit unpopular—which may be right, but may

CHAPTER THREE

The Cult Leader Profile

In April 2017, a group of distinguished psychiatrists and mental health professionals convened at Yale School of Medicine to discuss an extraordinarily delicate conundrum: the mental health of the president of the United States. Alarmed by the way Donald Trump conducted his campaign and also by his communications and actions as president, and feeling a strong duty to warn the public, they decided to publish their views in a book, edited by Yale forensic psychiatrist Bandy X. Lee, called *The Dangerous Case of Donald Trump*. Although they stopped short of making a formal diagnosis, the authors found abundant evidence that Trump exhibited a disturbing and dangerous psychological pattern: narcissistic tendencies, impulsivity, delusions, paranoia, xenophobia, misogyny, inability to take ownership of errors, pathological lying, and extreme hedonism.

"Aren't all presidents narcissists?" some may ask. The office selects for, and may even require, a certain amount of narcissistic behavior.[1] That may be truer of recent presidents.[2] To deal with the constant pressure and scrutiny of the office, as well as handle the weight of responsibility for the health and safety of millions of Americans, presidents need a strong, if not inflated, sense of self. They must be driven by the belief that they are the best person to run the country. It takes enormous confidence, boldness, and bravado—as well as focus and persistence—to realize that dream. Small wonder that the job selects for a kind of flamboyance and assertive and interpersonal style—what might be called "grandiose narcissism." A recent study ranked past presidents according to their degree of grandiose narcissism. Lyndon Johnson came out on top, followed by Teddy Roosevelt, Franklin Roosevelt, Andrew Jackson, John F. Kennedy, and Bill Clinton.[3]

Narcissism is not a disorder by itself—everyone may have a streak of it. We all want "to stand out from the rest of the seven billion people on the planet," writes Craig Malkin, clinical psychologist and lecturer in psychology at Harvard Medical School. Healthy narcissism—the desire to feel appreciated and special—can even be beneficial. It can make people feel less anxious and depressed and more effective in the world. It becomes pathological, Malkin writes, when a person becomes so addicted to feeling special that they'd do anything to get their high, including lie, cheat, steal, betray, or even hurt those closest to them.

There is an even more dangerous kind of narcissism, one defined by a darker and more destructive pattern. It is fittingly called "malignant narcissism" and arises when narcissism combines with other psychopathological traits. According to Malkin, political leaders such as Hitler, Vladimir Putin, and Kim Jong-un exhibit malignant narcissism. As Robert Jay Lifton notes in *The Dangerous Case of Donald Trump*, such narcissism in a leader can lead to a "malignant normality"—a term Lifton coined while studying Nazi doctors, who carried out terrible experiments but were able to justify and normalize them through a kind of "adaptation to evil." Lifton's point is that people can come to accept aberrant and even pathological behavior as the new norm, especially when it is exhibited by an authority figure. He applies this to Trump. "Because he is president and operates within the broad contours and interactions of the presidency, there is a tendency to view what he does as simply part of our democratic process."

This process of rationalizing and adapting to a "new normal" happens all the time in destructive cults, and it does so, as I have said, through a systematic indoctrination process. But it all starts with the leader. Like Putin and Kim, cult leaders such as Sun Myung Moon, L. Ron Hubbard (Scientology), Jim Jones (Peoples Temple), David Koresh (Branch Davidians), Warren Jeffs (Fundamentalist Church of Christ of Latter-Day Saints, or FLDS), Bhagwan Shree Rajneesh (Rajneesh Movement), and Keith Raniere (NXIVM) display many traits associated with malignant narcissism. They all fit a similar pattern: grandiose, arrogant, bombastic, supremely confident, demanding of attention and admiration, rarely admitting a mistake. They were known to lie, cheat, and steal without apparent conscience and even empathy. The question is, to what extent does Trump exhibit the malignant narcissistic profile of a destructive cult leader?

MALIGNANT NARCISSISM

It was the social psychologist Erich Fromm who, in 1964, first coined the term malignant narcissism. He did so to describe what he thought was the most severe mental sickness, one that represented the "quintessence of evil," mostly because of the lack of empathy and morality on the part of the patient. Though the diagnostic bible of the American Psychiatric Association—the *Diagnostic and Statistical Manual of Mental Disorders, 5th Edition* (DSM-5)—does not recognize malignant narcissism as a distinct type of narcissism,[4] researchers suggest that it combines narcissistic personality disorder with three additional psychopathologies: antisocial behavior, self-affirming sadism, and paranoia.[5]

NARCISSISTIC PERSONALITY DISORDER

People with narcissistic personality disorder display a characteristic pattern of traits: 1) grandiose self-centered behavior; 2) fantasies of power, success, and attractiveness; 3) a need for praise and admiration; 4) a sense of entitlement; and 5) a lack of empathy, which can lead them to exploit, bully, shame, and demean others, without guilt or remorse.[6] Yet, as Philip Zimbardo and Rosemary Sword write in *The Dangerous Case of Donald Trump,* "What lies underneath this personality type is often very low self-esteem."[7] Below the surface, they are plagued by feelings of inferiority, emptiness, and boredom, which in turn help to fuel the first pattern of traits. Cult leaders seem to be especially prone to this vicious cycle.

GRANDIOSITY:
EXAGGERATION OF TALENTS AND ACHIEVEMENTS

Sun Myung Moon claimed that he was the greatest man who ever lived—greater than Moses, Buddha, and Muhammad and "ten times greater than Jesus." "Out of all the saints sent by God, I think I am the most successful one already," he said at one of his meetings.[8] He also claimed to possess superior military prowess. "I am a master tactician or strategist. When I plan, I execute the plan. And when I execute a certain battle plan, I will always come with a better result than any other tactician in history. The Korean government learned many tactics from me. And America is going to be learning much from my strategies."[9]

Jim Jones made only slightly less grandiose claims. "At various times, he claimed that he was either Lenin, Jesus Christ, or one of a variety of other religious or political figures," said Deborah Layton Blakey, a close aide of Jones, who fled Jonestown before the mass murder in 1978. She remembers him talking incessantly. "He claimed that he had divine powers and could heal the sick. He stated that he had extraordinary perception and could tell what everyone was thinking. He said that he had powerful connections the world over, including the Mafia, Idi Amin, and the Soviet government."[10]

Trump has also claimed a powerful and special relationship with the Soviet Union, in particular leader Vladimir Putin, not to mention other authoritarian leaders such as Recep Tayyip Erdogan and Kim Jong-un. As president, he actually does have those relationships but, according to his claims, that was true before he ever met these leaders. Even then, he intimated that his relationships were much more powerful and special than those held by previous occupants of the office. In his dealings with Kim, in particular, he depended on his personal charisma and self-proclaimed prowess as a dealmaker to negotiate a nuclear disarmament, with disappointing results.

Domestically, he exaggerated and embellished his expertise and abilities from the start of his campaign, in interviews, tweets, and rallies. "Nobody will be tougher on ISIS than me. Nobody," he said during his campaign announcement speech on June 16, 2015. "There's nobody bigger or better at the military than I am," he stated a few days later. The following month came this memorably hypnotic line, one that echoes Moon's language: "I know more about offense and defense than [the generals] will ever understand, believe me. Believe me. Than they will ever understand. Than they will ever understand." It's a classic example of Trump's tried-and-true habit of lulling his audience through repetition. A few months later came another infamous claim: "I know more about ISIS [the Islamic State militant group] than the generals do. Believe me."

It turns out Donald Trump has claimed to know more than anyone else about many things—renewables, social media, debt, banking, Wall Street bankers, money, the U.S. government, campaign contributions, politicians, Senator Cory Booker, trade, jobs, infrastructure, defense, the "horror of nuclear" [sic], and the visa system.[11] The expression is typically, "Nobody knows more about [fill-in the blank] than I do," with a few notable embellishments:

- "I know our complex tax laws better than anyone who has ever run for president and am the only one who can fix them."—tweet from October 2, 2016
- "I would build a great wall, and nobody builds walls better than me, believe me, and I'll build them very inexpensively, I will build a great, great wall on our southern border. And I will have Mexico pay for that wall. Mark my words."—presidential campaign announcement speech, June 16, 2015
- "Nobody has ever done so much in the first two years of a presidency as this administration. Nobody. Nobody."—political rally in Biloxi, Mississippi, November 26, 2018

FANTASIES OF SUCCESS,
POWER, AND ATTRACTIVENESS

Narcissists spin self-glorifying fantasies—about their power, wealth, intelligence, looks—to help make them feel in control and special, and also to cope with stress. "Since reality doesn't support their grandiose view of themselves, narcissists live in a fantasy world propped up by distortion, self-deception, and magical thinking," psychologist and health writer Melinda Smith explains. "These fantasies protect them from feelings of inner emptiness and shame, so facts and opinions that contradict them are ignored or rationalized."[12] Narcissists have difficulty handling even the most constructive criticism and may feel shame and humiliation when criticized or rejected.

Keith Raniere, the founder of NXIVM, claimed to be one of the smartest people in the world. "We were told that Keith is a genius with an IQ of 240, who was speaking in full sentences at the age of one, that he was a concert pianist, he was the east coast judo champion at 11, he earned degrees in mathematics, biology, and physics," said Sarah Edmondson, a former NXIVM member who has now come out against the group.[13]

L. Ron Hubbard claimed to be a nuclear physicist, though he flunked a course in atomic and molecular physics before being suspended for deficiencies in scholarship. He also talked about having made "the greatest discovery in 50,000 years."[14] It is in some ways fitting that the science he is best known for is science fiction—and of course, Scientology.

Donald Trump has often bragged about his intelligence, power, sexual prowess, looks, and most of all, his wealth. He was proud of his looks in his youth and even now appears to take pride in what he sees in the mirror. "Other than the blond hair, when I was growing up, they said I looked like Elvis," he told a 2018 rally in Tupelo, Mississippi, Presley's birthplace. The audience cheered. In April 2016, then sixty-nine-year-old Trump told a crowd in Pennsylvania, "Do I look like a president? How handsome am I, right? How handsome?"

Trump also likes to boast about his personal power—a power so great that he could famously "stand in the middle of Fifth Avenue and shoot somebody" and still win votes. He has also boasted about his sexual conquests, most infamously on the 2005 *Access Hollywood* tape, in which he claimed that because of his celebrity, he could grab women by their genitals.

Wealth is what Trump likes to brag about most. And it is his wealth that is the most debatable, especially since, contrary to presidential norms, he has not released his tax returns. In 2015, as he entered the presidential race, Trump claimed he was worth $8.7 billion, more than double *Forbes* magazine's tally at the time of $4.1 billion. Trump often took offense if anyone questioned this number, as he did with Timothy O'Brien, author of *Trump Nation: The Art of Being the Donald,* who estimated Trump's wealth between $150 million and $250 million. (He sued O'Brien for defamation in 2006, but a judge dismissed the case.)[15]

In June 2015 he told *The Des Moines Register,* "I'm the most successful person ever to run for the presidency, by far. Nobody's ever been more successful than me. I'm the most successful person ever to run. Ross Perot isn't successful like me. Romney—I have a Gucci store that's worth more than Romney."[16] Whether or not any of this is true, Trump's calculation appears to have paid off. Many people claimed to have voted for him for his business savvy, a reputation conjured and cultivated during his fourteen seasons on *The Apprentice.*

EXCESSIVE ADMIRATION

Due to a lack of affection during childhood, narcissists crave not just approval but admiration to help bolster a fragile ego.[17] They will manipulate people in order to get that attention.[18] For some cult leaders the need goes beyond admiration to pure devotion.

Moon demanded that we bow and kneel in our small meetings with him. At meetings, he would sometimes bring a member onstage and kick or hit them with a stick and then ask: "If I did this to you, would you still follow me?" The audience would roar their approval.

L. Ron Hubbard used to rehearse what he called his "Affirmations," which included, "All men shall be my slaves! All women shall succumb to my charms! All mankind shall grovel at my feet and know why!"[19]

Lyndon LaRouche's need for devotion was so great that members of his cult were encouraged—"forced, if not physically, then psychologically"—to abort their babies so that there would be no "higher loyalty . . . than their loyalty to LaRouche.[20] "Making men in my own image was the conscious articulation of my central purpose from approximately 1946," he wrote in his 1979 autobiography.[21]

Trump may not go quite that far but his need for admiration was plain to see during his 2016 campaign rallies, where he seemed to implore his audience to cheer not just for his policies but for him. That need was also clear from the moment he stepped into the White House. Immediately after his inauguration, his press secretary Sean Spicer announced that the event attracted "the largest audience to ever witness an inauguration—period—both in person and around the globe." These were still early days, and many were perplexed that he could make such a blatantly false statement—there was photographic proof that it wasn't true. It is striking that the size of the audience would remain an issue for Trump long after his inauguration. He would continue to bring it up months later, displaying his narcissistic need for attention and glory.

Like Spicer, former Trump attorney Michael Cohen was willing to lie—and also cheat and steal—for his boss. "One man who wants to do so much good with so many detractors against him needs support," Cohen reportedly said about Trump, before he turned against him. "I'm the guy who protects the president and the family. I'm the guy who would take a bullet for the president."[22]

Cognitive neuroscientist Ian Robertson states that the need for admiration "makes the narcissist's ego a little like an electric car with a limited range before its batteries need recharging, making it dependent on the availability of charging stations."[23] For Trump, campaign rallies were those charging stations while on the road to the White House—so much so that Trump continued to hold rallies even after he became president.

Then there is the president's love affair with Fox News. The conservative network is part of the machine that praises everything that the president does and demonizes his perceived enemies—from former FBI director James Comey and other FBI agents, to Democrats like Hillary Clinton, former staff members, and women who have come forward to accuse Trump of sexual harassment.

But most of all Trump seems to have it out for former president Barack Obama. There are some who believe that he decided to run for president after being roasted by Obama at the White House Correspondents' Association dinner in 2011, though he denies it.[24] Others have suggested that Trump is jealous of Obama's looks, intelligence, and class, and even of the size of his inauguration audience. "Trump hates Obama because he can't measure up to him. Obama is younger, thinner, better-looking and smarter," writes Carolyn Banks in the *Austin American Statesman*. "Come on, wouldn't you then want all things Obama gone?"[25] Beyond his own personal issues, Trump—like many Republicans and the right-wing media—blames many governmental problems on Obama, and has spent much of his time in office trying to dismantle the former president's many accomplishments.

SENSE OF ENTITLEMENT

Narcissists believe that they are so exceptional that they are entitled to get whatever they want—wealth, sex, devotion, special treatment.

David Koresh, of the Branch Davidians, believed his power was so great that only he had the authority to "give the seed." In fact, he made that happen. Married couples were expected to remain celibate while he had sex with many female members, the youngest of whom was ten. Women claimed to be in the "House of David" when they were pregnant. Warren Jeffs, jailed leader of the Fundamentalist Church of Jesus Christ of Latter-Day Saints (FLDS), had seventy-four wives and fifty-three children.

Hubbard believed he deserved a Nobel Prize for his discovery of the "Purification Rundown," a program that supposedly purged the body of drug and radiation residues. "While feeling enormous entitlement for accolades regarding his own projects, he haughtily and arrogantly demeaned perceived enemies, especially psychiatrists, for their opposition," write Jodi M. Lane and Stephen Kent about Hubbard's malignant narcissism.[26]

Narcissists feel they are above the law. Regulations meant for the rest of us do not apply. As special counsel Robert Mueller's investigation into possible collusion between the Russian government and the Trump campaign loomed over the administration, Trump insisted that he could pardon himself—not that he would need to. On June 4, 2018, he tweeted, "As has been stated by numerous legal scholars, I have the absolute right to PARDON myself, but why would I do that when I have done nothing wrong?"

A sense of entitlement can lead to all kinds of financial infractions. Moon conspired to evade paying his taxes and was sentenced to prison for eighteen months.[27] Trump has bilked hundreds of people—underpaying or failing to pay them. He has been involved in more than 3,500 lawsuits during the last thirty years, many from everyday Americans who have accused Trump and his businesses for nonpayment. They include employees of his resorts and clubs, contractors, and real estate agents.[28] Then there is the question of Trump's taxes. Ignoring a forty-year protocol, Trump the presidential candidate refused to release his tax returns—and got away with it.

As is often the case with narcissists, Trump surrounds himself with successful people but can quickly shift from idealizing them to denouncing them. When Trump picked Rex Tillerson to be his first secretary of state, the latter seemed camera-ready for the role. He had been the chairman and CEO of Exxon Mobil and was a heavyweight in the oil industry. It turns out Tillerson's traditional persona was like water to Trump's oil. The relationship got off to a rocky start over disagreements concerning Russia, North Korea, and Israel but deteriorated rapidly when it was rumored that Tillerson had called Trump "a moron." Retribution was swift. Trump fired him via the communication method he likes best—tweet.

LACK OF EMPATHY

Narcissists exhibit a defining lack of empathy—they are unable to put themselves in someone else's shoes and imagine what they might be feeling. They may be good at reading people, and may even appear charming, but in actuality they care little for other people's pain or suffering. They use them to their own advantage, often with devastating consequences.

In 2017, after Hurricane Maria wreaked havoc on Puerto Rico, Trump challenged the mayor of San Juan, Carmen Yulin Cruz, who had criticized Trump's lack of help. Trump denied that the storm was a real catastrophe—all the while taking personal credit for the Federal Emergency Management Agency's response—questioned the death toll, and minimized aid to the island, which years later, is still reeling.

More recently, he pumped up the immigration crisis at the border between the United States and Mexico to justify the need for building a wall—and created a real humanitarian crisis by separating children from their parents. He minimized the plight of the 800,000 government employees who struggled to make ends meet during the thirty-five-day government shutdown. He claimed—without any evidence—that they would support him if the shutdown dragged on for months or even years, using their plight for his greater glory. He appeared to be unconcerned about the effect that the shutdown was having on all Americans—food and drug inspections were cut, raising alarms about safety; security at airports and borders was compromised, risking national security; and renters, homeowners, and farmers alike, who depend on federal housing subsidies and aid, were left short, some possibly facing eviction.[29]

During the campaign, he put politics far above compassion in his treatment of the Gold Star couple Khizr and Ghazala Khan, who lost their army captain son in combat, and who addressed the 2016 Democratic National Convention. Khizr Khan memorably offered his pocket copy of the Constitution to Trump, who responded by criticizing his wife, Ghazala, for quietly standing by as he spoke, suggesting it was her religion that was silencing her. And then there was his belittling treatment of Christine Blasey Ford, who accused Trump's Supreme Court nominee Brett Kavanaugh of sexual assault when they were teenagers. Trump actually turned her testimony—and her ordeal—into a joke, mimicking her at a Mississippi rally, actions that her attorney Michael Browich described as "vicious, vile, and soulless."[30] Trump has shamed, bullied, and belittled hundreds of people since taking office, notably his once-devoted follower, former attorney general Jeff Sessions, whom he called "mentally retarded" and "a dumb Southerner."

ENVY

Envy is a driving force for narcissists and probably arises from their fundamental feelings of low self-esteem. But it can express itself differently depending on the situation. L. Ron Hubbard was jealous of one of his own members, the South African Scientologist John Mc-Master, who was dubbed the "World's First Clear," having attained the highest state of consciousness, one that Scientologists pay lots of money to achieve.[31] Hubbard, in his book *Dianetics,* claimed that people who are Clear have superior abilities. Apparently, Hubbard did not actually possess these himself and sought to make McMaster's life miserable. David Koresh yearned to be a rock musician and was frustrated and envious of others who were successful.

Though Trump tries to appear self-confident, he does slip once in a while and reveal the current of jealousy that runs beneath the surface. In June 2018, after meeting with Kim Jong-un in Singapore, Trump reflected: "He's the head of a country, and I mean he's the strong head. Don't let anyone think anything different. He speaks and his people sit up at attention. I want my people to do the same."[32] He later claimed that he was kidding, but he has made no bones about his admiration for authoritarian leaders, especially Putin, who have more control over their people than he does. He also appeared to be extremely impressed, if not envious, of the military display put on by French president Emmanuel Macron during Trump's visit to Paris—and was even planning his own military parade, but canceled it, blaming local Washington, D.C., officials for inflating the cost.

Closer to home, some have commented that despite Trump's outsider image, he has, as NBC's Chuck Todd coined on his MSNBC daily show, "elite envy" because he "never was accepted by the upper crust of New York society . . . . For a guy who claims, you know, he's just a 'regular guy,' 'just folks,' he sure does think a lot about the elite."[33]

ANTISOCIAL BEHAVIOR

Until now, we have been discussing pathological narcissism. This form of narcissism is described as malignant when it is joined with other pathological behaviors—antisocial behavior, sadism, and paranoia. Antisocial behavior may be defined as an ingrained disregard, and even contempt, for morals, social norms, and the rights and feelings of others. This can lead malignant narcissists to persistently lie and to steal and mismanage their own and others' money. It also leads them to manipulate others for their own personal gain, often through fear and intimidation.[34] While pathological narcissists may lie and manipulate others, malignant narcissists elevate this to an art form.

LYING

Deception is the lifeblood of a destructive cult. Members are recruited and indoctrinated through lies and trickery. Lying has other intrinsic benefits for cult leaders—it creates confusion, which disrupts people's stable mental framework and makes them more susceptible to the indoctrination process. Cult leaders use a variety of confusion techniques but a major one is delivering a dizzying amount of information, much of it contradictory and false, so that it overloads and overwhelms critical thinking. When overloaded and confused, people begin to doubt their ability to distinguish truth from lies, right from wrong. Fundamentally, their sense of identity is left uncertain, giving the cult leader an opportunity to inculcate a new set of beliefs, feelings, and behaviors. A confused person can be easily manipulated and controlled. People who confront leadership with contradictory information, regardless of it being factual, are punished or even banished for speaking the truth.

Cult leaders lie about everything from the state of the world to the size and devotion of their following. Mostly they lie about themselves in order to bolster their image. Moon lied about not having sex with his female disciples. He lied when he said he was a hero while in a North Korean prison camp. Moon lied about his taxes and was convicted and sent to the federal prison in Danbury, Connecticut. Hubbard lied about his military service. He claimed that he was highly decorated and that he was left partially blind and lame from injuries sustained during combat. In fact, his navy career ended far more ignominiously. After he conducted an impromptu ammunitions practice, Hubbard was brought before a military tribunal, who judged him unqualified for command. He was dismissed from his command and relocated to a larger vessel, where he could be properly supervised.

Trump has also lied about his military service, claiming he was deferred because of a bone spur. A doctor provided the false diagnosis as a favor to Trump's father, Fred.[35] When it comes to lies, Trump seems almost peerless. He has projected his own disregard for the truth onto the outside world, claiming it to be filled with fake news, liberal propaganda, and phonies. It happened during his candidacy and it started immediately with his inauguration. Trump lied not just about the size of the crowd but also about the weather. He claimed it was great, though the National Weather Service said it was actually raining. And he repeated his claim over and over, possibly leading some to question their own observations.

It only got worse. According to *The Washington Post,* Trump told roughly 2000 lies in 2017, about five and a half lies a day. By March 2019, he had racked up more than 10,000 false statements. According to *The Atlantic,* Trump is the "most fact-checked president."[36] But not everyone goes to the trouble of fact-checking Trump. People want to seek congruency—to see a reality that makes sense. When someone with presidential authority makes a false claim—and states it over and over—people can become disoriented, especially if they are predisposed to trust him and especially if they are a supporter.

The bigger the lie, the greater the disorientation. Ultimately a person can begin to question their own perception of reality, a phenomenon known as gaslighting. "The ultimate power of the gaslighter is to make it impossible for his targets to imagine a reality different from the one he imposes," writes Paul Rosenberg.[37] This power move got its name from the 1938 play *Gaslight*, later made into a movie, in which a husband conducts psychological warfare against his wife to the point that she begins to question her sanity. The goal is to undermine a person's judgment and increase their reliance on the gaslighter. Trump and his administration are particularly good at this. Speaking to a veterans' group in July 2018, Trump told the crowd, "Just remember—what you are seeing and what you are reading is not what's happening." In August 2018, Rudy Giuliani went on *Meet the Press* to argue the case that Trump should not testify in Mueller's special investigation. "When you tell me that he should testify because he's going to tell the truth and he shouldn't worry, well, that's so silly because it's somebody's version of the truth. Not the truth," Giuliani said. "Truth isn't truth." He later tried to clarify, but his comments—like Kellyanne Conway's use of the term "alternative facts" to defend demonstrable falsehoods—are not easily forgotten.

"A lie once told remains a lie, but a lie told a thousand times becomes the truth," the infamous Nazi propagandist Joseph Goebbels memorably claimed. Lies used to cost politicians their careers but are now a common tactic for winning elections. In Trump's world, they are standard operating procedure. When lies are repeated, they have the effect of shutting down critical thinking—people turn a blind eye to the lie and to the truth. When once respected and trusted sources of news are called fake or the enemy of the people, people are put into a double bind. They are discouraged from trying to reality check—they might even feel it is a betrayal of their allegiance to Trump to try to do so.

Trump's lies appear to have pushed the same thought stopping buttons used by cult leaders—shutting down critical thinking; employing us versus them thinking; and using emotional manipulation to gain sympathy for the leader while at the same time drumming up animosity toward the media.

INTERPERSONALLY EXPLOITATIVE

Malignant narcissists exploit people for personal benefit, often for financial gain. Cult leaders are notorious for making money off their followers. Moon sent legions of members out on "mobile fund-raising teams"—basically selling flowers and candy for long hours, in terrible weather, and often in dangerous neighborhoods. They were told to lie to the public, to say the money was for Christian youth programs or drug rehab centers. Multilevel marketing groups sell vitamins, supplements, water, and other products, as well as lectures, courses, and retreats of dubious value, all in an effort to raise funds.

As we have discussed, Trump the businessman would hire contractors and small businesses and cheat them out of a fair wage, presumably without guilt since he did it over and over again. Trump's for-profit university was sued and eventually shuttered for its deceptive practices and aggressive methods that scammed would-be students into paying tens of thousands of dollars, sometimes giving up their life savings.

Trump's "charitable" organization, the Donald J. Trump Foundation, is currently under investigation for using funds illegally. Trump allegedly hired someone to place a high bid on a portrait of Trump at a fund-raiser at his Mar-a-Lago Club in Florida, presumably to inflate its worth in the public's eye, and then bought the painting back, using funds from his charitable foundation.[38] The painting was reportedly shipped to one of his golf clubs in Westchester County, New York.

To make his case for a wall at the southern border, President Trump asked relatives of victims killed by illegal immigrants to tell their stories, a move that was typically political but also clearly exploitative. He was less interested in their welfare and more in getting what he wanted—a wall.

Trump family-associated businesses continue to attract legal attention. As of October 2018, three Trump-associated companies—ACN, a multilevel telemarketing company; the Trump Network, a company that sold health products; and the Trump Institute, a traveling real estate lecture series—were targets of lawsuits. One of the complaints alleges that Trump and his children received millions of dollars in secret payments and "were aware that the vast majority of consumers would lose whatever money they invested."[39]

SADISM

For malignant narcissists, sadism manifests as a conscious ideology of aggressive self-affirmation, one that also serves as a kind of perverse defense mechanism. According to one study, "Individuals with malignant narcissism have a tendency to destroy, symbolically castrate, and dehumanize others. Their rage is fueled by the desire for revenge."[40] Narcissists are defined by their need for praise but their desire to not be insulted or criticized may be even greater. Such attacks on their sense of self are so threatening that they cannot be tolerated— malignant narcissists will lash out aggressively and sadistically at anyone and everyone who has wronged them.

Cult leaders use an arsenal of indoctrination techniques to ensure complete devotion and will reserve some of their harshest weapons— shunning, shaming, expulsion, and even physical punishment—for those who criticize or disobey them.

Trump has repeatedly proved that he is incapable of taking the high ground—he always hits back at anyone over any perceived wrongs. In his book *Think Big: Make It Happen in Business and Life*, Trump has a whole chapter devoted to revenge. In 2011, at the National Achievers Congress, he said, "Get even with people. If they screw you, screw them back 10 times as hard. I really believe it."[41] For him, it is a matter of principle. Melania Trump has described how, when provoked, he "will punch back ten times harder"—a lesson he learned from his father, Fred. According to psychologist John Gartner, Trump has a cruel streak a mile wide. "You see it in everything he does, from the separating of the children at the border to how Trump tortures anyone who doesn't give him what he wants. There's a way in which he takes a kind of manic glee in causing harm and pain and humiliation to other people."[42]

When President Trump first nominated former senator Jeff Sessions for attorney general in November 2016, he showered him with compliments: "A world-class legal mind and considered a truly great Attorney General and U.S. Attorney in the state of Alabama. Jeff is greatly admired by legal scholars and virtually everyone who knows him."[43] Sessions, one of Trump's earliest and most ardent supporters, was a darling of Trump—until he wasn't. Unhappy that Sessions recused himself from the special counsel investigation, Trump became relentless in the public stoning of Sessions, angrily tweeting jibes such as "Will Bruce Ohr, whose family received big money for helping to create the phony, dirty and discredited dossier, ever be fired from the Jeff Sessions 'Justice' Department? A total joke!" Then there was James Comey. He was in Los Angeles visiting a local FBI office when he saw a ticker on the TV screen that read "Comey Resigns." He thought it was a prank. "I thought it was a scam by someone on my staff. So I turned to them and I said, 'Someone put a lot of work into that.' And then I continued talking."[44] After firing deputy FBI director Andrew McCabe two days before he was to receive his pension after twenty-one years at the bureau, Trump tweeted that it was "a great day for the hard-working men and women of the FBI—a great day for Democracy."[45]

HARASSMENT AND SILENCING

Trump is not the first malignant narcissist to use the courts. Hubbard's church of Scientology made the legal system a weapon of oppression, as a 1993 U.S. district court memorandum decision made explicitly clear: "[Scientologists] have abused the federal court system by using it, inter alia, to destroy their opponents, rather than to resolve an actual dispute over trademark law or any other legal matter. This constitutes 'extraordinary, malicious, wanton, and oppressive conduct.'"[46] Hubbard himself is quoted in a 1955 manual as saying that the purpose "is to harass and discourage rather than win. The law can be used very easily to harass, and enough harassment on somebody who is simply on the thin edge anyway, well knowing that he is not authorized, will generally be sufficient to cause professional decease. If possible, of course, ruin him utterly."[47]

For journalist Paulette Cooper, author of *The Scandal of Scientology* published in 1971—the first book critical of Scientology—legal harassment was only the start. "They sued me 19 times, all over the world, put me through 50 days of depositions."[48] Scientologists then broke into her house, lifted her fingerprints, and used them to frame her for a bomb threat. Luckily, she avoided the fifteen-year jail sentence when an FBI raid uncovered evidence of the forgery.

Few individuals can compete with Trump in terms of lawsuits— he has been involved in more than 3,500 litigations, according to an analysis by *USA Today*.[49] He was the plaintiff in 1,900—more than half of them. Before becoming president, he would send his lawyers to sue real estate developers, small business owners, and even cities. "Since winning his party's nomination in July 2016, Trump has threatened dozens of lawsuits, often against vocal critics and news media companies," writes Alexis Sachdev in *Metro*. "He once vowed to 'open up' libel laws to make it easier to sue media outlets. He's also threatened to sue women: those who accuse him of sexual assault, criticize his golf courses, and a teenager who made a website" where users could virtually scratch Trump's face with kitten paws.[50] Trump issues these threats mostly to intimidate—he rarely follows up.

VIOLENCE

Malignant narcissists are also well known for violent behavior. "I pulled the wings off a fly so that it couldn't get away," Moon told an audience of followers. "I spent hours each day watching it. I watched it clean its legs. I loved it so much that I didn't want it to escape. That is why I pulled its wings off."[51] Allen Tate Wood, a former Moonie, once asked Moon about his views on homosexuals. Moon replied, "Tell them that if it really becomes a problem to cut it off, barbecue it, put it in a shoe box and send it to me."[52] He was referring to their penises.

Keith Raniere, leader of the coaching cult NXIVM, became notorious when it was learned women were being branded. "We took turns holding one another down—three would be on them and the fourth would be filming," said ex-member Sarah Edmondson. "The first woman laid on the table and then the other women and I were sitting on her holding her legs down. With the first cut of her flesh—they burned her flesh—we were crying, we were shaking, we were holding one another. It was horrific. It was like a bad horror movie. We even had these surgical masks on because the smell of flesh was so strong . . . imagine someone taking a lit match to your crotch and drawing a line with it."[53]

Sexual abuse is another commonality.[54] The children in "Moses" David Berg's Children of God cult, for instance, had sexual activity forced upon them at a very early age, some as young as two years old.[55] Women were turned into "Happy Hookers for Jesus" and sent out to get new recruits as well as earn money and favors for the group.[56]

Dozens of women have made allegations of sexual assault against Trump, a situation that was brought to the fore by the *Access Hollywood* tape and also by the #MeToo movement.[57] But sexual abuse is most often committed behind closed doors, with only the perpetrator and the victim as witnesses. Divorce documents filed by Trump's first wife, Ivana, allege "cruel and inhuman" treatment, with verbal and physical abuse, including rape. Ivana has since made statements recanting her sworn testimony, saying that she does not want the rape to be considered in a "literal or criminal sense."[58]

Many of history's dictators were malignant narcissists. A thorough examination of their sadism and cruelty is beyond the scope of this book. But it is clear that when a malignant narcissist obtains power, they gain a platform for inflicting enormous harm. A simple review of history is filled with sobering reminders of the danger of violent leaders—Hitler, Stalin, Mao, Pol Pot . . . the list goes on.

PARANOIA

In his 1975 book, *Borderline Conditions and Pathological Narcissism,* renowned psychiatrist and professor Otto Kernberg describes paranoia as the root cause of the malignant narcissist's need for self-inflation. "The paranoid tendencies in malignant narcissists reflect their projection of unresolved hatred onto others whom they persecute. They have a deep sense of mistrust and view others as enemies/fools or idols, either devaluing or idealizing them. They have disorganized superegos and consequently lack the capacity for remorse, sadness or self-exploration. They are preoccupied with conspiracy theories. Their pathological grandiosity is a defense against paranoid anxiety."[59] In short, paranoia is the driving force behind malignant narcissism, the fear that people are judging you, and working and conspiring against you.

As we have seen, Trump's approach is to fight fear with fear, to return to that telling quote: "Real power is, I don't even want to use the word, fear."[60] Interestingly, Trump's fear of assault extends to the invisible—he is a germaphobe. So too was Hubbard, who demanded that his clothes be washed multiple times. "His clothes had to be washed in pure water thirteen times, using thirteen different buckets of water to rinse a shirt," said Tonja Burden, a former Scientology member.[61] Hubbard, she said, "frequently exploded if he found dust or dirt or smelled soap in his clothes." Trump washes his hands multiple times a day, as he acknowledged to radio host Howard Stern in an interview.[62] His love of fast food arises, in part, from a fear of being poisoned, which is "one reason why he liked to eat at McDonald's—nobody knew he was coming and the food was safely premade," reports former White House insider Michael Wolff in his book, Fire and Fury.[63]

ALLIES

One of the more tragic features of malignant narcissism is an inability to trust friends and subordinates. Their loyalty must be continually tested, often in abusive and humiliating ways. Trump is notorious for record-setting staff turnover and his preoccupation with perceived disloyalty and leaks.[64] Once-valued associates become villains and "idiots" overnight.

The brilliant 2004 film Downfall is notable for its three-dimensional portrayal of Hitler. The climactic scene, where Hitler rages and curses at his subordinates for failing and accuses them of sabotaging him is all too true to life. Malignant narcissists see enemies and danger everywhere and will lash out at allies. By the end, Hitler was so racked by anxiety that he even wanted his toilet bowl's water boiled and analyzed for traces of poison.[65] Joseph Stalin's purges—born from political paranoia—were just as lethal for his allies and followers. At a 1937 conference of the Communist Party in the Soviet Union, Stalin's people applauded him for eleven consecutive minutes, fearing that the first to stop would be killed or sent to prison. Finally, one man stopped, the director of a paper factory. "To a man, everyone else stopped dead and sat down," writes Nobel Prize winner Aleksandr Solzhenitsyn in *The Gulag Archipelago*. That same night the director of the paper factory was arrested and sent to prison for ten years. "Authorities came up with some official reason for his sentence, but during his interrogation, he was told: Don't ever be the first to stop applauding!"[66]

ENEMIES

Another great constant for the narcissist is his or her obsession with perceived enemies. We have seen this over and over again with Trump—the mainstream media, Democrats, globalists, the deep state, immigrants, Muslims, and really, any critic. As former White House aide Cliff Sims reveals in his memoir, *Team of Vipers*, soon after becoming president, Trump summoned him to help draw up a list of staffers he thought could not be trusted. "I was sitting there with the President of the United States basically compiling an enemies list—but these enemies were within his own administration. If it had been a horror movie, this would have been the moment when everyone suddenly realizes the call is coming from inside the house," Sims wrote.[67] It was only in retrospect that this struck Sims as remarkable. While in the White House, this bizarre cultlike behavior apparently seemed normal.

Trump might have had reason to be suspicious—his White House was notoriously leaky. But he clearly took it to an extreme. This is generally true of malignant narcissists. There is always a powerful

enemy to be vanquished—an urge that stems from both their paranoia and their need for attention. According to psychologist Craig
Malkin, "The greatest danger . . . is that pathological narcissists can
lose touch with reality in subtle ways that become extremely dangerous over time. When they can't let go of their need to be admired or
recognized, they have to *bend* or *invent* a reality in which they can
remain special, despite all messages to the contrary. In point of fact,
they become *dangerously* psychotic. It's just not always obvious before it's too late."[68]

Narcissists project their fears and anxieties outward. By external-
izing their fears—often onto people—they believe they can destroy
those negative emotions. They gain a feeling of safety from identifying and attacking enemies. To narcissists, admitting vulnerability,
especially personal vulnerability, is far more terrifying than any foe.

For the political cult leader Lyndon LaRouche, conspiracy theories
and paranoia were defining traits. "To say that Lyndon was slightly
paranoid would be like saying the *Titanic* had a bit of a leak,"[69] according to Jim Bakker, a disgraced televangelist who shared a prison
cell with LaRouche. Former cult insider Yves Messer has an excellent
website, LaRoucheplanet.info, which details LaRouche's obsession
with international bankers, British royalty, Jews, and a long list of
other enemies. LaRouche spent the latter part of his life ensconced in
a fortified compound out of fear of assassination, believing that his
ideas were so threatening to the established order that they put his
life in danger, though there is no indication that there were any assassination attempts against him. In addition to the enormous amount of
vitriol he directed at his ever-shifting political enemies, much of his
abuse was directed at former members whom he saw as dangerous
traitors.[70]

Most distressingly, a cult leader's paranoia and vindictiveness
toward enemies can become a self-perpetuating cycle. Hubbard in-
stitutionalized his paranoia with his Fair Game policy, which was a
blueprint for how to treat perceived enemies of Scientology—so-called
Suppressive Persons, people who criticize Scientology, including myself. "I never forget it, always even the score," Hubbard once wrote.[71]

The policy states that any Suppressive Person "may be deprived of property or injured by any means by any Scientologist . . . [they] may be tricked, sued or lied to or destroyed."[72] While officially the church canceled the Fair Game policy in 1968 because of bad press, there is ample evidence that the practice continued. Hubbard's vindictiveness would allow no less: "There are no good reporters. There are no good government or SP group agents. The longer you try to be nice, the worse off you will be. And the sooner one learns this, the happier he will be."[73]

Sadly, paranoia can drive malignant narcissists to harm their allies as well as their enemies. Jim Jones told his followers that they were all victims of a "profound conspiracy."[74] Fearing loss of control over his people—or possibly believing his worst paranoid fears—Jones chose to kill himself and, tragically, to bring his followers with him.

A FINAL WORD

What goes into the making of a malignant narcissist—how much is nature and how much nurture? Interestingly, malignant narcissists are at least seven times more likely to be men.[75] They are also more likely to have biological relatives—siblings and other family members— with antisocial personality disorders, though it is not clear how much of that is due to the common familial environment. According to researchers Mila Goldner-Vukov and Laurie-Jo Moore, people with antisocial personality disorders may be more likely to raise children with malignant narcissism. "The attitude of parents of children who will develop malignant narcissism is controlling and sadistic. They demand that their children be tough, tolerate pain, show no emotion and learn to manipulate others. Parental figures are cold and spiteful but over-admiring of their children's talents and charms."[76]

As we have seen, there is evidence that cult leaders and dictators may have experienced insecure or disorganized attachment in the first two years of their lives as a result of absent or authoritarian parenting. Such parenting can interrupt the bonding process, depriving a young child of the opportunity to feel safe and loved, and ultimately of developing a healthy sense of well-being. As they grow into adulthood, they may try to compensate for that lack of a healthy sense of self by seeking praise and accolades from devotees in the outside world—sometimes at all costs. It becomes almost a matter of survival.

With his cold and distant—indeed absent—mother, and his hard-charging and authoritarian father, Trump appears to fit this pattern. Of course, having such parents is no guarantee that one will become a narcissist. It is merely one more factor in Trump's life. Another would be his early and intense exposure to the teachings of Norman Vincent Peale, with his take-no-prisoners, the world is your oyster, harbor no doubts, think-it-and-it-will-happen ethos. I have counseled people who suffered debilitating delusions as a result of their involvement with Peale's school of thought. While positive thinking can be beneficial, it has to be balanced by critical thinking, humility, and a social support system that is willing to say when a person is off base. The danger is when it veers off into magical thinking—that if you believe fully, the universe will manifest. If it doesn't happen people often blame themselves—they aren't believing or praying hard enough. Faith healings are a variant of this kind of thinking—and they can be deadly if a person forgoes medical treatment. Faith and prayer can be helpful when dealing with an illness, but seeing highly trained doctors is a wise choice.

For what is most likely a combination of reasons, "Trump felt compelled to go to war with the world. It was a binary, zero-sum choice for him: You either dominated or you submitted. You either created and exploited fear, or you succumbed to it," said Trump's ghostwriter Tony Schwartz.[77]

And yet narcissists are highly dependent—they can't survive without other people to admire, serve, and prop them up. At the same time, Trump may address a need in his followers. As Barack Obama memorably claimed in a speech at the University of Illinois in September 2018, Trump is a "symptom not the cause" of the current political and cultural climate.[78] The question is—what has made such a large swath of Americans so susceptible to Trump?

CHAPTER FOUR

America, a Country
Wired for Manipulation

On February 27, 2019, at the annual Conservative Political Action Conference (CPAC) in Maryland, Donald Trump stood before his audience in all his riffing glory. Ten minutes into the speech, he told them what they might already have suspected. "You know, I'm totally off script right now. This is how I got elected, by being off script."[1] Not that long ago, during the GOP primaries, many in the audience might have viewed him with suspicion, if not disdain—a brash and unseemly outsider trying to horn in on the Grand Old Party. Now his remark earned him one of many standing ovations. Trump was supposed to speak for forty-five minutes but he went on for two hours, his longest speech ever. Almost nobody got up to leave. They were rapt. Trump had them in the palm of his hand.

Trump has not only taken over the Republican Party, he has transformed it into its own opposite: the party that used to be concerned about deficit spending but has racked up a trillion-dollar federal deficit since Trump took office. The party that was outraged when Bill Clinton lied about his relationship with Monica Lewinsky but turned a blind eye to—and maybe even believed—Trump's thousands of lies, including about his alleged affairs with a porn star and a former *Playboy* playmate. The party that loved John McCain—the late great war hero and stalwart Republican senator who dared oppose Trump on health care—but said almost nothing when Trump insulted and denigrated him.

How did this happen? How did people—politicians and ordinary citizens—fall in line to support a man who stood for everything they despised a few short years earlier? How did they lose their moral compass, override their conscience, and throw good judgment and common sense out the window?

To find answers ultimately means looking at how the mind works. While its machinations are still a mystery, much progress has been made in understanding how we, as individuals, take in and process information, and also how our collective minds can be manipulated and controlled. We go through our days thinking we are rational beings, but we are much more susceptible to manipulation than we think. That may be truer now than ever before. The sheer amount of information coming our way and the speed with which we receive it—coupled with our fast-paced, overworked, overscheduled world—has created a perfect storm of vulnerability.

Cults proliferate when a society is undergoing rapid change and particularly when there is a breakdown in trust between people and major institutions. The Great Recession of 2008 created economic hardships so severe that many people have not fully recovered. This is especially true in the American heartland, where Trump has many supporters. Many feel betrayed by government, religion, science, and big business. Every day the headlines are filled with news of clergy sexual abuse, political corruption, corporations caught lying and cheating, and pharmaceutical companies pushing drugs with terrible side effects, and in the case of opioids, creating a national crisis. Meanwhile, the mass media—TV and magazines as well as Facebook, Instagram, and Twitter—are filled with news about the rich and famous, chronicling their every movement, and even their meals. Celebrities, often vacuous and defined by their access to money, are rushing in to fill the cultural void, capturing our attention and our loyalty, engaging the public through subtle and not-so-subtle influence techniques. Many people are drawn to them, vicariously experiencing their wealth and fame. We live in a celebrity culture, with a celebrity president. With social media, it has become possible for ordinary citizens to become celebrities in their own right, using some of the same influence techniques that people like Trump exploit.

WE AREN'T REALLY THAT RATIONAL—
A BRIEF HISTORY OF PSYCHOLOGY

What makes the human mind so vulnerable to such manipulations? To answer that question requires going back to the turn of the twentieth century and the work of Sigmund Freud. Until Freud, many viewed human beings as rational creatures, a view epitomized in Descartes's famous maxim, "I think, therefore I am." Freud theorized that below the surface of conscious awareness lies a well of urges and feelings—often sexual and aggressive—that may be latent or repressed but that, under the right circumstances, can erupt. Freud saw World War I, with its horrific acts of inhumanity, as a battle waged by dark forces within us that we didn't know we possessed. So the assault on rationality began. Human beings couldn't be trusted to make rational decisions.[2]

Some thinkers of the time argued that a new elite was needed to control the public—the "bewildered herd," in the words of leading political writer Walter Lippmann.[3] During World War I, the U.S. government, wanting to sway public opinion in favor of the war, called in Freud's nephew, Edward Bernays, who had previously worked as a theatrical press agent to help promote the war and its message of making "the world safe for democracy." After the war, Bernays, fascinated—like his uncle—by what drove people's thoughts and actions, realized that the best way to get people to buy something—a war, but also an idea or a product—was to appeal to their emotions and desires. He would be the first to apply psychological principles to the area of public relations. In his 1928 book, *Propaganda,* he spelled out in stark detail techniques for scientifically shaping and manipulating public opinion, which he called "the engineering of consent."[4]

The following year, hired by the tobacco industry to promote cigarette smoking among women, he paid women to light and smoke cigarettes—he called them torches of freedom—as they walked in the New York Easter Parade and touted it as a bold act of defiance. Bernays's powerful theory of selling—that products should be sold not as necessities but as fulfilling human desires—spawned the modern era of consumerism. Ultimately, it would help define an American ideology, one that equated success with material objects—a fancy home, car, makeup, and clothes.

When Wall Street crashed on October 24, 1929, so too did Bernays's approach to selling—people could barely afford to buy food. Then came World War II, with acts of inhumanity that eclipsed those of World War I. Millions of people—Jews, blacks, gays, gypsies, communists—were killed in Nazi concentration camps that were run by "ordinary" Germans. This mass collaboration provoked great interest among psychologists.[5] How, they asked, could ordinary people help carry out murders on such a scale? Freud's belief that, deep down, humans are more carnal, even savage, and need to be controlled, was for many as good an explanation as any.

Rather than true peace, the end of World War II was followed by the Cold War, which pitted the United States and its European allies against communist countries like the Soviet Union and China. By the late 1950s, both the United States and the Soviet Union were ramping up nuclear testing. Images of another war culminating in a world-ending mushroom cloud scared every American. To allay their fears and to promote their own interests, the U.S. government once again called on Bernays, who would, among his many public relations campaigns, spin a 1954 coup in Guatemala as the "liberation of a country from the jaws of Communism."[6]

THE CIA AND MIND CONTROL

Whether he knows it or not, Trump—the salesman—owes many of his techniques to Bernays. But the work on influence and mind control intensified dramatically in the 1950s. With the rise of communism, and fearing that the Soviets were devising techniques to alter people's minds, the U.S. government, and in particular the Central

Intelligence Agency, set up secret experiments to explore the limits of human behavioral control. As described by John Marks in his book *The Search for the Manchurian Candidate* and by Alan W. Scheflin and Edward M. Opton Jr. in *The Mind Manipulators*, the CIA conducted mind control research from the late 1940s through the early 1960s. Code-named MK-ULTRA, their research program was a clandestine and illegal program of experiments on human subjects in a quest to find ways to manipulate people's mental states, alter their brain functions, and control their behavior. The techniques used in their experiments ranged from LSD and other psychotropic drugs to brain surgery, electroshock therapy, sensory deprivation, isolation, hypnosis, and sexual and verbal abuse. Other researchers attempted to follow up on this work but the CIA, in violation of many federal laws, destroyed almost all of its relevant files, claiming the research had not been productive.[7]

SOCIAL PSYCHOLOGY RESEARCH

The U.S. government raced to uncover the secrets of mind control by also helping fund academic research by social psychologists who were realizing that our thoughts, feelings, and behaviors can be deeply influenced by the actual, imagined, or implied presence of another person or persons. Their work would yield surprising insights about the power of group conformity, authority, and human suggestibility.

Among the most remarkable discoveries is that people are hardwired to respond to social cues. Consider these key experiments, which I cite when I am counseling and teaching:

- *The Asch Conformity Experiments.* In 1951, Solomon Asch conducted his first conformity experiment with a group of eight Swarthmore College students. All but one were "actors." The students were shown a card with three lines of different lengths and then asked to say which line was closest to the length of a target line on another card. The actors agreed in advance which line they would choose, even if

THE CULT OF TRUMP

it was obviously not the correct answer. Asch ran eighteen trials with the group. In twelve of them, the actors intentionally gave the wrong answer. Even when their answers were blatantly incorrect, the unwitting student would occasionally agree with the rest of the group. Asch repeated this experiment with multiple groups of eight students. Overall, 75 percent of the students conformed to the group consensus at least once, while 25 percent never conformed.[8] The results demonstrated that most people will conform when placed into a situation of social pressure.

- **The Milgram Experiment.** In 1961, inspired by the concentration camp horrors of World War II, where ordinary Germans carried out horrific acts, Yale University psychologist Stanley Milgram undertook an experiment to test the limits of obedience to authority. He did not believe it was only "authoritarian personalities" that were to blame for conscienceless obedience. He was curious to see whether ordinary Americans could be made obedient like German citizens had been. He recruited male volunteers and paired them with another subject, actually an actor, for what they thought was a memory and learning experiment. They were instructed to teach a task to their partner and to administer what they thought was a shock, ranging incrementally from 15 to 450 volts, each time the learner made a mistake. Tape recordings of the learner feigning pain or even screaming when receiving the punishment at higher shock levels were played. If the subject refused to administer a shock, the experimenter would order them to do so. Milgram found that all of the subjects administered shocks of at least 300 volts, though some were visibly uncomfortable doing so. Two-thirds continued to the highest level of 450 volts. Milgram wrote, "The essence of obedience consists in the fact that a person comes to view himself as the instrument for carrying out another person's wishes, and therefore no longer regards himself as responsible for his own actions." This experiment showed how people will follow orders from someone they think is a legitimate authority figure, even against their conscience.

■ *The Stanford Prison Experiment.* In 1971, Dr. Philip Zimbardo conducted a world-famous prison experiment in the basement of the psychology building at Stanford University. He wanted to explore the psychological effects of roles and perceived power, as might exist in a prison setting. Twenty-four healthy young men were randomly divided into two groups: prisoners and prison guards. Prisoners were mock "arrested" at their homes and brought to the so-called prison, where they encountered the guards, who were dressed in uniforms, including mirrored sunglasses, and equipped with batons. In very little time, the subjects adopted their roles with disturbing results. The experiment was supposed to last two weeks but it had to be called off after only six days because some of the guards had become sadistic, and some of the prisoners had psychological breakdowns. Good people started behaving badly when put in a bad situation and were unaware of the mind control forces at work. Even Zimbardo got pulled into the power of the situation. It took graduate student Christina Maslach, later Zimbardo's wife, to shock him out of his role as warden and to realize that young men were suffering—and that he was responsible.

Both the Milgram and Zimbardo studies led to the establishment of strict ethical review board requirements for doing experiments with human subjects.

Why do we bow to social pressure? According to Nobel Prize–winning author psychologist Daniel Kahneman, when it comes to making choices, we have two systems in our brains. As he writes in his 2016 book, *Thinking, Fast and Slow*, the first system is fast and instinctive and the second system more deliberate. The fast system relies on unconscious heuristics, and makes decisions based on instinct

and emotion—a kind of "sensing"—without consulting the more analytic, critical "slow" system. It's the part of the mind that you use
when you're "thinking with your gut," that looks to others in your
environment when it gets confused, and that defers to authority figures. When a person is unsure, they do what the tribe is doing—they
conform. We unconsciously look to someone who promises security
and safety. In short, we are unconsciously wired to adapt, conform,
and follow to promote our survival.

FUNDAMENTAL ATTRIBUTION ERROR

Other discoveries were showing the limits of human rationality. In
1967, two researchers, Edward Jones and Victor Harris, conducted
an experiment in which subjects were asked to read essays either for
or against Fidel Castro. When the subjects believed that the writers
freely chose their positions, they rated them as being correspond-
ingly pro- or anti-Castro. But even when subjects were told that the
writer had been directed to take their stance, subjects still rated the
pro-Castro writers as being in favor of Castro, and the anti-Castro
speakers against him.

This psychological bias—known as the fundamental attribution
error—is important to understand before we go any further in explaining the science of mind control. When we see a negative behavior in another person (for example, joining a cult), we might explain
it as an expression of a personality defect in that person (they are
weak, gullible, or need someone to control them). When we see such
a behavior in ourselves, we tend to attribute it to an external situation
or contextual factor (I was lied to or pressured). The fundamental
attribution error refers to this tendency to interpret other people's
behavior as resulting largely from their disposition while disregarding
environmental and social influences.[9] When I was in the Moonies,
people probably assumed that I was weak, dumb, or crazy to join such
a group. I thought I was doing something good for myself and the
planet. At the same time, I might have looked at a Hare Krishna devo-
tee and thought they were weird. The truth is, we were both being lied

to and manipulated. We also see it at play in our country—between Trump supporters and anti-Trumpers, each assuming the other is dumb, stupid, or crazy. We are all affected by situational factors, including our exposure to influence. By understanding the fundamental attribution error we are encouraged not to blame other people but rather to learn about the influences that have led them to adopt their position and work to expand the sharing of information and perspectives.

COGNITIVE DISSONANCE

In their classic book, *When Prophecy Fails*, Leon Festinger and his colleagues Henry Riecken and Stanley Schachter describe their studies of a small Chicago UFO cult called the Seekers. The leader of the group had predicted that a spaceship would arrive on a particular date to save them, the true believers, from a cataclysm. The big day came—without a spaceship. To Festinger's surprise, rather than become disillusioned, members of the group claimed that through their faith, the catastrophe had been averted. "If you change a person's behavior," the authors observed, "[their] thoughts and feelings will change to minimize the dissonance"[10]—a phenomenon Festinger called "cognitive dissonance."

Dissonance is psychological tension that arises when there is conflict between a person's beliefs, feelings, and behavior. We think of ourselves as rational beings and believe that our behavior, thoughts, and emotions are congruent. We can tolerate only a certain amount of inconsistency and will quickly rationalize to minimize the discrepancy. This often happens without our conscious effort or awareness. What this means is that when we behave in ways we might deem stupid or immoral, we change our attitudes until the behavior seems sensible or justified. This has implications for our ability to accurately perceive the world. People who hold opposing views will interpret the same news reports or factual material differently—each sees and remembers what supports their views and glosses over information that would create dissonance. Trump campaigned on the promise of a wall along the border with Mexico and even guaranteed that the Mexicans would pay for it. Today the wall has not been built and Mexico has made it clear that they will not pay for any such thing. Here is how Trump dealt with the cognitive dissonance. "When, during the campaign, I would say, Mexico is going to pay for it. Obviously, I never said this and I never meant they're going to write out a check. I said, 'They're going to pay for it.' They are. They are paying for it with the incredible deal we made, called the United States, Mexico, and Canada (USMCA) Agreement on trade."[11] Apparently, many of his supporters believe him. People tend to look for congruence and avoid discordance, which can create emotional distress. Beliefs often shift to fall more in line with a person's emotional state.

THE PSYCHOLOGY OF MIND CONTROL

In 1961, Massachusetts Institute of Technology psychologist Edgar Schein wrote his classic book *Coercive Persuasion*. Building on a model developed in the 1940s by influential social psychologist Kurt Lewin, he described psychological change as a three-step process. Schein, like Lifton, Singer, and others, had studied the Chinese communist programs and applied this model to describe brainwashing. The three steps are: *unfreezing*, the process of breaking a person down; *changing*, the indoctrination process; and *refreezing*, the process of building up and reinforcing the new identity. It's a model that could apply to the millions of Americans who have fallen under the sway of Trump and his administration.

UNFREEZING

To ready a person for a radical change, their sense of reality must first be undermined and shaken to its core. Their indoctrinators must confuse and disorient them. Their frames of reference for understanding themselves and their surroundings must be challenged and dismantled.

One of the most effective ways to disorient a person is to disrupt their physiology. Not surprisingly, sleep deprivation is one of the most common and powerful techniques for breaking a person down. Altering one's diet and eating schedule can also be disorienting. Some groups use low-protein, high-sugar diets, or prolonged underfeeding, to undermine a person's physical integrity. Former Trump inner circle member Omarosa Manigault Newman reports that while working closely with Trump, she adopted many of his habits—working all hours of the night, eating fast food, often at Trump's insistence.

Unfreezing is most effectively accomplished in a totally controlled environment, like an isolated country estate, but it can also be accomplished in more familiar and easily accessible places, such as a hotel ballroom. When they were not all in the White House, Manigault Newman and other Trump aides would vacation together at Trump-owned resorts, either Mar-a-Lago or at his golf course in Bedminster, New Jersey.[12]

Hypnotic techniques are among the most powerful tools for unfreezing and sidestepping a person's defense mechanisms. One particularly effective hypnotic technique involves the deliberate use of confusion to induce a trance state. Confusion usually results when contradictory information is communicated congruently and believably with an air of certitude. For example, if a hypnotist says in an authoritative tone of voice, "The more you try to understand what I am saying, the less you will never be able to understand it. Do you understand?" the result is a state of temporary confusion. If you read it over and over again, you may conclude that the statement is simply contradictory and nonsensical. However, if someone is kept in a controlled environment long enough, they will feel overwhelmed with information coming at them too fast to analyze. If they are fed disorienting language and confusing information, they will zone out, suspend judgment, and adapt to what everyone else is doing. In such an environment, the tendency of most people is to doubt themselves and defer to the leader and the group, as in the Asch and Milgram experiments.

Trump is a master of confusion—presenting contradictory information convincingly. We saw it earlier in the way he explained the funding for his wall. He will say something, "Mexico will pay," then say he never said it: "I never said Mexico will pay." And then say it again, "Mexico will pay," but in a new context: "with the incredible deal we made." He does it all in an assured tone of voice, often with other people present—for example, at rallies—who nod in agreement. And so do you.

Sensory overload, like sensory deprivation, can also effectively disrupt a person's balance and make them more open to suggestion. A person can be bombarded by emotionally laden material at a rate faster than they can digest it. The result is a feeling of being overwhelmed. The mind snaps into neutral and ceases to evaluate the material pouring in. The newcomer may think this is happening spontaneously within themselves, but it has been intentionally structured that way.

Other hypnotic techniques, such as double binds[13]—in which a person receives two or more contradictory pieces of information—can also be used to help unfreeze a person's sense of reality. The goal is to get a person to do what the controller wants while giving an illusion of choice. For example, cults will often tell a person that they are free to leave whenever they wish but that they will regret it for the rest of their lives. A double bind commonly used by controlling people is to tell a person that they are free to go but that they will never find anyone who will love them as much as they do. In short, they will be miserable. An example of a hypnotic double bind—one that Keith Raniere reportedly used—is "you will remember to forget everything that just happened." Whether the person believes or doubts the controller, confusion and emotional distress often ensue.

Once a person is unfrozen, they are ready for the next phase.

CHANGING

Changing consists of creating a new personal identity—a new set of behaviors, thoughts, and emotions—often through the use of role models. Indoctrination of this new identity takes place both formally—through meetings, seminars, and rituals (or at Trump rallies)—and informally—by spending time with members, recruiting, studying, and self-indoctrination through the internet (watching Trump videos, communicating on social media with Trump supporters). Many of the same techniques used during unfreezing are also repeated in this phase.

Repetition and rhythm create the lulling hypnotic cadences with which the formal indoctrination can be delivered. The material is repeated over and over (and Trump is a master of repetition). If the lecturers are sophisticated, they will vary their talks somewhat in an attempt to hold interest, but the message remains the same. The goal is programming and indoctrination, not real learning. Often recruits are told how bad the world is and that the unenlightened have no idea how to fix it. Ordinary people lack the understanding that only the leader can provide (a common theme for Trump: the world is a mess that only he can fix). Recruits are told that their old self is what's keeping them from fully experiencing the new truth: "Your old concepts are what drag you down. Your rational mind is holding you back from fantastic progress. Surrender. Let go. Have faith."

Behaviors are shaped often subtly at first, then more forcefully. The information that will make up the new identity is doled out gradually, piece by piece, only as fast as the person is deemed ready to assimilate it. The rule of thumb is to tell the new member only enough that they can swallow. When I was a lecturer in the Moonies, I remember discussing this policy with others involved in recruiting. I was taught this analogy: "You wouldn't feed an infant thick pieces of steak, would you? You have to feed a baby something it can digest, like formula. Well, these people [potential converts] are spiritual babies. Don't tell them more than they can handle, or they will choke and die."

Perhaps the most powerful persuasion is exerted by other cult members. For the average person, talking with an indoctrinated cultist is quite an experience. You'll probably never meet anyone else who is so absolutely convinced that they know what is best for you. A devoted cult member also does not take no for an answer because they have been indoctrinated to believe that if you don't join, they have failed to save you. Often, members are told that if they do not get converts, *they* are to blame. This creates a lot of pressure to succeed.

Human beings have an incredible capacity to adapt to new environments. Charismatic cult leaders know how to exploit this strength. By controlling a person's environment, using behavior modification to reward some behaviors and suppress others, and by inducing hypnotic states, they may reprogram a person's identity.

Once a person has been fully broken down through the process of changing, they are ready for the next step.

REFREEZING

The recruit's identity must now be solidified, or refrozen, as a "new man" or "new woman." They are given a new purpose in life and new activities that will enable their new identity to become dominant and suppress the old one.

Many of the techniques from the first two stages are carried over into the refreezing phase. The first and most important task is to denigrate their previous "sinful self" and avoid anything that activates that old self. During this phase, an individual's memory becomes distorted, minimizing the good things in the past and maximizing their failings, hurts, and guilt. Special talents, interests, hobbies, friends, and family usually must be abandoned—preferably through dramatic public statements and actions—especially if they compete with a person's commitment to the cause.

During the refreezing phase, the primary method for passing on new information is modeling. New members are paired with older members who are assigned to show them the ropes. The "spiritual child" is instructed to imitate the "spiritual parent" in all ways. This technique serves several purposes. It keeps the older member on their best behavior while gratifying their ego. At the same time, it whets the new member's appetite to become a respected model so they can train junior members of their own.

After a novice spends enough time with older members, the day finally comes when they can be trusted to recruit and train other new-comers by themselves. They are taken out with a senior member and encouraged to enlist new members. Thus the victim becomes a victim-izer, perpetuating the destructive system.

The group now forms the member's "true" family; any other is considered their outmoded "physical" family. In my own case, I ceased to be Steve Hassan, son of Milton and Estelle Hassan, and became Steve Hassan, son of Sun Myung Moon and Hak Ja Han, the "True Parents" of all creation. In every waking moment, I endeavored to be a small Sun Myung Moon, the greatest person in human history. As my cult identity was put into place, I was told to think, feel, and act like him. This is not unique to my cult. When faced with a problem, Sci-entologists are encouraged to ask, "What would Ron [Hubbard] do?"

In an interview with CBS News, Republican Ron DeSantis—who won the Florida governor's race with Trump's help—claimed that Trump was a role model for his own children. "We all have our faults and what-not," DeSantis said. "But even [Trump's] worst critics would say he is someone who is determined to keep his word."[14] At the time of the interview, Trump had been on record as having made well over six thousand false or misleading claims.

BITE MODEL

Trump has had extensive experience helping to create environments that regulate people's behavior, information, thoughts, and emotions. On The Apprentice, the show he worked on for fourteen seasons, contestants lived communally, in a highly controlled environment where their actions were tightly circumscribed. (Interestingly, show creator Mark Burnett had significant military training, having served in the British army in the Falklands and Northern Ireland in the early 1980s.) Contestants tried to please a harsh mercurial leader (Trump), who would punish failure with banishment and exile. Those who re-mained might be rewarded lavishly, but the fear of failure was om-nipresent, and trust toward fellow members practically absent. The artificial nature of reality TV does not make it any less of a window into the fundamental levers of mind control. If anything, reality TV brings to the fore mind control's power—how else could people do such crazy things if they were not in an environment that systematically manipulated them?

Mind control is not an ambiguous, mystical process but instead a concrete and specific set of methods and techniques. The BITE model, which I briefly outlined in chapter 1, identifies the main techniques cult leaders use to control behavior, information, thoughts, and emotions—all in an effort to make followers dependent and obedient. It is not necessary for every single item on the list to be present for a group to be judged destructive. In fact, only a few items under each of the four components need be present to raise red flags about an organization or leader. For reference, I have identified in boldface aspects of the BITE model that people—including former *Apprentice* contestant and promoter Omarosa Manigault Newman—have described in association with Trump.

Behavior Control

- Regulate an individual's physical reality
- Dictate where, how, and with whom the member lives and associates or isolates
- Dictate when, how, and with whom the member has sex
- **Control types of clothing** and hairstyles
- **Regulate diet—food and drink, hunger, and/or fasting**
- **Manipulate and limit sleep**
- Financial exploitation, manipulation, or dependence
- Restrict leisure, entertainment, vacation time
- Major time spent with group indoctrination and rituals and/or self-indoctrination, including the internet
- Require permission for major decisions
- Report thoughts, feelings, and activities (of self and others) to superiors
- **Use rewards and punishments to modify behaviors, both positive and negative**

- Discourage individualism, encourage groupthink
- Impose rigid rules and regulations
- Encourage and engage in corporal punishment
- Punish disobedience. Extreme examples done by pimps are beating, torture, burning, cutting, rape, or tattooing/branding
- Threaten harm to family or friends (by cutting off family/friends)
- Force individual to rape or be raped
- Instill dependency and obedience

Information Control

- Deception
  - Deliberately withhold information
  - Distort information to make it more acceptable
  - Systematically lie to the cult member
- Minimize or discourage access to noncult sources of information, including:
  - Internet, TV, radio, books, articles, newspapers, magazines, other media
  - Critical information
  - Former members
  - Keep members busy so they don't have time to think and investigate
  - Exert control through a cell phone with texting, calls, and internet tracking
- Compartmentalize information into Outsider versus Insider doctrines
- Ensure that information is not easily accessible
- Control information at different levels and missions within the group
- Allow only leadership to decide who needs to know what and when
- Encourage spying on other members
- Impose a buddy system to monitor and control member
- Report deviant thoughts, feelings, and actions to leadership

- Ensure that individual behavior is monitored by the group
- Extensive use of cult-generated information and propaganda, including:
  - Newsletters, magazines, journals, audiotapes, videotapes, YouTube, movies, and other media
  - Misquoting statements or using them out of context from noncult sources
- Unethical use of confession
- Use information about "sins" to disrupt and/or dissolve identity boundaries
- Withhold forgiveness or absolution
- Manipulate memory, possibly implanting false memories

Thought Control

- Require members to internalize the group's doctrine as truth
- Adopt the group's "map of reality" as reality
- Instill black and white thinking
- Decide between good versus evil
- Organize people into us versus them (insiders versus outsiders)
- Change a person's name and identity
- Use loaded language and clichés to constrict knowledge, stop critical thoughts, and reduce complexities into platitudinous buzzwords
- Encourage only "good and proper" thoughts
- Use hypnotic techniques to alter mental states, undermine critical thinking, and even to age-regress the member to childhood states
- Manipulate memories to create false ones
- Teach thought stopping techniques that shut down reality testing by stopping negative thoughts and allowing only positive thoughts. These techniques include:
  - Denial, rationalization, justification, wishful thinking
  - Chanting
  - Meditating

□ Praying
□ Speaking in tongues
□ Singing or humming
- Reject rational analysis, critical thinking, constructive criticism
- Forbid critical questions about leader, doctrine, or policy
- Label alternative belief systems as illegitimate, evil, or not useful
- Instill new "map of reality"

Emotional Control

- Manipulate and narrow the range of feelings—some emotions and/or needs are deemed as evil, wrong, or selfish
- Teach emotion stopping techniques to block feelings of hopelessness, anger, or doubt
- Make the person feel that problems are always their own fault, never the leader's or the group's fault
- Promote feelings of guilt or unworthiness, such as:
  □ Identity guilt
  □ You are not living up to your potential
  □ Your family is deficient
  □ Your past is suspect
  □ Your affiliations are unwise
  □ Your thoughts, feelings, actions are irrelevant or selfish
  □ Social guilt
  □ Historical guilt
- Instill fear, such as fear of:
  □ Thinking independently
  □ The outside world
  □ Enemies
  □ Losing one's salvation
  □ Leaving
- Orchestrate emotional highs and lows through love bombing and by offering praise one moment, and then declaring a person is a horrible sinner

- Ritualistic and sometimes public confession of sins
- **Phobia indoctrination: inculcate irrational fears about leaving the group or questioning the leader's authority**
  - No happiness or fulfillment possible outside the group
  - Terrible consequences if you leave: hell, demon possession, incurable diseases, accidents, suicide, insanity, 10,000 reincarnations, etc.
  - Shun those who leave and inspire fear of being rejected by friends and family
  - **Never a legitimate reason to leave; those who leave are weak, undisciplined, unspiritual, worldly, brainwashed by family or counselor, or seduced by money, sex, or rock and roll**
- **Threaten harm to ex-member and family (threats of cutting off friends/family)**

As the BITE model shows, mind control isn't the thuggish, coercive activity portrayed in film—of being locked up in a dark room and tortured, though that is possible. Instead, it is a much more subtle and sophisticated process. Often, a person may regard their controller as a friend or peer, and will unwittingly cooperate with them, for example by giving them private and personal information that they do not realize may later be used against them.

Mind control may involve little or no overt physical coercion, though obviously there is psychological abuse. There may be physical and sexual abuse as well. On their own, hypnotic processes—especially when combined with group dynamics—can create a potent indoctrination effect. A person is deceived and manipulated, though not directly threatened, into making prescribed choices and may even appear to respond positively, at least in the beginning. Manigault Newman enjoyed the "spoils of success" first as a contestant on *The Apprentice* and later as part of the Trump Organization and then the White House, only later to wake up to the systematic deception and indoctrination she had experienced. Though hers is a prominent case, I believe it is happening all over America. Trump, with the aid of

the greater media machine, is using mind control techniques to recruit, indoctrinate, and maintain his base, speaking to them through
tweets and at rallies but also through his executive orders, judicial
appointments, and policy decisions, which are essentially call-outs, or
political dog whistles, to his followers—"I did this for you, I expect
loyalty in return"—all the while drawing them deeper into his cult of
personality.

THE REAL WORLD

Okay, you may be saying to yourself, I see these points. But aren't
cults usually relatively small fringe groups? How might the Cult of
Trump exert control over tens of millions of Americans?

Let's look at the media that we consume today. I have already
mentioned the documentary *The Brainwashing of My Dad,* in which
Jen Senko shows how her father, Frank, was transformed from a Democrat to an ultraconservative Republican by being exposed to hours
of right-wing media, in particular Rush Limbaugh and Fox News. She
found many others who had loved ones in similar situations and uses
their personal stories, along with interviews with experts, to educate
the public about how conservative media uses social influence techniques to manipulate their consumers.

One such expert is Frank Luntz. A PR consultant and author of
the book *Words That Work,* Luntz spells out how propaganda techniques used by right-wing media bypass critical thinking and hit
people emotionally, especially through the use of fear. (A longtime
Republican advisor, Luntz openly criticized Trump during the 2016
campaign but is now working in the White House, advising Trump
on messaging.)[15] On Fox News, everything is created to maximize
patriotic feelings. The settings are glitzy and compelling, with red,
white and blue colors, and attractive female and male hosts who espouse their conservative views, often with passion but little evidence.
"Fox trades in stories about the venality of big government, liberal
overreach and little-guy heroes of the heartland. A large share of Fox
stories deftly push emotional buttons," writes William Poundstone in

Forbes magazine.[16] Their segments often promote views that play on tribal tendencies that ratchet up a kind of fear and hatred of "out-groups," such as immigrants, Democrats, and ethnic groups such as blacks, Latinos, and Muslims. And then there is the hypnotic scroll of the news ticker and general graphic excess, which can leave people feeling overwhelmed but addicted to finding out what comes next—in the same way that they look at their Instagram, Twitter, or other social media to assuage their fear of missing out.

Most of what happens in our minds occurs in our unconscious, as Freud observed. Our conscious minds can only process a limited amount of information at a time. It has been estimated that the average American sees 4,000 to 10,000 ads a day.[17] When there are so many messages coming at us, often simultaneously, we can easily become overloaded. We are not as rational and logical as we think, and today's society is further dimming our capacity for sound judgment. Due in part to the informational overload, our attention spans have become shorter. The quality of education has dipped in many areas of the country, and for a variety of reasons, students are underperforming compared with the past. With TV shows streaming at all hours and with internet access at our fingertips; with our smartphones practically an extension of our arms, we are being bombarded and manipulated, often unwittingly, by people and organizations who want to influence how we think, feel—and buy.

Critical thinking is an effortful activity—one that our 24/7 society makes very difficult in other ways. Take, for example, sleep deprivation. The average adult needs somewhere between seven to nine hours of sleep a night, though this can vary between individuals. Currently 40 percent of Americans get less than seven hours of sleep a night—the national average is 6.8 hours, down more than an hour from 1942.[18] Sleep deprivation is linked to many health issues including cognitive impairment.[19] Critical thinking is hard enough when you're not exhausted. Yet sleep deprivation is not the only force eroding our mental abilities.

Consider the ease with which Facebook, Google, Apple, Amazon, and other technology companies are affecting our behaviors not just as a society but at a very personal level: people are addicted to their devices.[20] The average American spends eleven hours a day looking at screens.[21] Facebook addiction is a well-studied phenomenon[22]—articles with titles like "Facebook Addiction 'Activates Same Part of the Brain as Cocaine' "[23] are more explanatory than alarmist. Cal Newport, author of *Deep Work,* argues that "the knowledge economy is systematically undervaluing uninterrupted concentration and overvaluing the convenience and flexibility offered by new technologies . . . [If people are bombarded] with email and meeting invitations, their cognitive capacity will be significantly impeded."[24] This awareness is not just bubbling up from the rank and file; CEOs across the tech sector are speaking out and cutting back technology use in their own lives.[25]

Trump watches at least four hours of television daily and often much more, eats fast food at many meals, and sleeps a reported three or four hours a night. He might be able to handle it but many Americans cannot. Whether we're looking at the effects of adverse nutrition, poor education, climate change, economic disparity, job insecurity, high rates of divorce, along with the alarming rise of drug abuse in this country—the overload of everyday stress and outside forces is affecting the cognitive functioning of our brains.

One of the most damaging factors to us, as individuals and as a society, is poor parenting, and in particular child abuse. In his book, *The Holocaust Lessons on Compassionate Parenting and Child Corporal Punishment*, social worker and child protection advocate David Cooperson describes the negative effects of corporal punishment on childhood development. The title of his book refers to studies by Samuel and Pearl Oliner and others on people who rescued Jews during World War II in Nazi-occupied countries, often at great risk to themselves. They found that rescuers received negligible physical punishment as children—compared to those who did not attempt to rescue Jews—suggesting, among other things, that corporal punishment may play a role in whether a person becomes susceptible to authority. Studies by Harvard Medical School psychiatrist Martin Teicher and others have also shown that physical, sexual, emotional, and even verbal abuse can produce lasting changes in the brain. It can also lead to psychiatric disorders such as anxiety, depression, bullying, and post-traumatic stress disorder.[26]

Add to this volatile mix the breakdown in trust between people and institutions, the rise of celebrity culture, and the explosion of social media—we're looking at a staggering number of negative influences on our ability to concentrate, think clearly, and make decisions, both individually and collectively.

The 24/7 digital age has made us wired for manipulation—literally. But there are many other factors at work. As someone who has experienced life in a totalitarian group, I know firsthand how cults work— how they target people at vulnerable moments and use well-honed psychological techniques to manipulate and indoctrinate their members. I also know firsthand how cult leaders work—how they distort, confuse, and manipulate their followers, in their one-on-one interactions and on a larger stage. Some may think that Trump is a buffoon who does not know what he is doing when he repeats himself over and over again at rallies or goes on for hours at a CPAC conference. While I do believe that he is failing in his mental health, he is also a longtime student of influence techniques with a need for attention and control over others. He would not be where he is without that knowledge and—let's call it what it is—talent.

CHAPTER FIVE

The Persuasiveness of Trump

n the summer of 2015, more than a year before the presidential
election, *Dilbert* cartoonist Scott Adams made what sounded like
an outrageous prediction—that Donald Trump had a 98 percent
chance of becoming president. With a still wide-open field of Republican candidates, and almost all the polls tilting heavily toward Democratic candidate Hillary Clinton winning the general election, Adams
was ridiculed and even attacked. He later admitted that he had exaggerated Trump's chances in order to attract attention—a key method
of persuasion.[1] But Adams, who claims to be a trained hypnotist, did
believe that Trump—with his media savvy, his fourteen seasons on
The Apprentice, and his extensive experience in business—had a high
likelihood of winning. What gave Trump the edge, said Adams, were
his superior powers of persuasion.

In his classic 1936 book, *How to Win Friends and Influence People*, Dale Carnegie outlined six principles of persuasion: smile, listen,
show genuine interest in people, make them feel important, remember their name and use it frequently, and talk about their interests.
Carnegie's principles sound almost homespun. In fact, they still work,
but the science of persuasion has moved far beyond his insights. First,
with mass media—radio and television—and then the digital age,

influence techniques have become much more sophisticated. According to Adams, Trump has masterfully exploited many of these techniques to his advantage.

In his book *Win Bigly: Persuasion in a World Where Facts Don't Matter*, Adams describes one of the fundamental principles of Trump's rhetorical style. "Persuasion is all about the tools and techniques of changing people's minds, with or without facts or reason," Adams writes. When Trump claimed that Mexican immigrants are rapists, we may have recoiled in disgust but we remembered it. And we talked about it. Adams would argue that Trump didn't mean all Mexican immigrants—he was intentionally exaggerating. He was using hyperbole, a persuasive tactic that provokes controversy and captures people's attention and emotions.

"An emotional speaker always makes his audience feel with him, even when there is nothing in his arguments; which is why many speakers try to overwhelm their audience by mere noise," Aristotle wrote in his classic work on persuasion, *Rhetoric*. By his own account, Trump seems to know what he is doing. "I play to people's fantasies," Trump says in *The Art of the Deal*. "That's why a little hyperbole never hurts. . . . I call it truthful hyperbole. It's an innocent form of exaggeration—and a very effective form of promotion." According to Adams, even at his most blustery, Trump has a strategy, one that should not be underestimated. He is a master manipulator of the media and of people's minds.

A LITTLE MORE ABOUT
MIND, LANGUAGE, AND HYPNOSIS

The human brain has been described as an incredibly complex and sophisticated biocomputer, one that is designed to learn survival patterns. It is remarkable in its ability to creatively respond to a person's physiological and psychological needs, as well as to their environment. Our brains filter out the floods of information that come our way every second so that we can cope with those things that we consider important. The latest research describes how the right hemisphere of our brains takes in the big picture and the left hemisphere concentrates on details.[2]

Our minds are filled with enormous reservoirs of information—images, sounds, feelings, tastes, and smells. All this information is systematically connected in meaningful ways and stored as memories. These memories help develop our sense of self. Our beliefs about ourselves in turn serve as a filter for processing new information. They also help to determine our behavior. Yet only a small part of our behavior is under our conscious control. The unconscious does the rest, including regulating our bodily functions. Imagine having to tell your heart to beat seventy-two times every minute—there would be no time for anything else.

In addition to controlling our bodily functions, the unconscious plays a large role in shaping our conscious minds. It is the primary manager and keeper of information. It's where our multitude of beliefs, judgments, feelings, and behaviors are processed and stored. Think of our conscious mind as the tuner on an AM/FM radio. You can put your attention on one "station," but all the AM/FM frequencies are going all the time in the human mind. We're just not aware of it. We're working off what Nobel Prize–winning behavioral economist Daniel Kahneman calls "unconscious heuristics."

It is our unconscious that allows us to make mental pictures and experience them as real. Your perceptions of the world are "simply electrical signals interpreted by your brain," to quote the classic movie *The Matrix*. Try this experiment. Allow your mind to transport you to a beautiful beach—bask in the warmth and brightness of the sun, the cool breeze, the smell of the ocean. Hear the sounds of waves crashing, feel the grit of the sand between your toes. Did you go somewhere else for a moment? Imagination can be a powerful tool. Top professional basketball players learn to visualize the ball leaving their fingers and going through the net before they shoot. We all do it: imagining what we will say at a presentation, or when we meet the "one" and fall in love.

Trump does it, too—he is a master of getting our attention and manipulating people's imaginations. You can see it in his use of hyperbole. His exaggerations are simply vivid images designed to scare or delight—usually both at the same time. In his 2017 inauguration speech, he spoke of abandoned factories, failed schools, rampant crime, and a decrepit military that only he could fix. "This American carnage ends right here and right now," he claimed. "I'll be able to make sure that when you walk down the street in your inner city or wherever you are, you're not going to be shot." Over the course of Trump's first year, 112 people died in ten separate mass shooting events.[3] The following year, the number of fatalities reached over 300.[4] Even his insults—Lyin' Ted, Pocahontas, Crazy Bernie—play upon our imaginations, conjuring up images and associated emotions that, once heard, can be triggered over and over again at a mere mention.

The mind is powerful but it has its vulnerabilities. It requires a stream of coherent information to function properly. Put a person in a sensory deprivation chamber and within minutes they will start to hallucinate and become incredibly receptive to another person's suggestions. Likewise, put a person in a situation where his senses are overloaded with contradictory incoherent information and the mind will typically go numb as a protective reaction. It gets confused and overwhelmed—critical faculties no longer properly work. In this overloaded state, people can become vulnerable to hypnotic suggestion and trance.

You may associate hypnotism with a bearded doctor dangling an old pocket watch in front of a droopy-eyed subject, or a stage hypnotist who makes people believe that they are a chicken or Elvis Presley. While those images are stereotypes, they point to a central feature of hypnotism: the trance. In trance, critical thinking and other mental processes are diminished, leaving the highly suggestable unconscious imagination more in control.[5] People are less able to critically evaluate information received in a trance than when in a normal state of alert consciousness. The altered state does not need to be deep or long-lasting. It happens to all of us multiple times a day—when someone says, "pass the salt," do you analyze the communication, or do you just pass the salt while your focus remains on the meal or who you were speaking with?

The mind needs frames of reference in order to structure reality. Beliefs, past experiences, or points of information provide the filters. Change the frame of reference and the information coming in will be interpreted in a different way. If someone approaches you in the mall and says, "You look like an adventurous person who likes to try new things, a real free thinker who doesn't let conventions constrain you. Would you like to try some chocolate covered ants?" you're much more likely to agree than if that person approaches you and says, "You look like a sensible person who thinks carefully before acting."

When people are subjected to a systematic mind control process, most do not have any frame of reference for the experience and will often unconsciously accept the frame given to them by the leader or the group—for example, that they are special, chosen, or smart, and therefore deserving of what you are about to impart to them. Trump does that when he greets his audiences at rallies and tells them how much he loves them, as he did at a rally in El Paso. "I love this state. I love the people of this state. We've had a great romance together, you know that."[6] What they also know is that the love extends only to his supporters. One of Trump's favorite lines when meeting powerful men is to tell them how "handsome" they are. In 2017, when interviewing Kevin Warsh as a possible chairman of the Federal Reserve, the first thing he said was, "You're a really handsome guy, aren't you?"[7] He has even used it on himself. While campaigning in April 2016, he addressed the crowd, "Do I look like a president? How handsome am I, right? How handsome?" These may sound like harmless compliments or the endearing—or laughable, depending on your perspective—ravings of a vain and superficial narcissist but they are highly strategic. He is telling the audience—whether it is an individual or a crowd—that they are "worthy" of attention and that they are in this together. By framing the audience's experience from the outset, Trump makes it much more likely that they will lap up whatever he dishes out. As behavioral scientist Robert Cialdini shows in his book *Pre-Suasion: A Revolutionary Way to Influence and Persuade*, when a frame is set first, audiences become receptive to a message before they even hear it.

When we make decisions, we usually base them on information we believe to be true. We don't have the time or ability to stop, think, and fact-check every observation or statement that comes our way. We often trust what we're seeing and being told. If we distrusted everyone, we might become debilitatingly paranoid. If, at the other extreme, we were to trust indiscriminately, we would open ourselves to exploitation. Most people tend to maintain a healthy balance between skepticism and trust. Destructive mind controllers and con artists try to upset that balance to their own advantage.[8] Their goal is to size up their mark, tell them what they want to hear, give it to them—while picking their pocket—and then move on, says Pulitzer Prize winner David Cay Johnston, author of *The Making of Donald Trump* and *It's Even Worse Than You Think*. According to Johnston, Trump is "the greatest con artist in the history of the world, by conning his way to the White House."[9]

NEURO-LINGUISTIC PROGRAMMING (NLP)

In the 1970s, Richard Bandler and John Grinder developed a systematic approach to dial into another person's worldview—to understand how they make sense of reality—in an effort to help them be more effective. They called it Neuro-Linguistic Programming, or NLP. Bandler and Grinder developed the approach based on the revolutionary work of psychiatrist Milton Erickson—in particular his process-oriented hypnosis—and of others such as therapist Virginia Satir, anthropologist and linguist Gregory Bateson, and the body awareness expert Moshe Feldenkrais.[10] Bandler and Grinder saw how therapists like Erickson and Satir were achieving great results—what they called therapeutic "magic"—with their clients and set out to model them and discover how they were so effective.

They realized that people experience the world subjectively, through their five senses—vision, hearing, touch, smell, and taste. When we perform mental operations—recall an event or anticipate or rehearse a future one—we do so in terms of visual images, sounds, tactile sensations, smells, and tastes. Some people are more visual, while others might be more auditory. The goal of the therapist is to understand how their client subjectively experiences the world. Bandler and Grinder found that by using a set of techniques—mirroring a person's posture or vocal patterns, responding to eye movements, as well as observing nonverbal behaviors—they could elicit greater trust, which allowed them to get to the heart of their client's mindset, thereby helping them to change. They did this by creating a set of experiences for their clients, which often included imagining future states of being, that would help them be more effective—make teachers better at teaching, salespeople better at selling—as well as helping people in conflict or pain.

When I first encountered NLP in 1980, I was fascinated—I was so impressed that I moved out to Santa Cruz to study with Grinder. What he and Bandler did was to identify and explain many of the techniques I had used in the Moonies to recruit and indoctrinate people—and that had been used on me. In a sense, NLP teaches in a systematic way what many cult leaders and con artists do. Though it was originally developed for therapists and educators to help people, its techniques have been used to influence people in destructive ways.

Of course, influence techniques have been used by persuaders for thousands of years. With NLP, they just became systematized in such a way that they could be taught on a mass scale. Let's look at some of the more common techniques.

HYPNOTIC TRANCES AND HALLUCINATIONS

People go in and out of trance all day long. It's a natural feature of consciousness. We daydream. We get in a car and realize we spaced out for the last ten miles while driving. Our attention is not always in the here and now, with our analytic mind engaged. Milton Erickson found that he could help his patients overcome psychological problems through a dynamic process of naturalistic hypnosis, in which he monitored when patients went in and out of consciousness. He believed that the unconscious mind was always listening and that, through his own careful and strategic use of words and suggestions, he could help patients change unhealthy beliefs, feelings, and behaviors. Whether or not a person was in trance, suggestions could be made that would have a hypnotic influence as long as they found resonance at the unconscious level.

Of course, Erickson was a psychiatrist—people were coming to him for help. He had a therapeutic ethical frame but his work on hypnosis provided an extremely important addition to the mind-control arsenal. Hypnotic mind control techniques are not in themselves negative. In fact, they can be very beneficial as long as the locus of control is inside the person and the external influencer does not have an agenda to impose their own beliefs and expectations.

Cult leaders and high-demand groups always have an agenda—they seek to control people for power, money, and sex. An ethical mental health professional might use hypnotic suggestions to help you be your most effective and authentic self and will tell you that they are doing so. Unethical people and cults almost never tell members they are using hypnotic techniques, which makes it easier for them to enact their agenda. In a high-demand group or cult, the external influencer wants to make you into a true believer, one who has internalized the new ideology and code of conduct. They want you to die to your old self and be reborn. This is true in many cults—Scientology, Hare Krishnas, Moonies, and NXIVM, Christian shepherding groups, and others.

Scientology is notorious for its use of hypnosis. It employs hypnotic techniques in its initial communications course all the way through to its more advanced Training Routines, or TRs, which are part of what Scientologists call the "Bridge to Total Freedom."[11] The first hypnotic step is to make a person sit for long periods of time without moving; next they are commanded to stare into the eyes of another Scientologist, possibly for hours. At some point, the other Scientologist will try to get them to react—it is a sign of advancement to be able to sit there maintaining the stare but what it requires is a dissociation from themselves. Essentially they are being pushed into an altered state of deep trance where the goal is to develop a Scientology self that is obedient to Hubbard and the group. Members are indoctrinated to believe that the Training Routines will help them be more effective in their lives—earn more money, be better communicators, get better jobs. Later they are told that by performing these routines they will help clear the planet of poverty, crime, disease—indeed, of all of humanity's problems. At the highest level, members are told that they can control matter, energy, space, and time. The truth is, they are the ones being controlled.[12]

In extreme hypnotic states, people might see things that aren't there or make things disappear. These are referred to as positive and negative hallucinations, respectively. They are especially common in some Bible and shepherding cults, and in particular in the ministries belonging to the Christian right movement known as the New Apostolic Reformation (NAR), which believes in demon possession and puts a heavy emphasis on Satan. Believers are taught to perform visualizations and undergo various altered states and hypnotic experiences that can lead them to believe that they are being attacked by evil entities. Likewise, they can believe that they are being filled with the holy spirit and act "drunken for God." You can see videos online of people looking like they drank a fifth of scotch but it's their belief in the holy spirit that allegedly animates them. It turns out the NAR—with its millions of adherents—has become one of Trump's biggest supporters. They are told, and many believe, that Trump was picked by God to lead the nation. They are Trump's true believers. They view themselves as "spiritual warriors" who think they are helping Trump carry out his God-given mission.

Some hypnotic mind control hallucinations can have positive effects. Before I was recruited into the Moon cult, I was introverted and very uncomfortable doing public speaking. In the group, I was taught to use a variation of a hypnotic technique that included praying and telling myself that God was using me as a vessel. I imagined God was speaking through me, so I had no ego. After I left the cult, I needed to reconfigure my belief system, but realized I could still behave confidently, as I had as a Moonie leader. Also, I started applying some techniques when I started giving lectures about my cult involvement. For example, I would use another positive hallucination technique:

I would imagine my family and friends in the audience. This way, I wouldn't feel alone talking to strangers. When I did my first few television interviews, I used a negative hallucination technique to make the cameras in front of me disappear. All I saw was the interviewer.

Hypnotic techniques are not inherently good or bad. It depends on who is using them and for what purpose. Norman Vincent Peale—Trump's mentor during his childhood—taught hypnotic techniques in his church and in his book *The Power of Positive Thinking*. There is an aspect to Trump's positive self-talk that sounds almost self-hypnotic. During the campaign, after the second Republican debate, when Trump was slipping in the polls, he would talk about all the positive signs—referring only to polls that showed him gaining ground, and talking about how "amazing" things were going on. He was so insistent on the hugeness of his inaugural crowd that one might wonder if he actually hallucinated that it was that huge.

While Peale's methods might be a boon for some, they can also lead to psychological problems. I worked with a young man who was a true believer in the art of positive thinking—he was a high school football player and was practicing Peale's techniques, visualizing himself in a particular football position and being successful. It turns out his coach didn't want him to play that position and told him to do another. The young man did the program and believed 100 percent and thought if he just kept believing, the coach would magically change his mind. Instead the coach kicked him off the team. He had a breakdown and thought there was something wrong with him.

One needs to be able to use reality-testing strategies and be open to feedback and adjust accordingly. Believe all you want, but if you don't have the talent, no matter how much positive thinking you do, you are not going to become a baseball legend, a rock star, or a computer genius.

So far, I have mostly talked about techniques that are used one-on-one but hypnotic techniques can be used on large crowds, like at a Trump rally. Of course, all political rallies—or rock concerts—have the potential for inducing a kind of trance state, but Trump's repetitions, his rhythmic vocal cadences, his vivid imagery are unusual. He

keeps returning at his rallies to the same images—of the Wall, dangerous foes, and even now, the size of his inaugural crowd. None of these
exist and yet some of his followers believe that they do—they can
even visualize them. They have become real in many people's minds.

It is a fact that some people are more susceptible to trance and
may even be born with that ability. Hypnosis experts call them "high
hypnotizables." These people have a high capacity for imagination
and concentration, so much so that some can intentionally change
their skin temperature just by imagining holding ice cubes. We've all
felt ice, many of us have made snowballs, so we carry in our memory
and in our neuronal patterns what it feels like to be cold. It's really
about accessing your imagination and your reservoir of experiences
and applying them in a concentrated way. An ethical therapeutic treatment by health-care professionals trained in hypnosis can help people
avoid migraine headaches. People are taught to visualize as well as
have kinesthetic hallucinations that can dilate and constrict the blood
vessels in their heads. They practice first with making their hands
warm and cold.

Hypnosis is a powerful method almost anyone can learn if they
want to invest the time and effort. Ethical professional groups will not
train just anyone. Two organizations that I belong to, The American
Society of Clinical Hypnosis and The International Society of Hypnosis, require at least a master's level in health care. But it's important to
be careful. There are countless videos online by dubious individuals
with no credentials or code of ethics.

There is a famous British entertainer named Derren Brown who
delights his audiences by performing what I consider unethical social influence experiments. On his TV series *Mind Control* he has
demonstrated some amazing feats—fooling people into turning over
their watch, cell phone, and wallet within minutes of talking to him.[13]
Brown has also done several potentially dangerous hypnotic experiments as part of his show, like making someone believe they had no
choice but to kill a kitten or creating a "Manchurian Candidate." The
volunteer, believing a toy gun to be real, was commanded to shoot
a famous actor onstage. A hidden red dye pack exploded when the

trigger was pulled. The actor collapsed, frightening everyone in the audience. The hypnotic subject had no memory of the act until he was shown the video recording later.[14]

The hugely popular self-help guru Tony Robbins[15] has built a media empire of bestselling books, sold-out retreats and seminars, and infomercials by optimizing what he learned from NLP methods of persuasion. He's done seminars for top corporate executives around the world, as well as former president Bill Clinton[16] and tennis star Serena Williams, who is a Jehovah's Witness. *Dilbert* cartoonist Scott Adams said Robbins is the "best working hypnotist in the world." He is most probably among the richest and most influential. In an interview with *The Daily Beast,* Robbins said that he was the first person to give Trump his first big speaking gig. "He'd never done a big speech before and he thought he was coming to give it for 300 people but it was 10,000. And he got hooked."[17]

A BRIEF WORD ABOUT MEDITATION

There are hundreds if not thousands of ways to meditate—no one way is best for everyone. I have done a number of different meditation practices with a variety of teachers. My understanding is that the fundamental goal of meditation is to train the mind to overcome restless and unsettling thoughts—what meditation teachers call "monkey mind"—and, in some practices, to let go of ordinary consciousness and reach a higher state of awareness. Some meditation practices involve sitting still and watching your thoughts, or attending to the inflow and outflow of your breath, or walking and focusing on your steps. The locus of control is inside you. Focusing on a flame or repeating a word, or mantra, are also forms of meditation.

In my opinion, guided meditation and visualization are not, strictly speaking, forms of meditation. Listening to someone prompt you through a series of thoughts, feelings, and experiences is closer to a hypnotic, trance-inducing process than it is to meditation. Guided visualizations can be healthy and therapeutic, depending on who is doing it and why. For example, if at the end of a yoga class, you are lying on your mat, and the instructor asks you to visualize walking on warm sand at a beach or to feel your body melting into the mat and you feel better, that is fine. If it is ethical and empowers people to think for themselves and be more functional, with an internal locus of control, I am all for it. Be careful! So much of what is being promoted on the Web as meditation is actually hypnosis.

Some forms of meditation can actually be detrimental for certain people, provoking feelings of anxiety and even panic. This can be especially true if a person gets drawn deeply into a meditation-based group like Transcendental Meditation (TM), which encourages its members to meditate for hours at a stretch. In his book *Transcendental Deception: Behind the TM Curtain*, former ten-year TM teacher Aryeh Siegel describes how the group uses a "veneer of science" and celebrity endorsements—from people like filmmaker David Lynch—to peddle their own brand of Hinduism. According to Siegel, TM claims to promote a science-backed form of meditation, but members can be drawn into a whole set of beliefs and practices which they are told will lead to supernatural powers—flying, invisibility, and immortality—all for a price.

I have met and worked with many people who have been harmed by TM. One young man I counseled told me he had intense headaches, involuntary tics, and even began barking like a dog while a member of TM. He went to his supervisor, who told him that he was de-stressing and should meditate more. After suffering a serious breakdown, he stopped doing TM and sought my help. I taught him about cults and mind control and explained the history of the group—that the late founder, Maharishi Mahesh Yogi, who claimed to be an enlightened master, was a womanizer and a fraud. Maharishi said he was ordained by a group of holy gurus in India, known as Shankaracharaya, but the ordination never happened. He claimed to give people their own special mantras but in fact assigned them based on the year a person was born.[18] He also claimed that for three thousand dollars he could teach someone to levitate, which no one ever experienced. The best they managed was a cross-legged version of hopping. Ex-member Robert Kropinski—who suffered from an anxiety and dissociative disorder after practicing TM for more than eleven years—visited the Shanka-racharaya in India to ask about Maharishi. They effectively said that anyone who charges money for a spiritual practice is a fraud.[19]

I have encountered many ex-members of meditation cults over the decades. Often they are afraid to try a meditation practice of any type again. After they understand cult mind control and process their experiences, they come to trust their ability to evaluate healthy and unhealthy practices, people, and organizations.

ANCHORING

Anchoring is essentially using a cue—a touch, sound, a visual image—to trigger an associated thought or feeling. The cue, or anchor, can come from any of the five senses so long as it connects to an experience or a memory. Words can be anchors, so too a tone of voice or a touch. A gesture, a saying, an image—all of these serve as anchors when they are used purposefully to trigger an emotional response in someone. These triggers can be used quite intentionally and right in the open without people even realizing it. Once you are made aware of these techniques, you are far more likely to identify them when they are being used. To me, they seem obvious and pop into my conscious mind like a waving red flag. Much like the conditioning experiment conducted by Russian physiologist Ivan Pavlov on his dogs, a person who is subjected to the trigger is "trained" to respond in a prescribed way. As the famous case goes, Pavlov's dogs would hear a bell ring when given food, and the dog would salivate seeing the food. After several meals, Pavlov noticed that the dog would salivate just hearing the bell. As the psychologist B. F. Skinner showed, a similar kind of conditioning can be effective with humans who are capable of learning faster than dogs, even if they are unaware of the trigger.

There are thousands of anchoring examples—think of really successful logos like the Nike Swoosh, or the Apple's iconic partially eaten apple, or the American flag and the patriotism it conjures up. The pink hats made for the Women's March of January 2017 in Washington, D.C., elicit an emotional response for its participants.

For Trump supporters, red MAGA hats or T-shirts may act as anchors. They bring about a feeling of identity and solidarity and may elicit memories of past Trump rallies. Make America Great Again is a linguistic anchor. This phrase triggers a kind of positive nostalgia and idealization of a moment in history that may never have happened—an imaginary golden age. Each person might have a different image or movie in their mind when they hear this phrase. For some people, it may have less benign associations, possibly harkening back to a time when America was a less diverse, more repressive country. They hear the phrase and may think, Make America White Again.[20]

FRAMING

As we have already seen, framing occurs when we set a psychological context for an experience in a way that biases the outcome—like a person's willingness to eat chocolate-covered ants, as we saw earlier. Trump also uses it to identify his rally audiences as loyal followers. It's a way to direct and focus attention and, for Trump, to gain the upper hand. In the Fox presidential debate in 2015, moderator Megyn Kelly said to Trump: "You've called women you don't like fat pigs, dogs, slobs, and disgusting animals."[21] He cut her off: "Only Rosie O'Donnell." Trump turned the tables and reframed Kelly's accusation, taking all the power out of her statement and getting a chuckle out of the crowd to boot.

Trump also sets the linguistic frame for whoever happens to be his nemesis at the moment—calling Marco Rubio "Little Marco" and Ted Cruz "Lying Ted." It's what Scott Adams calls the "linguistic kill shot," like Low-Energy Jeb Bush, Crooked Hillary Clinton, Pencil-Neck Adam Schiff. Once you hear the nicknames, you can't help but focus on Bush's energy levels, or Schiff's neck. They are difficult to get out of your mind.

Withdrawing from the Paris climate accord, Trump called climate change a "hoax" and redirected attention to China and India, who he claimed were the real winners in the accord. He reframed the debate from saving the planet to an economic and political contest with two superpowers.

STORYTELLING

Stories are the primary way we communicate with ourselves and others in our ongoing experience to make meaning of our lives. They are how we learn and how we teach. Engaging a person in a compelling narrative creates vicarious experiences that elicit powerful emotional responses, accessing memories and creating new perspectives.

Stories can be told to help, heal, instruct, guide, inspire, create, and move people to actions that help them and their communities. But stories can be used to entrap, manipulate, and control. Scientology's L. Ron Hubbard was a science fiction writer before he became a cult leader. It is no wonder that at the heart of Scientology lies a fantastic secret narrative, one that members spend many years and tens of thousands of dollars to finally learn. They are told that they will die if they discover this information before they are prepared for it. The story goes like this: 75 million years ago, a galactic dictator named Prince Xenu (or Xemu) wanted to solve the overpopulation problem plaguing the galaxy, so he sent millions of beings from seventy-six different planets to Teegeeack—now known as Earth. He forced the beings, or "thetans," into volcanoes and then dropped hydrogen bombs on the volcanoes. According to Hubbard, everyone alive today is a mass of thousands of "clusters" of these "body thetans," which influence our every thought and action. We are all possessed and controlled by demons, according to Hubbard. Only Scientology can rid us of these invisible body thetans. Once freed—which usually requires six extremely expensive levels of "processing"—Scientologists are told they will have super powers, including complete control over matter, energy, space, and time. (Although Hubbard's courses have been available since 1967, no Scientologist was able to claim the million-dollar prize offered, until 2016, by famous magician James Randi to anyone able to demonstrate supernatural powers.)

White nationalist storytelling describes a global conspiracy of Jewish bankers, Muslims, and terrorists who want to destroy the white race. They create vivid narratives portraying Hitler as a great savior and hero who tried to restore the white race to its rightful dominant place. They rouse people who have felt economically or culturally deprived by blaming and even attacking the "other"—Jews, Blacks, Hispanics, Muslims—for taking what is rightfully theirs. It's a classic villain-versus-hero narrative pattern. The meme #WhiteGenocide is a kind of shorthand for the story, one that Trump has retweeted many times.[22]

Trump is not a brilliant storyteller—he can be clumsy, and lacking in subtlety. But in his campaign slogan—Make America Great Again—he had a simple and brilliant story, one that he told over and over again, in rally after rally. According to author and filmmaker Randy Olson, it won him the presidency: "How could this country elect a reality TV show host as its President? Trump had a story. Hillary had none. 'America was once great. America is no longer great. I will make America great again.'"[23] Now that he is president, Trump tells an updated version—*Keep* America Great. But the message is similar: "I have made American great again, but it can all come crashing down if the liberal Democrats are elected into office."

One might say that Donald Trump, the successful businessman, is himself a story crafted by Tony Schwartz, his ghostwriter on *The Art of the Deal*—one that was furthered through the propaganda efforts of Mark Burnett for fourteen seasons on American reality television. People who have worked on *The Apprentice* have talked about how important the editing process was to crafting a story that reinforced the image of Trump's greatness. Fans of *The Apprentice* would be influenced hour by hour, week after week, and year after year to think of him as a great business leader. It may not have been a leap to think of him as president.

MODELING

Young people look to model themselves after influential people—a parent or family relative, a scientist or inventor, an athlete or celebrity, historical figure, a president. It's an important aspect of identity formation. Trump had several role models—his father, and his military academy instructor, Colonel Theodore Dobias. Norman Vincent Peale was also influential, as was Roy Cohn. Looking for role models doesn't end with childhood—adults often emulate people they respect and may try to embody certain of their characteristics. The whole self-help movement is based on the premise that by following the advice and example set by successful people, we can improve our lives.

One of the key techniques of NLP is to create internal mental models of success. Often that involves finding a "true" role model of success—an actual person. The danger comes when our role models turn out to be unethical, unscrupulous people, who promise one thing and deliver another and who seek followers for their own gain. Cults are built on a foundation of role-modeling—followers model themselves in the image of false prophets, gurus, or messiahs. It seems ludicrous to me today that I once tried to be like Sun Myung Moon—a paunchy, middle-aged Korean arms dealer who lied, humiliated followers, had multiple extramarital affairs, and foisted his delusions of grandeur on his hundreds of thousands of followers.

This is often the case in religious cults. While most Bible cults claim to be following Jesus, their leaders are often promoted as role models for followers—even when they ignore the words and practices taught by Jesus Christ. Jesus minimized the importance of money and wealth and yet so-called prosperity preachers tell their followers that their faith will be rewarded by material riches. Often these preachers live luxurious lifestyles while their followers get poorer and poorer. Jesus taught his followers to "turn the other cheek," and yet Trump, who is held up by many of these groups as a man of god, preaches revenge.

To prepare herself for her role on *The Apprentice*, Omarosa Manigault Newman read everything she could about Trump. She wanted to learn all she could to impress him, but modeling herself after him may have made her more susceptible to his influence. In *The Art of the Deal*, Trump promoted himself as a kind of business role model. Now he touts himself as a kind of political savior who will help rescue

America. We saw earlier how Florida governor Ron DeSantis said he can't think of a better role model for his own children than Trump.

RAPPORT AND TRUST-BUILDING TECHNIQUES: MIRRORING, MATCHING, PACING, AND LEADING

Mirroring is a relatively easy and common persuasive technique: copy the other person's body language, speech patterns, and mannerisms. Make that person feel comfortable with you and they will let down their guard. When I was being trained in NLP, we were taught to mirror someone's body posture but not too overtly; otherwise it could have the opposite effect. Arms folded? Fold yours, but not too obviously. Legs crossed, cross yours. We were even trained to match people's breathing rates. These behaviors occur quite naturally with those you feel close to. NLP practitioners are taught to speed up the get-to-know-you process by mirroring and matching someone's speech patterns, accents, words, mannerisms, and beliefs.

Trump has his own style, to be sure, and he exploits it to full effect—essentially announcing that "I am not like the rest of Washington." He is always gesturing, striking power poses, and making faces to press his points. He plays to his audience's expectation that he is not like other politicians—an expectation that he helped to cultivate in the first place. At the same time, he is extremely responsive to his audiences, in some ways encouraging them to match him in emotion and intensity. He bobs his head vigorously when he is listening, which is a kind of positive reinforcing behavior. Perhaps most of all, he mirrors people's expectations that he be an authority figure—with his dominance stance, his fierce handshake, his strutting, and on one memorable occasion, his almost threatening posturing. This was during a 2016 debate with Hillary Clinton, when he stood—or rather loomed—directly behind her while she was speaking. The effect for many viewers was breathtaking and scary.

Trump has also used the mirroring technique on the international stage. In January 2018, as North Korea was ramping up its nuclear program and threatening to unleash a missile on the United States,

Trump threatened back verbally, saying that he could destroy Kim and his country with "fire and fury." Kim said he has a nuclear button on his desk. Trump told Kim that his button was bigger than Kim's button, and that his nuclear arsenal actually worked.

He switched tactics at a later point and flattered Kim and, some would say, "wooed" him into talks. Obviously, Kim was the one with the most to gain by a meeting with Trump—the leader of a small pariah nation meeting with an American president. Trump walked away from the meeting with no deal, though he did receive international media attention. Diplomats said it was a squandered diplomatic opportunity. But it gave Trump temporary bragging rights: he could say he had averted a nuclear showdown. Never mind that his earlier rhetoric—which included giving Kim his own nickname, Rocket Man—actually helped create the crisis in the first place. Braggadocio aside, the method that Trump used to engage the Korean dictator was effective. Narcissistic cult leaders can often be manipulated by flattery. It takes one to know one.

CONFUSION TECHNIQUES

Among the most effective persuasion techniques are those designed to create confusion. Our conscious minds can only attend to a limited amount of information at any moment—they can get overwhelmed very easily. When there is incongruity between information and how it is delivered—for example, someone telling you bad news while smiling—the situation is exacerbated. People often go into a mild trance to resolve the conflict. In that trance state, they are more susceptible to being programmed with false beliefs, phobias, and conspiracy theories. Confidently lying while your facial and body language says you are telling the truth is an especially effective confusion technique. Con artists and pathological liars know that they need to occasionally say some true things, which can reassure people but also confuse them. What is the truth?

This is one of Trump's favorite techniques—he tells lies about a lot of things, some of them quite extreme. It turns out "the big lie" is an effective persuasion technique, one used often by Nazi propagandist Joseph Goebbels. Goebbels found that the bigger the lie, the more it is likely to be believed—people think, "This is such a huge and outrageous claim, it must be true." Repeating the big lie—as Trump did with his claims that Obama wasn't born in the United States or that he is a Muslim—reinforces the validity of the falsehood that a person has just accepted. Trump does this all the time.

Once a frame is set that the person lies a lot to make a point, there is usually less confusion. Many Trump followers excuse his behavior by saying he is prone to exaggeration but is not a liar, or that all politicians lie. Or that he lies but they support and love him anyway.[24] Such a dizzying amount of false and contradictory information, with the occasional kernel of truth, overloads and overwhelms critical thinking. Making matters worse is when a person gaslights—utters a lie and then says they never said it, as Trump did when he denied that he ever claimed that Mexico would pay for the Wall.

PATTERN INTERRUPTION

A pattern interruption occurs when there is a violation of a norm or social script. Cursing and swearing is something that some Scientologists like to do to throw people off guard, especially when asked critical questions about their group.[25] Trump does this frequently—his presidency is defined by pattern interruptions. While most politicians show some modicum of political decorum, Trump does the opposite—he is bold and disruptive. He uses politically incorrect words and actions to reaffirm in his followers that he is not a politician. He is an outsider. He lies, as we have abundantly seen, and distracts. His tweets disrupt the normal mode of political communication and can come at any hour of the day or night (and Trump sleeps only a few hours). His followers love him for it but it also creates a disconnect for those who expect a president to be honest, trustworthy, and respectful. His actions call into question not just the executive branch but the whole structure of government.

Another pattern interrupt Trump has used is the handshake—and in hypnosis, there is a technique known as a handshake induction. The norm is to reach out your hand, grasp the other person's—not too tightly or loosely—and shake and release. Trump would famously not let go, even pulling the other person toward him, inducing a moment of confusion and disorientation, demonstrating that he is in control—until Portuguese president Marcelo Rebelo de Sousa turned the tables on him as he was greeted by Trump at the White House. De Sousa yanked Trump's outstretched arm before Trump could assert his dominance.[26]

Trump's self-avowed grabbing of women's genitals—if true—could be considered another pattern interruption technique. Most women would consider such behavior invasive and highly disturbing and go into an immediate confusion state—especially if Trump were to make eye contact, smile, and say something like "You are so beautiful. I want to get to know you." His celebrity, power, and money would add to the confusion. Of course, if a woman had been abused previously or was taught about this abusive behavior, they might get angry, move away—and, ideally, report the incident.

DOUBLE BINDS

As we have seen earlier, a double bind forces a person to do what the controller wants while giving an illusion of choice. I once heard a tape of now-deceased cult leader Bhagwan Shree Rajneesh (known now as Osho) hypnotically say, "For those people who are having doubts about what I am telling you, you should know that I am the one putting those doubts inside your mind so that you will see the truth, that I am the true teacher and come back to me." Whether the person believes or doubts the leader, they are usually left confused and vulnerable—unless they understand what a double bind is.

Sometimes a double bind can be used for a person's benefit. For example, the psychiatrist Milton Erickson is quoted as having said to a client, "I think your unconscious mind knows more about this than your conscious mind does, and if your unconscious mind knows more about this than your conscious mind does, then you probably know more about this than you think you do." Either way, the person is smarter than they believed!

Trump uses double binds to control situations to his own advantage. Charlie Houpert, founder of Charisma on Command and a YouTube personality, cites several examples of Trump using double binds during the Republican primary debates. In one of the debates, Trump taunted Jeb Bush about having low energy, saying, "I know you're trying to build up your energy, Jeb, but it's not working." As Houpert astutely observed, "With this, Jeb Bush has two options: either up his energy level or bring it back down. If he chooses to go after Trump full-throttle, he'll look defensive and [like he's] putting Trump in the control seat. If he tries to diffuse it, he perpetuates [Trump's] taunt."[27] It's a catch-22. Trump 1, Jeb, 0.

PROJECTION

Projection is one of the most powerful techniques used in social psychology. It occurs when a person projects their own behaviors, traits, or beliefs onto other people. For example, when confronted, a cheating husband might turn around and blame his wife, saying it was she who wanted to cheat, has cheated, or is somehow responsible for him cheating. Jim Jones ordered his followers to drink poisoned fruit punch but said that enemies of the group were coming to kill them. I have been the recipient of a fair amount of cult projection. Cults accuse me and other countercult activists of trying to gain fame and money, when in fact that is exactly what the cult leader is doing.

Trump is a master of projection. His twisted use of the "birther" lie is one example. For years he claimed that President Obama was not born in the United States, earning a lot of publicity in the process. When the birth certificate was produced, he accused Senator Hillary Clinton of spreading the rumor. In September 2015, he tweeted, "The birther movement was started by Hillary Clinton in 2008. She was all in!"[28] Why would he do this? Projection is a powerful psychological defense mechanism, one that is a hallmark of malignant narcissism. But it is also an incredibly powerful technique of psychological manipulation.

Projection is Trump's consistent response to criticism.[29][30] When he was accused of being misogynistic, he immediately defended himself, claiming no one respects women more than him. He then deflected the accusation, accusing Bill Clinton of abusing women. "There's never been anybody in the history of politics in this nation that's been so abusive to women. So you can say any way you want to say it, but Bill Clinton was abusive to women. Hillary Clinton attacked those same women and attacked them viciously," Trump said.

Often Trump's projections will entail an elaborate pattern of deflection. When he was accused of criticizing the Gold Star couple, Kihzr and Ghazala Kahn, he actually tried to blame the death of their son on Hillary Clinton. "Captain Khan is an American hero, and if I were president at that time, he would be alive today, because unlike her, who voted for the war without knowing what she was doing, I would not have had our people in Iraq. Iraq was a disaster. So he would have been alive today."[31] From a general psychological perspective, people with undeveloped personalities, such as occurs in narcissistic personality disorder, are unable to tolerate criticism; they need to be viewed as brilliant and wonderful, and will go to great lengths to bury or project the criticism and blame onto someone else.

Social influence expert Anthony Pratkanis demonstrated in his 2000 study, "Projection as an Interpersonal Influence Tactic: The Effects of the Pot Calling the Kettle Black," that projection is a surprisingly effective persuasion tool. In the first experiment, Pratkanis was able to verify the most obvious case: that projection exonerates the accuser at the expense of the accused. Later experiments showed that projection continued to be an effective technique even when suspicions were raised about the projectionist. Participants in the experiment still saw the "accused" as guilty. "The vast majority of participants thought that projection would not work and would boomerang to increase the perceived guilt of the accuser," writes Pratkanis. Even more surprising, being skeptical of projection as a persuasion technique had little effect on how well the technique worked and was in fact negatively correlated.

USE OF FEAR

In his 1954 book, *The True Believer*, Eric Hoffer wrote about the use of fear—the most basic of human emotions. It hits at the heart of our drive for survival. According to Hoffer, followers of mass movements need not believe in a god, but they must believe in a devil. He actually talked about the strength of a mass movement being measured by the vividness and tangibility of its devil. Hatred and fear always unify believers against a common enemy. We have seen how Trump does this: drumming up fear of the "other" and of what will happen to the country if he is not in power. Trump is not alone. Many political candidates, in their speeches and negative ads, create an image of dire consequences if their opponent wins. If you vote for the other candidate, you and the country will suffer—jobs will be lost, crime will rise, family values will erode, and your very freedoms will be stripped away.

Yet few candidates have stoked fear quite like Trump does—fear is the way he holds onto power. It was the basis of his presidential campaign, and it is the basis of his bid for reelection. He frequently cites the same old cast of enemies to maintain his position and to keep his followers stoked and ready to defend him. Even with a seemingly strong economy he needs to fuel the drama. Trump is the "candidate of crisis," as Richard Wolffe colorfully writes in *The Guardian*. "For most politicians, this would be a frabjous day of well-nigh full employment and fatter paychecks. But there are no calloohs or callays in this Trumperwocky. There are just rock-wielding caravans of disease-plagued murderers invading a fragile nation at risk of imminent collapse from the enemies within: notably the media and a bunch of leftwing mobs in cahoots with a suspiciously Semitic man named [George] Soros."[32]

Parody aside, creating fear of imaginary threats is dysfunctional and dangerous. It is especially dangerous when the fear is directed toward a group of people, a phenomenon known as scapegoating. Hubbard blamed psychiatrists and journalists for society's ills, claiming they were part of a global conspiracy to undermine the "clearing" of the planet. Like Trump, he demonized the press and even had a word for information that was critical of him or the group, "entheta." He claimed that if we could get rid of his enemies, Scientology could save the world. Moon blamed the communists for all the world's problems. Most notoriously and tragically, Hitler blamed the Jews for Germany's economic and social woes and suggested they were vermin needing to be exterminated. Trump has used similar terms for undocumented immigrants: "You wouldn't believe how bad these people are. These aren't people, these are animals."[33]

REPETITION

Want to get a point across? Repeat it. Repetition, as we have seen, can be very effective in everyday speech and in advertising. Hearing words and phrases multiple times is a way to get across a message and have it stick in people's heads. As mentioned earlier, Trump's father, Fred, repeated over and over again to his sons, "You are a killer. You are a king. You are a killer. You are a king." Trump would absorb these words, developing, as we have seen, a predator versus prey mentality. His brother, Fred Jr., took a more self-destructive path, dying at a young age due to alcoholism.

In everyday life, too much repetition may backfire. A classic study by J. T. Cacioppo and Richard Petty showed that low to moderate levels of repetition often create greater agreement with the message, while too much repetition can have an adverse effect.[34] And yet the content of the message, as well as how it's conveyed, and also its context, can affect how a repeated message is received. Messages that resonate with a person's prior beliefs may be more likely to be believed. With cult members, it is akin to programming.

When I was in the Moonies, we would hear the same lectures over and over—the goal was to get us not just to remember and accept what we were hearing but to reinforce it and have it become part of our mindset. It was part of our mind control programming. Repetition is standard operating procedure for many cults—from Scientology, to

Aum Shinrikyo, Lyndon LaRouche's organization, the World Mission Society Church of God, NXIVM, and numerous others. In some cults, members would be forced to watch endless videos. As we saw in an earlier chapter, it is part of Pratkanis and Aronson's formula for becoming a cult leader: "Repeat your message over and over and over again. Repetition makes the heart grow fonder and fiction, if heard frequently enough, can come to sound like fact."

Trump uses this technique a lot, both with his truthful statements and with his numerous falsehoods and lies. According to his biographer David Cay Johnston, repetition is the key to Trump's success. Trump boiled his platform down to just a few key slogans—Make America Great Again, Drain the Swamp, Build the Wall, Lock Her Up—and then repeated them over and over, and eventually had his followers repeat them at rallies. Like my Moonie programming, the constant repetitions reinforced the Trump platform in the minds of his followers.

Trump also repeats individual words and phrases—repetition is part of his idiosyncratic speech pattern. Shortly after he was inaugurated, he complained about his legacy from former president Obama. "To be honest, I inherited a mess," he said. "It's a mess. At home and abroad, a mess . . . I inherited a mess."[35] Do you see the mess? Even for Obama lovers, who might be enraged by the insults and believe them to be totally false, it's hard not to see a "mess."

Trump loves to remind the public how smart he is:

- December 11, 2016, on Fox News: "I'm, like, a smart person. I don't have to be told the same thing in the same words every single day."
- January 6, 2018, tweet (defending himself against material in Michael Wolff's *Fire and Fury*): "My two greatest assets have been mental stability and being, like, really smart."
- April 26, 2016, Trump Tower event: "I'm not changing. I went to the best schools, I'm, like, a very smart person. I'm going to represent our country with dignity and very well. I don't want to change my personality—it got me here."[36]

He also loves the word "winning." He repeated it throughout his campaign. "We don't win anymore. We don't win anymore in our country. We used to win. If I win, we'll win, we'll all win," he said during an interview on Fox News. Nor has he stopped using it since he won the presidency. "Winning is such a great feeling, isn't it? Winning is such a great feeling. Nothing like winning—you got to win. . . . Victory, winning—beautiful words, but that is what it is all about," he said during a 2018 address to the U.S. Naval Academy.

Beautiful words, indeed—they helped get Trump elected. Repetition is effective at persuading people of the credibility of a statement for several reasons. It leads the recipient, through a primarily unconscious and memory-based process, to "mistakenly believe that he/she has already heard the statement from another source," according to researchers Nicole Ernst, Rinaldo Kuhne, and Werner Wirth. Second, it may "increase the 'processing fluency,' which is defined as the metacognitive experience of ease during information processing. The easier and more fluently that information can be processed, the more credible the information appears, regardless of the statement's content."[37] Trump's often outrageous claims may also cause confusion—crowding out analytical thinking and causing the mind to retreat into a kind of trance, especially when the repeated phrase is a lie, falsehood, or otherwise contradicts what you already know.

SOCIAL PROOF

One of the six universal techniques described by behavioral scientist Dr. Robert Cialdini in his 2009 book, *Influence: The Psychology of Persuasion,* social proof describes how people are influenced by the actions or opinions of others. Cialdini writes that "we determine what is correct by finding out what other people think is correct." Especially if there is uncertainty, people, like, sheep, will follow the herd. It is based on our ancient instincts for survival—if everyone is eating this berry, it's probably a safe berry to eat.

Think about it: if someone looks up at the sky, others will look up as well. Do you check Yelp.com for a restaurant's ratings before making a reservation? That's social proof. Today it is used in advertising and marketing campaigns all the time. Instagram "sponsorships" are impossible to miss. In our information-laden, time-strapped world, we tend to be overwhelmed, making us even more likely to default to the herd's opinion. The Moon cult was famous for having mass weddings in stadiums with tens of thousands of members getting married to people selected by Moon, a striking testament to their faith. Tom Cruise, John Travolta, and dozens of other celebrities are often used by Scientology to promote how great the group is. NXIVM and Aum Shinrikyo both made large donations in order for leaders to have a meeting with as well as a photo opportunity with the Dalai Lama.

President Trump uses social proof to dispel criticism. As Jason Hreha observes in *Medium*, during the third Republican primary debate, when Trump was getting pushback on his tax plan, he cited Larry Kudlow. "Larry Kudlow is an example, who I have a lot of respect for, loves my tax plan." He thrives on showing how popular he is. "During rallies he will often heckle the cameramen, saying they never show the full crowd. 'They don't turn 'em. They don't turn 'em. Go ahead, turn 'em. Look. Turn the camera. Go ahead. Turn the camera, ma'am. Turn the camera . . . Show them how many people come to these rallies.'"[38]

HYPNOSIS FOR HARM

We remember from George Orwell's *1984* that language can be manipulated and convoluted so that freedom becomes a synonym for slavery. Orwell called it doublespeak—using language in a way that deliberately obscures, distorts, disguises, and even reverses the meaning of words. The result was to promote in the citizens of *1984* a kind of doublethink—the ability to hold contradictory statements in one's mind without noticing the discrepancy, "knowing them to be contradictory and believing in both of them, to use logic against logic, to repudiate morality while laying claim to it," in Orwell's words. I believe a similar thing can happen with the techniques included in NLP. Though Bandler and Grinder may have developed their approach with good intentions—to help people be their best selves—their techniques can take on an almost opposite meaning when they are used to subvert people's free will and to indoctrinate, control, and enslave them. Instead of bringing out a person's best self, they can promote a cult self.

The cult group NXIVM is an example of NLP used unethically. Its president, Nancy Salzman, was trained in NLP by Tad James, a protege of Richard Bandler. She evidently trained the group's leader, Keith Raniere, to use hypnotic techniques, which I believe created dissociative states in his followers. He would tell stories with embedded commands in them, essentially programming members. The group used those techniques to recruit and keep members in line, and to lure women and girls to have sex with Raniere. Followers of NXIVM did not realize that hypnotic techniques were being used on them and that they were using them on others. This is often true in destructive groups—members do not realize what they are doing or what has been done to them. It was certainly the case for me when I was in the Moonies.

In my opinion, this kind of use of covert hypnotic techniques is amoral and dangerous. It's one thing if you're a trained mental health professional who abides by an ethical code to do no harm and has a professional body that holds them accountable. But when hypnosis is used by unscrupulous people to make money, solicit sex, wield power, or otherwise further their own ends, without supervision or strict ethical guidelines, great harm is often done.

When I first saw Richard Bandler in 1980 doing a hypnotic trance with someone, a light went on in my head. I thought to myself, "I used to talk like that when I was a Moonie leader." I've since talked to former members of NXIVM about their experiences during private meetings with Raniere. Some of their meetings lasted between two and four hours and yet they told me they have no memory of what happened. According to former members, Raniere was likely using hypnotic techniques. Programming amnesia is not difficult for someone skilled in hypnosis with no ethical principles.

Destructive cults use hallucinations to their advantage and commonly induce trances in their members through lengthy indoctrination sessions. Repetition, boredom, and forced attention provide favorable conditions for inducing a trance. Looking at a group in such a setting, it is easy, as a leader, to see when the trance has set in with most people. Audience members exhibit slowed blink and swallow reflexes; their facial expressions appear rapt in attention or relaxed into a blank, neutral state. When they fall into such a state, it is possible for unscrupulous leaders to implant irrational beliefs. I know many intelligent, strong-willed people who were hypnotized in such settings, usually without knowing it, and made to do things they would never normally do.[39]

Nefarious use of covert hypnosis is not limited to cults. Hypnotic techniques are taught as "go-to tricks" for mastering human connection in a multitude of areas—from personal development programs to business management seminars. Methods of NLP were taught in Neil Strauss's 2005 bestselling book on pickup artists, *The Game*. The book describes how to master the art of seduction using hypnotic techniques and triggers, which raises the question: are these merely tricks for picking up women or are they methods for controlling their minds—something altogether darker?

Something was definitely dark in the case of former Ohio divorce attorney Michael W. Fine who, in 2016, pleaded guilty to five counts of kidnapping and one count of attempted kidnapping. Instead of using brute physical force, Fine hypnotized female clients for sexual purposes.[40] The first victim to step forward, Jane Doe 1, contacted police after she realized that she was unable to recall large portions of her meetings with Fine, and that her clothes and bra were out of place. When a second woman stepped forward, the claims against Fine were examined more thoroughly and an investigation was opened. Eventually, the police caught Fine in the act. After news of the case was made public, twenty-five more of Fine's victims came forward with similar claims. Before entering into a twelve-year plea agreement, he was charged with multiple counts of kidnapping, rape, sexual battery, gross sexual imposition, possessing child pornography, and engaging in a pattern of corrupt activity.[41] It was a precedent-setting case—it showed that a person can be put into a trance, made to do something they would normally not agree to, and develop amnesia about those events. In 2018, Fine was ordered to pay Jane Doe 1 $2.3 million.[42]

Human beings are incredibly susceptible to well-honed powers of persuasion—sometimes to our benefit. But with the internet and 24/7 streaming of images and messages from anonymous, often ill-meaning sources, the opportunity for harm has greatly increased. The Russians who manipulated social media during the 2016 presidential election clearly knew how to use hypnotic techniques and other methods of persuasion. Almost all politicians use persuasion techniques but Trump has used them in a way that is both brazen and insidious. Clearly they have been effective—he was elected president.

Trump, of course, did not engineer his presidential victory all by himself. He had enormous help—from advisers, wealthy donors and corporations, internet companies, religious leaders, and a vast and powerful conservative media behemoth that found in Trump a willing mouthpiece for its own agenda.

CHAPTER SIX

Manipulation of the Media

Everyone is entitled to his own opinion,
but not to his own facts.

—Daniel Patrick Moynihan

Early on Easter Sunday morning in 2018, Donald Trump tweeted out a simple message: "HAPPY EASTER!" The holiday spirit didn't last long. Over the course of the next few hours, he sent out a barrage of tweets railing against U.S. immigration policy. In his tweets, which became ever more agitated, he would blame "ridiculous (Democrat) laws like Catch & Release" and stoke fears of "more dangerous caravans coming." He threatened to use the "Nuclear Option"—the congressional procedure that allows an issue to pass by a simple majority vote—to get tough laws passed and concluded with a familiar refrain: "NEED WALL."

Though the volley bore Trump's trademark bluster, what was striking was the way he echoed words spoken earlier that morning on the TV show *Fox & Friends*. "Our legislators actually have to stand up, and the Republicans control the House and the Senate; they do not need the Democrats' support to pass any laws," said border patrol agent and frequent Fox News guest Brandon Judd. "They can go the nuclear option, just like what they did on the [Supreme Court] confirmation. They need to pass laws to end the catch-and-release program."[1] Of course, Judd was reiterating what Trump had been saying. He might have even suspected that Trump would be watching. It was as though Trump were speaking to—and inflaming—himself.

The New York Times would later describe it as "a public mind meld" between Fox and the president. In The New Yorker, Jane Mayer describes Fox News as a kind of state-run television.[2] She quotes Nicole Hemmer, an assistant professor at the University of Virginia and author of Messengers of the Right: " 'Fox is not just taking the temperature of the base—it's raising the temperature,' [Hemmer] says. 'It's a radicalization model.' For both Trump and Fox, fear is a business strategy—it keeps people watching." Mayer goes on to describe how the "White House and Fox interact so seamlessly that it can be hard to determine, during a particular news cycle, which one is following the other's lead." Fox News host Sean Hannity speaks to Trump nearly every weeknight,[3] and Fox owner Rupert Murdoch is like a member of the administration, according to Mayer. Former copresident of Fox News Bill Shine was appointed director of communications and deputy chief of staff at the White House, though he resigned to advise the 2020 Trump campaign. His job description—to sell the president—is not that different from his job at Fox News. "[I]t's a fact: [Fox News] is the closest we have come to having state-run media," said former CBS anchor and journalist Dan Rather, "a straight up propaganda outlet."[4]

Trump is not the first president to exploit the power of the bully pulpit or to explore a new media platform, like Twitter. Nor is he the first to have a favorite media organization. As Mayer points out, "James Madison and Andrew Jackson were each boosted by partisan newspapers." But rarely has a president used his media partnership to such partisan ends. Teddy Roosevelt, Woodrow Wilson, and Franklin D. Roosevelt were presidents who explored new media platforms but they did so to address and benefit the whole nation rather than to speak directly to their own partisan base, or to fill the coffers of their chosen media partner. Trump is perpetually campaigning, kicking up political dust, creating crises. It's all good business—and not just for Fox. As Les Moonves, former president of CBS, famously said, Trump's candidacy "may not be good for America, but it's damn good for CBS."[5] The same could be said of cable networks like CNN and MSNBC.

Trump did not bring about his presidency single-handedly, as much as he might like us to believe he did. He was in the right place at the right historical moment. To paraphrase Obama, he is the symptom of a celebrity-promoting media culture based on corporate greed, manipulation of public opinion for personal gain, and marketing by wealthy corporations and elites using every influence trick in the book to get what they want—to cut corporate taxes, boost the use of fossil fuels, and promote right-wing political and religious views. The rise of the conservative media empire has been many decades in the making and so has Trump's Fox-inspired, Twitter-fueled bully pulpit. In its broad outlines, the Cult of Trump was taking shape long before Trump stepped into the shoes of leader. To get a fuller understanding of how that happened, we must cast a backward glance at the intertwining history of the media and the presidency.

THE BEAUTIFUL PULPIT

The term "bully pulpit" may seem practically designed for Trump, who has used his office to insult, deride, and humiliate people. But when President Theodore Roosevelt coined the phrase, "bully" had an altogether different meaning. It was an adjective, not a verb, meaning "wonderful" or "superb"—as in "bully for you!" What made the pulpit of the presidency so bully for Roosevelt was the way it could be used to persuade people of a particular agenda.

Like Trump, Roosevelt was a convention-defying president who came to Washington with the goal of shaking things up. A dynamic speaker, he would often cast aside the microphone at rallies, projecting his voice to its limit in order to speak to tens of thousands of people. More remarkable was the way he seemed to emotionally connect with them. He courted publicity aggressively. He frequently invited the Washington press corps to the White House, monitored the whereabouts of photographers at events, hired the first government press officers, and staged publicity stunts, like riding ninety-eight miles on horseback to defend new navy regulations that officers be required to take a ninety-mile riding test. "It was bully," he was reported to say as he bounded into the White House after finishing his ride. Though he loved the attention, and many would agree he had a strong streak of narcissism, according to David Greenberg writing in *The Atlantic,* most of his stunts were done "not simply to boost his ego but also to effect his vigorous reform."[6] He understood the power of publicity in furthering his agenda. "Roosevelt ushered in an age in which presidents would be perpetually engaged in the work of publicity and opinion management—the work of spin."

PRESIDENTIAL PROPAGANDA

The need for opinion management increased dramatically during World War I when President Woodrow Wilson created a new federal agency, the Committee on Public Information (CPI), that "put the government in the business of actively shaping press coverage" while waging "a campaign of intimidation and outright suppression against newspapers that continued to oppose the war."[7] At the time, most Americans got their news through newspapers—in New York City, nearly two dozen papers were published every day in English alone; dozens of weeklies served ethnic audiences. Through the work of people like Edward Bernays, the CPI would become a full-scale media organization, creating its own media—newspapers, newsreels, broadsheets, posters, and speeches—to recruit soldiers, sell war bonds, and stimulate patriotism. It would promote a grand narrative—that "the nation is involved in a great crusade against a bloodthirsty, antidemocratic enemy" and "making the world safe for democracy"—at the same time that it curtailed one of the pillars of democracy, freedom of the press.[8]

With the rise of radio in the 1920s, news could be disseminated much more quickly—indeed, almost immediately—and it could be conveyed in a new way, by an actual human voice. Between 1933 and 1944, President Franklin Delano Roosevelt would masterfully exploit this more intimate medium in a series of thirty "fireside chats," talking the country through the dark days of the Depression and World War II. Speaking in a confident and reassuring voice, he tried to calm the fears of an anxious nation, explaining his policies in an effort to prevent rumors and fearmongering from dividing the American people.[9] Roosevelt's fireside chats may seem a relic of a bygone time, especially in the age of the Trumpian Twitter storm, but they were "a revolutionary experiment with a nascent media platform," according to Adrienne LaFrance, writing in *The Atlantic*. "Imagine if Roosevelt had used his radio access to relentlessly criticize individual Americans by name."[10]

Yet, as Roosevelt was trying to soothe and unite, some were using radio to sow discord and fear. During the 1920s, a Roman Catholic priest named Father Charles Coughlin took to the airwaves to preach directly to his millions of followers. Coughlin had been a fan of FDR but had come to see him as too friendly with Jewish "money-changers" and capitalists. He would later use his radio show to broadcast anti-Semitic conspiracy theories and to praise the fascist policies of Hitler and Mussolini as an antidote to the growing threat of communism. He would tout isolationist views with slogans—"Less care for internationalism and more concern for national prosperity"—that sound remarkably modern. Coughlin's views clearly resonated with many Americans. By 1939, when he was forced off the air, he had an audience of 30 million people.

Coughlin's show had especially disturbed the members of a new watchdog group, the Institute for Propaganda Analysis (IPA), who had been alarmed by the use of what they saw as wartime and foreign propaganda in the United States. They formed the IPA to promote free thought and the spirit of democracy by educating the public about the dangers of propaganda. Toward that end, they commissioned a book, *The Fine Art of Propaganda: A Study of Father Coughlin's Speeches*, outlining seven of his techniques, many of which are being used today by Trump and his conservative media supporters:[11]

   1. *Name-calling:* Attaching negative or derogatory labels to a person or idea can make us reject and condemn them without examining the evidence. Trump, along with Fox hosts

Sean Hannity and Laura Ingraham, make extensive use of this, turning words like "liberal" and "socialist" into insults; assigning nicknames to opponents; pinning words like "stupid," "weak," "dangerous," "disgraceful," and "bad" on people or ideas that they disagree with.

2. *Glittering generalities:* Associating positive virtuous words with a person or idea can make us accept and approve them without examining the evidence. Trump uses words like "smart," "tough," "great," "amazing," "terrific," and "classy" to describe people whom he likes—including dictators.

3. *Transfer:* Associating an admired, respected, or revered person, institution, or idea with another in order to make the latter attractive. The converse is also true: being associated with a disrespected, disgraced, ridiculed, or scorned person, institution, or idea can cause us to reject it.

4. *Testimonial:* Having a respected person say that a given idea or program or product or person is good or bad can lead us to accept it. Endorsements are common in American political life, as popular candidates support and lend legitimacy to less popular ones.

5. *Plain folks:* This occurs when a speaker attempts to persuade his audience that their ideas are good by claiming that he or she is just like them—of the people, plain folk. Trump is a brash billionaire who has nonetheless fostered a sense of identification with his audience by promoting an outsider, nonpolitician image and by mirroring their issues and emotions, taking their struggles—for example, the closing of coal mines—as his own cause.

6. *Card stacking:* Selectively citing facts or falsehoods, illustrations or distractions, and logical or illogical statements in order to give the best or the worst possible case for an idea, program, person, or product. Trump's vilification of immigrants—using faulty data and outright lies—is a prime example, where the group is blamed for the actions of a small handful of rogue individuals.

7. *Bandwagon:* Claiming that all members of a group accept a policy, idea, or action in an effort to encourage others to follow—essentially, to jump on the bandwagon. According to Trump, if you're not with him trying to "make America great," then you are part of the problem.

FAIRNESS DOCTRINE: BIRTH AND DEMISE

The size of Coughlin's audience showed there was a market for a variety of listener niches. As radio grew in popularity, a dilemma arose. There were only so many frequencies designated for wireless communication and a lot of people were competing for airspace. In 1934, the U.S. government established the Federal Communications Commission (FCC) to regulate interstate communications. Broadcasters had to receive FCC licenses in order to broadcast, which is still the case today. The advent of licensing raised a question: if radio waves are a public asset, should they be used for the public good? The FCC thought so and in 1940 issued the Mayflower Doctrine, which stated clearly that the public interest is not served by partisan programming: "Radio can serve as an instrument of democracy only when devoted to the communication of information and the exchange of ideas fairly and objectively presented. A truly free radio cannot be used to advocate for the causes of the licensee. It cannot be used to support the candidacies of his friends. It cannot be devoted to the support of principles he happens to regard most favorably. In brief, the broadcaster cannot be an advocate. Freedom of speech on the radio must be broad enough to provide full and equal opportunity for the presentation to the public of all sides of public issues."[12]

Though noble in its goals, this near-total ban on partisan programming proved to be unworkably broad, and, after World War II, suffered multiple legal challenges. In June 1949, the Mayflower Doctrine was repealed. A few months later, the FCC established the Fairness Doctrine,[13] which allowed that the public interest "can only be satisfied by making available . . . varying and conflicting views held by responsible elements of the community."[14] This demand to air alternative views placed broadcasters and also the FCC in a difficult spot. Broadcasters were expected to determine how to apportion their air time when dealing with controversial issues, and how to arrange for fairly presented opposing views, while the FCC was expected to determine whether any individual stations ran afoul of this legislation. Taking advantage of the ensuing confusion, preachers and ministers, some of them wealthy and looking to become more so, rushed in to buy up slots previously reserved for more community-based religious programs. A new era of televangelism began.

Unsurprisingly, legal cases arose and were pretty much handled on a case-by-case basis. It was not a tidy system, and it would not apply to cable news. But despite its many issues, the Fairness Doctrine maintained a fragile balance, helping to set the tone for a "fair and balanced" media landscape—until 1987, when Ronald Reagan used his presidential veto to prevent Congress from codifying the doctrine into actual law and then directed the FCC to abolish the Fairness Doctrine altogether.[15] As Jonathan Mahler and Jim Rutenberg observe in a *New York Times* piece, "Planet Fox: Inside Rupert Murdoch's Empire of Influence," Reagan's actions "spawned a new generation of right wing radio personalities who were free to provide a different sort of opinion programming to a large, latent conservative audience that was mistrustful of the media in general."[16] Coughlin had already shown that many Americans were hungry for this kind of programming.

THE CONSERVATIVE MEDIA COMPLEX

During the 1960s, FM radio broadcasting had increased dramatically. FM radio's ability to better handle stereo audio made it an obvious choice for high-fidelity music and the market responded accordingly: by the end of the 1970s, FM's listeners outnumbered AM's. The audio limitations of AM radio made it a natural fit for talk and news programs—in fact, they were among the very small variety of programs that remained on AM frequencies. But in the late 1980s, with the Fairness Doctrine revoked, AM radio took off. Functioning now under wholly capitalist incentives, the AM radio stations suddenly had a new product: talk radio. Serving the public interest quickly transformed into interesting the public—sometimes with salacious, shocking, and highly opinionated content.

One man who did more than anyone else to usher in this new era was Rush Limbaugh, a modern-day Charles Coughlin. Moving from his Sacramento, California, station to New York City in 1988, he started *The Rush Limbaugh Show*, a nationally syndicated talk radio program that would soon become one of the most popular in radio history. Its mix of political commentary, news, and entertainment proved to be enormously influential, giving rise to a host of imitators who quickly filled the airwaves with conservative ideology.[17] Limbaugh's personal appeal is not to be discounted. David Foster Wallace, writing for *The Atlantic*, described Limbaugh as a "a host of extraordinary, once-in-a-generation talent and charisma—bright, loquacious, witty, complexly authoritative."[18] Limbaugh's "brilliantly effective" rhetorical genius was to label the rest of the media "biased," thus functioning as "a standard around which Rush's audience could rally, as an articulation of the need for right-wing (i.e., unbiased) media, and as a mechanism by which any criticism or refutation of conservative ideas could be dismissed."

By leveraging conservative dissatisfaction with mainstream media sources, Limbaugh created a loyal following and an audience hungry for supposedly "unbiased" media. The nascent conservative media complex grew, fueled by the 9/11 attacks, which led to a bevy of new radio shows hosted by outspoken, charismatic, and highly paid individuals like Sean Hannity, Laura Ingraham, and Glenn Beck. Like Limbaugh, they would cultivate their audiences using many of the same influence techniques that Coughlin used, and that are used by cult leaders—sowing confusion, distrust, and fear while providing a heavy dose of exaggeration along with black-and-white, us-versus-them thinking. It is interesting to note that Vice President Mike Pence, who in the early 1990s hosted a conservative radio show, studied

Limbaugh's radio persona and even referred to himself as "Limbaugh on decaf."[19] Pence remains close with Limbaugh and does interviews with him.[20]

They weren't the only ones to use radio to captivate and influence conservative America. Christian televangelists had become extraordinarily successful as well. In 1973, the Trinity Broadcasting Network was founded—the first of a number of evangelical media outlets. Much in the same way that talk radio served as an incubator for influential voices, so too did the Christian media network—Franklin Graham, Joel Osteen, Pat Robertson, and others became superstars. The Trinity Broadcasting Network would come under significant scrutiny for flagrant misuse of donated funds and would endure lurid scandals. Pastor John MacArthur, host of his own international radio show, would describe Trinity as a bunch of "religious quacks"[21]—a network "dominated by faith-healers, full-time fund-raisers, and self-proclaimed prophets" preaching the prosperity gospel. It appears to be a winning formula. Trinity is currently the country's third-largest broadcast group and the world's largest religious television network, with more than 18,000 television and cable affiliates and twenty-eight international networks, including the internet.[22] They are currently estimated to reach some two billion viewers. Like right-wing talk radio, Trinity forms an important pillar of support for Donald Trump.

FOX NEWS

As depicted in the documentary *The Brainwashing of My Dad*, Frank Senko's right-wing radicalization began when he started listening to Bob Grant and Rush Limbaugh's radio shows during his work commute, but the deal would be further sealed when he starting watching Fox News. Fox News would do for conservative television what Limbaugh did for radio—cultivate an audience that would thrive on the kind of anti-mainstream-media, antigovernment, racist, xenophobic, hate-filled, and fear-based messaging that Trump would later serve up. And it can be said to have begun with one man—the late Roger Ailes.

By all accounts, Ailes was a towering figure on the conservative media landscape, one who may have done more than anyone else to pave the way for Trump's presidency. He got his start in TV early and was one of the first to see how the future of the American presidency lay in television. As the story goes, in 1967, a twenty-eight-year-old Ailes approached Richard Nixon backstage on *The Mike Douglas Show*, where Ailes worked as an executive producer. Nixon, who had performed abysmally in his televised 1960 presidential debate with John F. Kennedy, and who was appearing on Douglas's show to drum up support, said to Ailes, "It's a shame a man has to use gimmicks like this to get elected."[23] Ailes shot back, "Television is not a gimmick." Ailes became Nixon's media consultant.

One of Ailes's greatest strengths was his insight into human nature: he understood that people like to think they are rational, but they are actually driven by emotions—anger, fear, nostalgia, even disgust.[24] The role of television was to provoke emotional reactions in the viewer. He also knew that television—at least primetime TV—was a shallow medium: "Television rarely tells the whole story," he famously said, in a speech entitled "Candidate + Money + Media = Votes." But superficial stories could be effective if they triggered the right emotions. He helped Nixon, a famously untelegenic presence, appeal to the public with what came to be known as the sound bite—a short phrase that would stick in people's heads. With Ailes's considerable help, Nixon won the presidency, as described in Joe McGinnis's book, *The Selling of the President 1968*.[25] (As it turns out, Nixon was also advised by consultant Roger Stone who, by then, had met Trump through lawyer Roy Cohn. Stone would remain friends with Trump for decades, advising him on his 2016 presidential campaign, and was eventually indicted for perjury and obstruction.)[26]

Ailes would later become a media consultant for Ronald Reagan. He also helped George H. W. Bush come from behind in 1988 to defeat his presidential opponent Michael Dukakis, using what he called his "orchestra pit theory." As he told TV host Judy Woodruff: "Let's face it, there are three things that the media are interested in: pictures, mistakes, and attacks . . . You have two guys on a stage and one guy says, 'I have a solution to the Middle East problem,' and the other guy falls in the orchestra pit; who do you think is going to be on the evening news?"[27] It's a theory we see play out every day in the Trump presidency. Ailes realized almost from the start that television would be the future of American presidential politics. As he told McGinniss shortly before Nixon's win, "This is the way they'll be elected forevermore. The next guys up will have to be performers."[28]

In 1996, Ailes teamed up with Australian media mogul Rupert Murdoch to create a cable television network—Fox News. Appealing to Limbaugh's ideological audience, Fox News soon towered over the television landscape and it would do so by using and adapting for a visual medium many of the techniques that Limbaugh used. In her book *Brainwashing: The Science of Thought Control,* neuroscientist Kathleen Taylor outline the tactics that Fox and other conservative media use to indoctrinate viewers:

1. lie and skew
2. confusion and doubt
3. blame and divide
4. brand and label
5. language and framing
6. fearmongering
7. bullying and shaming.

Ailes would use every trick in the book, but mostly he would use fear. A die-hard Republican, he flooded the media landscape with conservative messages and narratives designed to conjure up fear and ultimately to recruit followers—paving the way for Trump. "Fear, in fact, is precisely what Ailes is selling: His network has relentlessly hyped phantom menaces like the planned 'terror mosque' near Ground Zero," writes Tom Dickinson in a *Rolling Stone* piece, "How Roger Ailes Built the Fox News Fear Factory." "To watch even a day of Fox News—the anger, the bombast, the virulent paranoid streak, the unending appeals to white resentment, the reporting that's held to the same standard of evidence as a late-October attack ad—is to see a refraction of its founder, one of the most skilled and fearsome operatives in the history of the Republican Party."[29]

Ailes would also shape the internal culture of the network. "Roger Ailes is not on the air. Roger Ailes does not ever show up on camera. And yet everybody who does is a reflection of him," writes Dickinson. As it turns out, the Fox culture would include misogyny and outright sexual harassment, costing millions of dollars and leading to the resignation of Ailes and popular host Bill O'Reilly.

Meanwhile, Rupert Murdoch had his own agenda—namely, extending his global empire and making money. While he left the running of Fox mostly to Ailes, with Ailes's departure Murdoch would continue Fox's rightward push, indeed giving it a shove with the candidacy of Donald Trump. Though he initially considered Trump's presidential aspirations to be a joke, he would exploit Trump's candidacy and election to further his own goal of blurring the line between his media empire and governments around the world. Indeed, he would be a major influencer to help engineer the Brexit vote and elevate Theresa May to prime minister. "To see Fox News as an arm of the Trump White House risks missing the larger picture," write Mahler and Rutenberg. "It may be more accurate to say that the White House—just like the prime ministers' offices in Britain and Australia—is just one tool among many that [the Murdoch] family uses to exert influence over world events."

Today Fox's influence continues as Lachlan Murdoch takes the helm from his aging father. In 2018, according to *Adweek,* "Fox News averaged its largest prime time audience in the 22-year history of the network, and for the third year in a row, finished as the most-watched network on cable television."[30] This means billions of dollars in revenue each year.

THE RIGHT-WING PROPAGANDA FEEDBACK LOOP

Money may help to explain the rightward push, but according to Harvard scholars Yochai Benkler, Robert Faris, and Hal Roberts, there is something else at play. They analyzed millions of TV news stories, together with Twitter and Facebook shares and YouTube videos, and found that the right-wing media were much more likely to promote the disinformation, lies, and half-truths peddled by the Russian propaganda effort as well as conspiracy theories and misinformation coming from white supremacist and extremist sources like the neo-Nazi site *The Daily Stormer*. In their 2018 book, *Network Propaganda: Manipulation, Disinformation, and Radicalization in American Politics,* they argue that "the right-wing media ecosystem differs categorically from the rest of the media environment." In mainstream left and centrist media, there is a commitment to observing agreed-upon journalistic standards of honest reportage. Furthermore, there is a media ecosystem that has within it an error detection and correction mechanism in which other journalists and media entities point out mistakes and errors made by others. These should be acknowledged and corrected publicly. Retractions and apologies are the standard. This mechanism is absent in the right-wing media ecosystem, creating a kind of propaganda feedback loop, whereby uncorrected lies and distortions are circulated and promulgated from one media outlet to the next, for example from extreme sources, like conspiracy theorist Alex Jones's InfoWars site, to Breitbart to Fox. If a demonstrably false story gets a lot of world publicity, it might be taken down, but no public acknowledgment that it was wrong is given. "It's a pattern that is growing more pronounced as we move forward in the Trump presidency," said Roberts at a talk at Harvard.[31]

THE FAR RIGHT

One of the biggest suppliers of erroneous hate-filled rhetoric is Alex Jones. He's a popular figure who had more than 2.4 million subscribers on his YouTube channel,[32] more than 6.7 million people a month on his website, InfoWars, and two million listeners on his syndicated radio show.[33] In 2018, he was kicked off YouTube, Twitter, Facebook, Apple, and Spotify for violating their rules and because he was inciting his followers with hate speech to do violence, and to harass people like the parents of victims of the Sandy Hook school shootings.[34] A longtime conspiracy theorist operating out of his basement in Austin, Texas, he has argued that the U.S. government was involved in the 1995 Oklahoma City bombing, that 9/11 was "an inside job," that no one was actually killed at Sandy Hook, and that the Apollo 11 moon landing never happened. These sound like fringe ravings, akin to the lunatic theories put forth by notorious cult leaders like Lyndon LaRouche, who claimed there was a global conspiracy with the queen of England, the Freemasons, and the Jewish bankers to ruin the world, and Jim Jones, who claimed that the evil capitalists were out to kill him and his members.

Alex Jones has millions of followers including, it appears, Donald Trump. On December 2, 2015, Trump appeared on the show, praising Jones and promising that "I will not let you down."[35] During the campaign, Trump and Jones shared the same alternative facts—like the infamous birther claim that President Obama was born in Kenya, not Hawaii. He is also responsible, according to *Network Propaganda*, for taking and disseminating more than a thousand false propaganda stories from RT (the Russian state-run news organization), serving as the critical entry point for those false stories into the American media ecosystem. In 2018, Jones was sued by parents of children murdered in the shooting at Sandy Hook. He would later admit that the children had been killed[36] and blamed "psychosis" for his actions, though he refused to acknowledge that his actions added to the grief and distress of the families. Adding salt to their wounds—and true to his conspiracy-mongering leanings—he claimed that the lawsuits were retaliation for Hillary Clinton's failed presidential bid. His statement came only a few days after prominent Sandy Hook parent Jeremy Richman committed suicide.[37]

Nor is Jones the only peddler of conspiracy theories in the right-wing media firmament. Breitbart News began as a conservative news and opinion website in 2007 by Andrew Breitbart, a conservative commentator who also cofounded *The Huffington Post*. When Breitbart died in 2012, Robert and Rebekah Mercer bought the company and installed Stephen K. Bannon, a former investment banker for Goldman Sachs, as head. Under the new leadership, Breitbart News moved further right, veering into conspiracy-theory territory with outrageous headlines about Democratic politicians, including Barack Obama and Bill and Hillary Clinton.[38]

Breitbart has also been instrumental in radicalizing the anti-immigration wing of the Republican Party—and the change has been dramatic. It is worth remembering that Republican presidents Ronald Reagan and George H. W. Bush were strong supporters of immigration. During the 1980 GOP debate, candidate Reagan said of Mexico, "Rather than talking about putting up a fence, why don't we work out some recognition of our mutual problems?"[39] That Republicans are now talking about a Wall instead of a fence is a measure of how far they have come, with help not just from Breitbart News but also from Fox News and other conservative media outlets who have trumped up fear of invaders to sell Trump—and their own products.

CORPORATE INFLUENCE

Even mainstream media is not immune to biased and misleading reporting. In 1988, media critic and scholar Edward S. Herman and linguist and activist Noam Chomsky wrote a scathing critique of the idea that the mass media objectively informs the public. As they laid out in their book, *Manufacturing Consent,* instead of acting as a check on the three branches of government—the *fourth estate*—mass media is carrying out a kind of state propaganda function by promoting the capitalist ideology of the media companies' powerful owners.[40] They identified five factors that may contribute to distorting the news:

1. *Ownership:* Media firms are part of huge conglomerates, many of which have interests far outside the journalistic sphere. In cases where journalism might interfere with the conglomerate's profit, the interest of the conglomerate takes priority over the interest of journalism or the public.

2. *Advertising:* Advertising creates perverse incentives for media companies, transforming their audience's attention into a product. As the media companies are ultimately beholden

to whoever pays them, their priority is to hold the audience's attention above all else, with little regard for their audience's well-being. Without regulations guiding ethical activities, people have little recourse against corporate malfeasance.

3. *Sourcing:* Journalism cannot be an effective check on power because the very system encourages complicity with governments, corporations, and other newsworthy institutions. Journalists rely on access to important sources, which might be limited or revoked if critical pieces are published. Often they are implicitly encouraged to simply repeat the information they receive.

4. *Flak:* Powerful institutions might try to divert attention from unfavorable stories by discrediting and demonizing their source. Flak—a term that derives from the German word for anti-aircraft fire—can be directed at journalists, whistleblowers, or sources, and is a way for powerful people and organizations to manage public information.

5. *Common enemy:* To manufacture consent, you need an enemy—a target, a villain to fear: communism, terrorists, immigrants. It helps corral public opinion. According to Herman and Chomsky, this is done "partly to get rid of people you don't like but partly to frighten the rest. Because if people are frightened, they will accept authority.[41]

Today the largest corporations operate internationally and no longer feel obligated to one country, like the United States. The world has become increasingly interconnected and complex. However, those who hold the key to power are an elite minority. It is safe to assume that they can be counted on to make decisions that will perpetuate their power.

MONEY TALKS

As David Foster Wallace wrote in a 2005 *Atlantic* piece, "It is a fallacy that political talk radio is motivated by ideology. It is not. Political talk radio is a business, and it is motivated by revenue. The conservatism that dominates today's AM airwaves does so because it generates high Arbitron ratings, high ad rates, and maximum profits."[42] The situation is exacerbated by the increasing homogeneity of the media landscape as media conglomerates solidify their hold. Today, more than 90 percent of all media in the United States is owned by just six companies.[43] Clear Channel Communications[44] owns more than 1,000 radio stations, and the Sinclair Broadcasting Group[45] owns almost 500 local channels. This consolidation was made possible by the Telecommunications Act of 1996,[46] which eliminated regulations on ownership that had been in place since 1934, and which allowed for "anyone to enter any communications business—to let any communications business compete in any market against any other."[47]

A blatant example of corporate influence is the Sinclair Broadcast Group. Among their hundreds of stations are many local ABC, CBS, and Fox affiliates. In early 2018, the company faced harsh criticism when it required local broadcasters to read from a company-generated script decrying the danger that mainstream outlets and "false news" posed to democracy. Timothy Burke, a video director at Deadspin, clipped together recordings of the announcers reading, in near unison, the mandated script, often without a trace of irony. The video went viral and quickly led to widespread criticism.[48] Former news anchor Dan Rather commented, "News anchors looking into the camera and reading a script handed down by a corporate overlord, words meant to obscure the truth not elucidate it, isn't journalism. . . . It's propaganda. It's Orwellian. A slippery slope to how despots wrest power, silence dissent, and oppress the masses."[49] Trump, evidently noting his own positive coverage by Sinclair, responded to the scandal: "So funny to watch Fake News Networks, among the most dishonest groups of people I have ever dealt with, criticize Sinclair Broadcasting for being biased. Sinclair is far superior to CNN and even more Fake NBC, which is a total joke."[50]

In March 2019, conservative Nexstar Media Group purchased Tribune Media in a $6.4 billion transaction, making it the single largest television group in the United States. Time will tell how much this

behemoth will influence American minds by dominating local programming.[51]

MOON: MEDIA MOGUL

Clearly, there is a lot at stake. After all, the average American household watches almost eight hours of television a day—and that's in
addition to other types of screen time.[52] That's a lot of time for TV
networks to get their messages across—which is why cults have been
so keen to enter the media market. Of course, the media surrounding
the Cult of Trump is vaster and more complex than that surrounding
most cults. The one cult group that comes anywhere close is my former group, the Moon organization, which has owned and operated
hundreds of businesses, including media companies. The Moonies
founded *The Washington Times* newspaper in 1982, but they have also
owned dozens of other media entities, such as United Press International, purchased in 2000.[53] In the 1990s, they owned TV broadcast
facilities in Washington, D.C., that were used by most of the major
networks including ABC and NBC. The organization has been heavily
involved in advancing right-wing media not only in the United States
but around the world. Their official line was that it is smart to invest
in communication and media. But the cult's ultimate goal was to take
over media companies so that they could control messaging. It was all
part of Moon's grand scheme to take over the world.

Before the fall of the Soviet Union, a strong political focus of
all of Moon's myriad organizations was the fight against communism, especially in North Korea and China. To put it in simple but
bizarre-sounding terms, the Moonies believed that Christians and
citizens of the free world were locked in a mortal struggle with the
satanic forces of "materialistic communism." If they failed to fight
communism, they would grow weak and fall. The true solution—
indeed, the world's salvation—lay in establishing a theocracy with
Moon at the helm: God would rule the world through him and his
minions. Working through *The Washington Times* and other media
companies was one way to get his message out. Though the newspaper

was controversial for some time, it eventually got a foothold in the media landscape. Most people don't know about its ownership or don't care. Among some conservative readers, it has enjoyed significant influence both inside Washington and internationally. Former president Ronald Reagan said it was his favorite newspaper and that he read it every day. So did George H. W. Bush and George W. Bush.

And yet there have been notable critics. The newspaper's founding editor, James Whelan, resigned in 1984 to protest what he claimed were attempts by the publisher to alter the news. Later that year, in a talk at the National Press Club, Whelan called the *Times* a "Moonie newspaper." The paper trashed him and insisted that it was not controlled by Moon. Another editor, William Cheshire, resigned in 1987 claiming that Unification Church executives were controlling the paper's editorial policy. Moon said in a 1991 speech that by then, nearly a billion dollars had been spent to run the *Times*. At least another billion has been spent since then though, according to *The Washington Post*, the total amount is closer to $2 billion. Why spend this kind of money on a paper that has not shown a profit? Where does the money come from? How could a convicted felon—Moon—be permitted to own a newspaper in American's capital in the first place? Presumably, for Moon, the benefits went beyond financial profit. They included political influence in the United States and other countries and the ability to gather information and intelligence under the guise of journalism.

THE SLIPPERY SLOPE

In a *New Republic* article titled "Fox News Is Officially Trump TV," Alex Shephard describes how far Fox News has slipped in journalistic principles since Ailes resigned in 2016. "Back in 2010, the network canceled a [Sean] Hannity appearance at a Tea Party rally, fearing that it would damage the institution's journalistic integrity. That integrity is long gone, at least for the network's late-night stars."[54] In November 2018, Hannity appeared on stage at a Trump rally, along with Fox News host Jeanine Pirro. Fox News had once promoted itself as "fair and balanced" but stopped using that motto in 2016.[55] "Fox News has always been more of a Republican propaganda outlet than a news organization. It's finally admitting it."[56]

Trump has filled numerous positions in his administration with people who once worked on Fox—Bill Shine, John Bolton, and Heather Nauert. Trump's ties to Fox have strengthened in ways that are, according to former FCC chairman Reed Hundt, "extremely unusual, and the only way to explain them is that they're pro-Fox, pro-Fox, and pro-Fox."[57] Jane Mayer describes the relationship between Fox News and the White House as a "revolving door," where the influence goes back and forth in a seamless fashion.[58]

New York Times columnist Ross Douthat has observed that television played a much bigger role in creating Trump than the internet did, even taking into account Russian and alt-right online interference. "It was television that convinced millions of Americans that Trump was a business genius despite his record of bankruptcy, and which gifted him countless hours of free advertising through unchecked coverage of his campaign rallies and Twitter feed."[59] Mark Burnett took a gamble when he asked Trump to do *The Apprentice*. It paid off hugely—for both of them. The same could be said of the conservative media machine, which provided Trump with a ready-made cult following, as well as a platform, and gained money and power in return. But they are not the only ones to be involved in a kind of quid pro quo with Trump. As candidate and president, Trump has been backed by an array of religious organizations for whom the stakes are even greater and include nothing less than turning our country into a nation run by and for Christians—a kingdom of heaven on earth.

CHAPTER SEVEN

The Influencers

I n early January 2017, as word was filtering out about Trump's choices for cabinet posts, the British newspaper the *Guardian* observed that Trump's list of picks revealed "a penchant for military brass, political outsiders, and Wall Street titans," and "no particular faith in the value of prior government experience."[1] As they reviewed the list of candidates, a more bizarre pattern started to emerge. At the top was Rex Tillerson for secretary of state, a man with no governmental experience and close business ties to Vladimir Putin. For secretary of the Treasury there was Steven Mnuchin, a hedge funder and Hollywood producer who was known as a "foreclosure king." Betsy DeVos, a critic of public education, was Trump's nominee for secretary of education. For energy secretary there was Rick Perry, who had claimed during his own 2011 presidential primary run that he would eliminate the Department of Energy. And finally, Scott Pruitt, a climate change denier and longtime critic of efforts to protect the environment, was Trump's pick to head the Environmental Protection Agency (EPA).

In those early days, some might have mistaken the outlandish array for a script for *Saturday Night Live,* or maybe Trump thumbing his nose at the establishment. Others might have seen them as the chaotic choices of a president-elect who never expected to win. But it was also possible to see in Trump's roster a kind of strategy, one first articulated by the Christian right, to delegitimize the very structure of government and destabilize American citizens' faith in facts, science, experts, and even democracy.

A STRATEGY OF DELEGITIMIZATION

Trump had questioned the legitimacy of government throughout his campaign. In speeches, tweets, and rallies, he described the Washington establishment as part of a rapacious "global power structure" with Hillary Clinton at the center. He would use Clinton's use of a private email server to undermine her candidacy, famously ask for Russia's help to further expose her, and claim that she was a felon who should be locked up. One of his most subversive moments came during the final presidential debate when he said that he might not accept the results of the general election if he lost. He was not simply attacking his opponent, he was attacking the legitimacy of a fundamental aspect of democracy—the electoral system.

It was an unprecedented—and breathtaking—moment. Some might have seen it as Trump at his most outrageously provocative. And yet he was taking a page out of a book written by two Christian right strategists, Paul Weyrich and William S. Lind, called *The New Conservatism*. Though it was published in 2009, largely to mobilize a right-wing movement against Barack Obama, Weyrich and Lind had been developing and writing about their approach for decades. Lind was a member of a team of analysts who, in the late 1980s, had written about a military approach that sought to collapse enemies from within by disrupting their mental, emotional, and moral foundations, an approach they called fourth-generation warfare (4GW).[2] Weyrich, a Christian right activist and cofounder of the conservative think tanks Heritage Foundation and Free Congress Foundation, believed the Christian right was engaged in an epochal struggle for dominance with an array of enemies—the left, secularists, gays, government, Jews, and anyone who opposed their vision of Christianity. They developed an approach to taking down perceived foes, one that used

THE CULT OF TRUMP

propaganda, confusion, a constant barrage of criticism, fearmongering, disruption, and other influence techniques, all aimed at undermining "the legitimacy of the dominant regime."[3]

Under their guidance, the Christian Right launched multiple
propaganda campaigns, often through television, radio, movies,
and documentaries—media that appeal to emotions rather than
logic. Interestingly, Weyrich met Roger Ailes in 1973, and, according to independent writer and retired senior civilian intelligence analyst James Scaminaci III, would help lay the groundwork for Fox
News. Of course, the internet opened up a whole new front for
fourth-generation warfare—one that has been exploited not just by
the Christian right but also by white supremacist and other alt-right
groups, libertarian followers of the novelist Ayn Rand, the Russian
government, and others. They have all been engaged in a massive effort to weaken, divide, disrupt, and delegitimize the U.S. government
and install their own version of reality. Fourth-generation warfare is
employed widely around the world. What is remarkable is that this
sophisticated approach to modern warfare has been so systematically
deployed by a powerful American religious faction against our own
country.

Just as Fox and the conservative media paved the way for Trump,
so too the Christian right—along with the alt-right and libertarian
groups—has provided Trump with messaging as well as a ready-made
following. In the case of the Christian right, we are talking about millions of followers belonging to megachurches as well as small ministries, some of them quite authoritarian. Their followers are politically
trained and ideologically educated to spread out, often with cultlike
zeal, and campaign for Trump, whom they see as helping them fulfill
their own mission of establishing a kingdom of heaven on earth.[4]

All presidents come into office surrounded by a web of influence—
donors, party officials, religious groups, political action committees,
and lobbyists. But never has a president been enmeshed with such antigovernment and antidemocratic interests. Notable among Trump's
donors in this regard are Robert Mercer and his daughter Rebekah
Mercer, who, like many wealthy elites, tend to put business before

country, and who rescued Trump's campaign in the eleventh hour by installing the norm-bashing, destabilizing, disruptive—if not outright antidemocratic—figure of Steve Bannon as campaign manager. As part owners of Breitbart, they also played a significant role in shaping the right-wing media that contributed to Trump's rise. A fuller discussion of the role played by wealthy billionaires and corporations is beyond the scope of this book. But as Jane Mayer observed in her authoritative book, *Dark Money*, they had a huge hand in getting Trump elected.[5]

PUTIN AND RUSSIA

Few delegitimization efforts have had the scope and depth of the campaign waged by Russia, which is to be expected from a country with such antidemocratic leanings—and such a robust and long-standing mind control apparatus. In his book *The Plot to Destroy Democracy*, counterterrorism expert Malcolm Nance describes how Russia deployed thousands of cyberterrorism agents to find ways to hack into the American psyche, systematically targeting individual Americans with lies, misinformation, and false narratives tailored to their interests and framed in ways that were intended to confuse, divide, and pit Americans against one another. Russia purchased Facebook ads for phony groups like "African-Americans for Hillary" that urged voters to tweet instead of going to the polls, in order to avoid the lines.[6] They created Facebook accounts in the names of nonexistent individuals, like "Melvin Redick," that directed people to links that provided false information about Hillary Clinton, George Soros, and other Trump "enemies."[7] They used many persuasion and mind control tactics that cults use—lying and deceiving (in fact, the whole enterprise was based on a grand deception, namely that the accounts were real); confusing and spreading doubt with alternative facts and narratives; blaming and dividing; branding and labeling; distracting and reframing; using loaded language;and most of all spreading fear by constructing false enemies.[8] As Nance describes, the Russian plan was to "destroy a democracy by using the democracy." Months before the 2016 election, members of the intelligence community—including the FBI, the CIA, and the National Security Agency—began investigating and concluded that Russian meddling took place during the 2016 elections. They presented their results on January 6, 2017.

In her 2018 book *Cyberwar: How Russian Hackers and Trolls Helped Elect a President*, the University of Pennsylvania's Kathleen Hall Jamieson[9] used statistical data to argue that, through their social media campaign, Russia influenced enough voters in key states to tip the election to Trump.[10] In addition, the Russians hacked the Democratic National Committee (DNC), the Democratic Congressional Campaign Committee (DCCC), and the Clinton campaign.[11] There is evidence that they infiltrated actual U.S. voting systems.[12] Some people pointed to other factors that may have played a role in Clinton's loss, including the way she waged her ground game, neglecting to campaign effectively in Michigan and Wisconsin.[13] [14]

THE MUELLER PROBE

In July 2016, then FBI director James Comey launched a counterintelligence investigation into possible ties between Russia and the Trump election campaign. Trump fired Comey on May 9 of the following year. About a week later, former FBI director Robert Mueller was appointed to lead the investigation and also to take over existing FBI investigations that Comey had been conducting before he was fired, including those looking into Trump campaign chairman Paul Manafort and former national security advisor Michael Flynn's ties to Russia.

On April 18, 2019, a redacted version of Mueller's report was released to the public. (This came several weeks after Trump-appointed Attorney General William Barr released a four-page summary that would make the report appear far less damning for the president than it actually was.) Any doubts about the effectiveness of the Russian interference campaign were laid to rest by the report, which laid out in unprecedented detail, across nearly 200 pages of the 448-page document, the steps Russia took to spread disinformation, divide the nation, and undermine the 2016 election in an attempt to get Trump elected. It confirmed—and expanded upon—what the intelligence community had discovered about fake social media accounts and hacked emails, and found evidence that at least one county in Florida had been hacked by the Russians. It also outlined the role played by WikiLeaks and its founder Julian Assange, and confirmed that he had received the emails from Russia, and not from a DNC employee, as he had claimed.

Though Mueller could not find conclusive evidence of "criminal conspiracy" between Trump's campaign and Russia, he found "numerous links" between Trump campaign officials and the Russians. He examined ten instances of possible obstruction of justice by Trump and though he was unable to convict, his report made it clear that Trump's obstruction of the FBI and special counsel investigation "crossed constitutional boundaries and could have merited criminal prosecution if not for a Justice Department policy against indicting sitting presidents," wrote Noah Bookbinder in *The New York Times*.[15] Even some in the conservative media agreed. "Depending on how you look at them, it might be enough to prosecute," said Fox News judge Andrew Napolitano. "But it did show a venal, amoral, deceptive Donald Trump, instructing his aides to lie and willing to help them do so."[16] In May 2019, over 980 federal prosecutors, including Republicans and Democrats, had signed a statement posted on *Medium* that Trump's conduct as described in the Mueller report "would, in the case of any other person not covered by the Office of Legal Counsel policy against indicting a sitting President, result in multiple felony charges for obstruction of justice."[17]

All along, Trump has repeatedly described the investigation as "a disaster," "a hoax," "a witch hunt," and "a disgrace" promulgated by the "fake news" media. His rants are reminiscent of cult leaders like Lyndon LaRouche, who would go on tirades about the conspiracy against him on the part of the CIA, the Jews, and the British government, and who think they are above the law. Trump described the Mueller investigation as a personal attack rather than a bipartisan investigation conducted by a Republican. Mueller and his colleagues would indict thirty-four people, including Flynn and Manafort, and also Trump campaign members George Papadopoulos, Rick Gates, and Roger Stone. In addition, Mueller indicted thirteen Russian nationals, three Russian companies, and twelve members of the Russian military intelligence agency, the GRU.[18]

Though Trump may not have criminally conspired, he has appeared, on occasion, to undermine American interests and institutions in favor of Russia. In July 2016, at a news conference in Florida, Trump made his famous request. "Russia, if you're listening, I hope you'll be able to find the 30,000 emails that are missing," he said, referring to deleted emails from the private account Hillary Clinton used when she was secretary of state. Later, as president, he would hold a private meeting with Vladimir Putin in Helsinki during which he would confiscate his translator's notes and take Putin's word over that of the CIA, FBI, and NSA regarding Russian interference. He would also compliment Putin's strength as a leader. Many have observed that Trump seems to be in Putin's thrall. It is worth asking the question, Why? Through much of his campaign, Trump was pursuing a lucrative deal to build a hotel in Moscow, as his former lawyer Michael Cohen revealed in testimony before Congress. In truth, Trump's ties to Russia go back decades.

TRUMP VISITS MOSCOW

When Trump first visited Russia, Putin was a low-level KGB agent in Germany, trying to recruit assets. According to author Luke Harding, Trump's first visit to Russia in 1987 was the result of just such a "fishing expedition."[19] Trump was invited to Moscow by the Soviet ambassador to the United States, Yuri Dubinin, at a time when the KGB was actively seeking recruits. It would be the first of several visits during which Trump was wined and dined—often under twenty-four-hour surveillance.

On September 2, 1987, not long after he returned from his first trip, Trump took out a full-page ad in *The New York Times*, *The Boston Globe*, and *The Washington Post*, blasting American foreign policy.[20] Framing it as an open letter, Trump made his case for "why

America should stop paying to defend countries that can defend themselves"—a foreshadowing of his later critique, as president, of NATO. The following month, he gave what sounded like a campaign speech in New Hampshire, one that seemed more congruent with the Kremlin's political goals than with America's.[21]

Trump's ties to Russia appear to have strengthened in the early 1990s. Two of his businesses, the Trump Taj Mahal casino and the Plaza Hotel, had gone bankrupt and the Trump Shuttle folded. He was massively in debt when Russian oligarchs, flush with cash, rescued him. "He could not get anybody in the United States to lend him anything. It was all coming out of Russia. His involvement with Russia was deeper than he's acknowledged," writes Michael Hirsh in his article "How Russian Money Helped Save Trump's Business" in *Foreign Policy*.[22]

Initially the bailout came in the form of real estate partnerships and the purchase of Trump condos. In the early 2000s, Trump began working with two Russians who would help him make his transformation "from builder to brander." As Hirsh observes, by 2015, when he announced his candidacy, Trump was already "enmeshed in this mysterious overseas flow of capital."[23]

A CLOSER LOOK

Some of Trump's policy decisions since becoming president appear to support or advance Russian objectives, including weakening NATO, slashing the State Department budget, loosening ties with our allies, and ultimately weakening America's power and prestige. Withdrawing from the Iran nuclear deal was yet another Trump move that appeared to serve Israel and Saudi Arabia more than it did our own or NATO's interests.

Trump has yet to take a stand against Russian aggression upon foreign territories, such as Ukraine, as well as Russia's continued support of Assad's regime in Syria. He has ignored, downplayed, or outright rejected the findings from the American intelligence community about how Russia infiltrated social media to influence the election. At the 2018 Russian–United States summit in Helsinki, he stood before the international press and sided with Putin, saying that the Russian leader "was extremely strong and powerful in his denial today," a stinging rebuke to the American intelligence community. He praised the Russian president as "very, very, strong" and pinned the tensions between the two countries on "years of U.S. foolishness and stupidity." It was at this same conference that Putin acknowledged that he had wanted Trump elected. Former George W. Bush speechwriter David Frum later commented in *The Atlantic,* "We still do not know what hold Vladimir Putin has on Donald Trump, but the whole world has now witnessed the power of its grip."[24]

We know what Putin wants—to destabilize democratic institutions and government in the United States and elsewhere. He wants to destroy the NATO alliance and get U.S. forces out of Europe so he can further pursue Russia's interests—possibly including future invasions—without international interference. He also wants Western-imposed sanctions lifted, not just on Russian trade but also on his own foreign bank accounts. With his sixteen years of KGB experience—he was an agent between 1975 and 1991—and years of using influence and mind control techniques on his own people as prime minister, Putin has the ability and knowledge to be creative about how to get it, including supporting the presidency of Donald Trump.

THE CULT OF PUTIN

Putin came to power in 1999, a relative unknown. One of the first things he did was stage a series of apartment block bombings and blame them on Chechen rebels, which created a sense of crisis and fear—and helped get him elected president. The second was to beef up his public persona. Back in 1992, while working for the mayor of St. Petersburg, he had commissioned a film about himself called *Vlast,* the Russian word for power. As president, he continued his personal mythmaking, releasing videos and photos of himself scuba diving and horseback riding—and even shirtless on vacation.

He would use other tricks in Pratkanis and Aronson's would-be cult leader's playbook to get the Russians to support, admire, and embrace him. Though Putin's rugged charisma and nationalist views—he promised to return Russia to its past glory, essentially to make Russia great again—initially won over the public, it led to an authoritarian style of governing, one that controlled many aspects of citizens' lives—their behavior, information, thoughts, and emotions. This included a crackdown on the press, the persecution (and poisoning) of political opponents, the suppression of personal freedoms and minority rights, and a surge of predatory foreign aggression.

Yet Trump appears to be smitten. Putin's toughness seems to play into Trump's vision of a true leader. According to Nance, Putin provides a blueprint for Trump. "DJT appears to literally have the checklist by Putin in how to solidify a nation into autocracy." It begins with information control—a "war on law enforcement intelligence and media. [It is] real, and will undermine our constitution."[25]

Like Trump, Putin is a malignant narcissist. He is charming but ruthless. He exaggerates his accomplishments, lies, and steals (he is a billionaire many times over). He also exhibits a seemingly KGB-bred paranoia and appears to lack empathy, judging by the way he treats dissenters, like Sergei and Yulia Skripal, the Russian father and daughter who were poisoned in Britain. Such attacks send a powerful message to anyone who dares to cross Putin, and are a powerful mechanism for controlling people, even if they don't live in Russia.

When Fox News host Bill O'Reilly asked Trump what he thought about Putin being a killer, Trump responded, "We've got a lot of killers. What do you think? Our country's so innocent?"[26] Again, we do not know what, exactly, accounts for Putin's grip on Trump, but it is often the case that cult leaders model themselves on other cult leaders. Sun Myung Moon was in a Korean cult before he started his own, and L. Ron Hubbard was involved with Aleister Crowley—the self-proclaimed Beast 666—and his occult group, Thelema, which was supposed to guide humanity to a new era, the Aeon of Horus.

There is also the possibility that Putin controls Trump through fear—that he will release compromising material. Though O'Reilly and other Fox commentators were bewildered by his defense of Putin,

Trump's embrace of Putin appears to be filtering down. Polls show that Republican approval of Russia has risen significantly. Part of it may be due to Trump's distraction campaign—he legitimizes Russia at the same time that he demonizes Democrats. In any case, it seems to be working. At a Trump rally in Ohio, a photo was taken of two friends wearing T-shirts that read: "I'd Rather Be a Russian Than a Democrat."[27]

THE CHRISTIAN RIGHT

Cult leaders often lie about their past. They embellish, distort, exaggerate, and invent to enlarge themselves in their own eyes and the eyes of their followers. While Trump does his fair share of self-mythologizing, the biggest myths of all are being told by others. Nowhere is that happening with greater gusto, flair, and audacity than on the Christian right. They have appropriated, reworked, and manipulated Trump's tale, using their own loaded language and imagery, for their own purposes. According to many Christian right leaders, Trump was chosen by God to lead America. He may be a sinner, but God has raised him up to turn America into a Christian nation. Theocratic theorist Lance Wallnau, in his 2016 book, *God's Chaos Candidate: Donald J. Trump and the American Unraveling*, compared Trump to the idol-worshipping Persian king Cyrus, who helped return the Jews to Jerusalem. Like Cyrus, Trump is seen as a figure of deliverance, an unwitting conduit, an unlikely vessel. And deliver he has—not just to the Christian right but also to the Jewish right. Israeli prime minister Benjamin Netanyahu, thanking Trump for moving the American embassy to Jerusalem, compared him to "King Cyrus the Great."[28]

At the CPAC meeting in February, Mark Lindell, the inventor and CEO of MyPillow, gushed about meeting with Trump in 2016. "I knew God had chosen him for such a time as this. We were given a second chance and time granted to get our country back on track with our conservative values and getting people saved in Jesus's name."[29]

As outrageous as such claims may seem, they are taken seriously

by millions of conservative religious believers. When a group's leader
is exalted and imbued with divinity, it is a short step to one who demands complete loyalty, devotion, and obedience. What is especially
concerning is that such views are being touted not just by pillow makers and proselytizers, but by a former White House press secretary. "I
think God calls all of us to fill different roles at different times and I
think that he wanted Donald Trump to become president, and that's
why he's there," said Sarah Huckabee Sanders during an interview on
the Christian Broadcasting Network.[30]

To think of the Christian right as a monolithic, Bible-thumping,
churchgoing bloc is a mistake. It's a dynamic movement fueled by
conservative factions and ministries—primarily Protestant evangelicals and Catholics. What unites them is a strong desire to see their
conservative positions—anti-abortion, antihomosexuality, antiscience
(including stem cell research and evolution)—become the law of the
land en route to achieving their grand theocratic vision. Their rallying
cry is "religious freedom," defined not as the First Amendment right
to believe differently from the rich and powerful, free from the undue
influence of government and religious institutions, but instead as the
right to deny constitutional rights to others based on one's own religious beliefs.

Christian right entities range in size, from the big megachurches led
by Rick Warren and televangelists like Pat Robertson to smaller congre-
gations. Most are small and not widely known. There are also religious
cults in the mix—Westboro Baptist Church, International Church of
Christ, as well as the Unification Church—that have theocratic ambitions. Here it is important to stress that most of mainstream Christianity, including the thirty-eight member denominations of the National
Council of Churches[31] and most Catholics, rejects the theocratic methods and goals of the Christian right. In fact, mainstream Christians are
considered to be heretics and apostates by many Christian right leaders, who may hold somewhat differing views but generally believe that
their fundamentalist versions constitute true Christianity.

Beneath the surface of these Christian right churches are powerful, sometimes secretive networks, whose goal is to exert influence

on powerful people—businessmen, celebrities, politicians, and even presidents like Trump—in order to bring about their vision of a Christian nation. One of these, known publicly as the Fellowship and privately as the Family, operates numerous front groups that keep its activities hidden. Another is the New Apostolic Reformation (NAR), which grows out of the Pentecostal and charismatic wing of evangelicalism and includes a wide range of large and small ministries. A third is the Catholic organization, Opus Dei. All are well-connected and ambitious. They believe that Christianity is under siege and must be restored to its rightful, central place by a theocratic takeover of American political and cultural institutions. As NAR leader Dutch Sheets said at CPAC in 2019, "We will expose the enemies of God, disrupt their plans, enforce Heaven's rule, and reform America."[32]

More mainstream Christian groups may evangelize and otherwise seek to influence politics and government. What distinguishes the modern Christian right is the idea that their theocratic takeover is ordained by God and, some believe, may lead to the return of Jesus. According to Frederick Clarkson, a senior research analyst at Political Research Associates and a longtime researcher of the Christian right, they believe that "regardless of theological camp, means, or timetable, God has called conservative Christians to exercise dominion over society by taking control of political and cultural institutions."[33] This theocratic doctrine, known as Dominionism, is "the ideological engine of the Christian Right" and has been driving Christian right ministries across the country—and, in the case of the Family, right in the heart of Washington, D.C.

THE FAMILY

No one has done more to shine a light on this group than Jeffrey Sharlet. In his book *The Family*, Sharlet, who is associate professor of literary journalism at Dartmouth College, traces the history of the group back to 1935. Abraham (Abram) Vereide, a Norwegian-born Methodist minister and founder of Goodwill Industries in Seattle, had a vision. "God spoke to him and told him that Christianity had been getting it wrong for 2,000 years by focusing on the poor and the weak and the down and out," said Sharlet.[34] "Only the big man was capable of mending the world. But who would help the big man?" Vereide organized a series of breakfast prayer meetings with civic and business leaders in Seattle—one of them would be elected mayor in 1938—and then across the Northwest and eventually across the country. By 1942, Vereide had sixty regular meeting groups. That same year, Vereide—living now in Washington, D.C.—held his first joint Senate-House prayer breakfast meeting. In 1953, he convened his first National Prayer Breakfast, which continues to this day, attracting the wealthy and powerful Washington elite—and every president since Eisenhower. It would become, as *The New York Times* reports, "an international influence-peddling bazaar, where foreign dignitaries, religious leaders, diplomats and lobbyists jockey for access to the highest reaches of American power"[35]—including Marina Butina, a Russian graduate student and gun rights activist. In 2017 she attended the breakfast, where Trump was giving the keynote speech, in hopes of establishing a back channel of communication with American politicians. She was later convicted of spying for Russia.[36]

Vereide would expand his vision over the years. He had what he called the Idea, writes Sharlet, "the most ambitious theocratic project of the American century, 'every Christian a leader, every leader a Christian.'" With the onset of the Cold War, amid claims that "godless communists" wanted to take over the world, he envisioned a "ruling class of Christ-committed men bound in a fellowship of the anointed, the chosen, key men in a voluntary dictatorship of the divine."[37] Though he would position the Family as, among other things, a Jesus youth movement, most of their dealings would be discreet. Today they lobby, recruit, and conduct private meetings and spiritual retreats in a red brick townhouse, C Street House, on Capitol Hill and in other buildings, including a gray colonial building in Arlington, called Ivanwald.

Sharlet lived at Ivanwald among young recruits—"high priests in training"—following a daily regimen that would sound familiar to many cult members: "no swearing, no drinking, no sex, no self. Watch out for magazines and don't waste time on newspapers and never watch TV. Eat meat, study the Gospels, play basketball: God loves a man who can sink a three-pointer."[38] He was told he was there "to learn how to rule the world."

Family member and Watergate felon Charles Colson called the Family "a veritable underground of Christ's men all through the U.S. government."[39] Though secretive about their membership, the list is thought to include Jeff Sessions, Betsy DeVos, Senators Chuck Grassley, Pete Domenici, and John Ensign, along with Vice President Mike Pence. Not all members are Republican. The Family's strategy is to cultivate people with money, power, or special skills by inviting them to their National Prayer Breakfasts—they have invited Muslims, Jews, foreign nationals, and even dictators of other countries, as well as Democrats. The Family thought Hillary Clinton might someday become president and began cultivating her years ago. She was reportedly an active participant in the Family (although not, apparently, a member) during her years in Washington, and described Doug Coe, the leader at that time, as "a genuinely loving spirit and mentor."[40]

Yet compassion does not seem to occupy a central place in the Family's philosophy. One of Vereide's most significant moves was to reimagine Jesus as a kind of strongman, one cast in the mold of authoritarian leaders like Adolf Hitler. "The bottom-line of Christ's message wasn't really about love or mercy or justice or forgiveness. It was about power," said Sharlet.[41] Though Vereide denounced Hitler, according to Sharlet "he admired fascism's cultivation of elites, crucial to what he saw as a God-ordained coming 'age of minority control.'"[42] Doug Coe would later add Stalin, Pol Pot, and Mao Zedong to the list. "[Coe is] quick to say these are evil men, but they understood power."[43]

It's not clear if the Family actively supported the authority-loving Trump, since they mostly operate behind the scenes. But in Mike Pence—who according to Sharlet was recruited into the Family by Charles Colson in 2009—they appear to have one of their own in the White House. Though Pence was brought up Catholic and Democratic, he underwent a conversion as a "born again" Christian in college. By the mid-1990s he would famously describe himself as "a Christian, a conservative, and a Republican, in that order."

As a member of Congress, he was known for his "unalloyed traditional conservatism,"[44] but most of all for his faith. He famously does not drink or associate socially with women unless his wife is present. "His evangelical Christianity is now the driving force behind his political agenda, whether it is working to deny federal funds to Planned Parenthood or to make it legal for religious conservatives to refuse to serve gay couples," write Jonathan Mahler and Dirk Johnson in *The New York Times*. "'Pence doesn't simply wear his faith on his sleeve, he wears the entire Jesus jersey,' as Brian Howey, a political columnist in Indiana, once put it."[45]

The Family, intentionally or not, took a huge leap toward fulfilling their central mission of creating, in Vereide's words, a "ruling class of Christ-committed men" when Pence took over as head of Trump's transition team. By the time he was finished, Trump's cabinet was filled with no fewer than nine evangelicals, including—in addition to Jeff Sessions—Rick Perry, Sonny Perdue (Agriculture), Ryan Zinke (Interior), Tom Price (Health and Human Services), Ben Carson (Housing and Urban Development), Elaine Chao (Transportation), and Betsy DeVos, who would soon begin pushing for charter schools and bringing prayer back into the classroom.

Zinke and Price were forced to resign amid scandal. Trump also replaced secretary of state Rex Tillerson with conservative evangelical Mike Pompeo, who has cast Muslim-Christian relations as a holy war, and who in his previous post as director of the CIA made speeches loaded with explicitly religious language. Trump would replace Jeff Sessions with William Barr. Though not an evangelical, Barr has close links—as we shall soon see—to the secretive conservative Catholic order Opus Dei, which, like the Family, has a theocratic mission. About a month after assuming his Justice Department post in 2019, Barr would write a four-page summary of the Mueller report that, according to many, whitewashed and cherry-picked the Mueller findings.

"What's interesting about Trump is that he's not really a believer, yet he's put together the most fundamentalist Cabinet in U.S. history," said Sharlet. "There never has been one like this. It's the most Family-friendly."[46]

THE NEW APOSTOLIC REFORMATION

On December 7, 2018, an unusual prayer was offered up in one of the grand ballrooms in the Trump International Hotel in Washington D.C. "In Jesus' name, we declare the Deep State will not prevail!" said Jon Hamill, head of Lamplighter Ministries, as dozens of worshippers held their hands aloft, engaging in glossolalia, referred to as "speaking in tongues." "We have governmental leaders throughout the Trump administration who love Jesus with all of their heart, and they are giving their all for this nation and for God's dream for this nation."[47] Hamill described how he and a group of religious leaders had been invited by former Kansas Republican senator Sam Brownback, U.S. ambassador at large for international religious freedom and a Family member, into his office to pray for evangelical pastor Andrew Brunson, who was imprisoned by Turkey's government. Brunson was later "miraculously" released.

Prayer can be powerful, according to many in the movement known as the New Apostolic Reformation (NAR). A contemporary movement of networks of ministries—each of which is led by modern-day "prophets" or "apostles" such as Hamill and his wife, Jolene—the NAR is united in their belief that intercessory prayer can work miracles. NAR originated in Pentecostal and charismatic movements and has roots in the so-called discipling and shepherding movements, which claim to model themselves on first-century apostolic Christianity. Through robust networking, savvy use of computers, aggressive grassroots tactics, and a mastery of influence techniques right out of the cult playbook, the NAR has grown into a movement with tens of millions of followers in America and a reported 300 million internationally, many of whom have been highly indoctrinated—rendered highly dependent and obedient to their leadership.

Many of the ministries and groups of the NAR—including the

International House of Prayer, Bethel Church, and Morningstar Church—fulfill criteria of the BITE model, such as deceptive recruitment, restricting access to critical information and people, and instilling phobias in members, as we will see in chapter 8. (The Australia-based Hillsong Church and its New York leader, Carl Lentz, recruited pop singer Justin Bieber and other celebrities.)

Followers are taught that God is working through their divinely appointed leaders, who receive revelations, speak in tongues, exorcise demons, and do faith healings. They believe that through prayer, they can perform miracles: in addition to freeing Andrew Brunson, they believe their prayers helped Brett Kavanaugh become a Supreme Court justice and put Trump in the White House. In the Cult of Trump, NAR followers are among the most fervent believers in the Dominionist vision and the idea that Trump was chosen by God to lead them.

Though they embrace Trump now, Ted Cruz was the preferred candidate of many NAR leaders during the Republican primaries. When it became clear that Trump was the likely Republican nominee, a steering committee of Christian right figures, including top NAR leader Joseph Mattera—whose website's tagline is "Influencing the Leaders Who Influence Culture"—organized a meeting at Trump Tower with more than a thousand evangelical and Christian right leaders.[48] Most of the attendees came out of the meeting feeling reassured that they could support Trump, despite his history of un-Christian indiscretions.

Once Trump arrived in the White House, he set to work making good on promises to the NAR and the broader Christian right. During their meeting with Trump, Christian right leaders had discussed their concerns about what they perceived to be the government's assault on religious freedom, defined as the right to practice their own brand of Christianity, even if it meant refusing to perform medical procedures, bake cakes, or perform services for people they might deem un-Christian. Trump delivered, signing religious freedom executive orders and making judicial appointments. Meanwhile, the NAR and other factions of the Christian right were making historic inroads at the state and local level. Several Christian right groups had organized a legislative campaign, called Project Blitz, providing state legislators with a manual outlining how to write laws that would further their goal of theocratic Christian dominion.[49] Included in the manual were a set of "model bills." In 2018, at least seventy-five bills were introduced in more than twenty states, many of which resemble these model bills. In five states bills were passed allowing, and sometimes requiring, that the phrase "In God We Trust" be posted in public buildings, schools, and vehicles, including police cars. They are only the tip of the iceberg. The goal is to introduce legislation governing issues from school prayer to gay marriage to a woman's right to choose and in this way advance their theocratic vision.

That vision was framed by Weyrich and Lind as a struggle between a theocratic insurgency against what they perceived to be an increasingly secular anti-Christian culture and government. In promoting their Dominionist vision, and their retooled concept of freedom of religion, the ministries of the NAR pit themselves against the Democrats, the establishment Republicans, and government in general. They even claimed that the FBI and Department of Justice were trying to destroy Trump's presidency. In a blog post, "Apostle" Dutch Sheets described how the NAR would use their "kingdom authority" to break "the back of this attempt to render President Trump ineffective. We will release favor over him, enabling him to accomplish everything for which God sent him to the White House—including the turning of the Supreme Court! President Trump will fulfill all of God's purposes for him," Sheets wrote.[50]

RALPH DROLLINGER AND CAPITOL MINISTRIES

Ralph Drollinger is a big man, over seven feet tall, with a sweeping reach. He is founder and director of the international Capitol Ministries, which has as its stated mission "to make disciples of Jesus Christ in the political arena throughout the world."[51] Once a week, Drollinger ventures from his office to a secret location where he conducts a Bible study meeting with members of the Trump Cabinet.[52]

At these meetings, Cabinet members like Rick Perry, Mike Pompeo,

Sonny Perdue, and Mike Pence study the Bible, verse by verse, and receive a lesson that Drollinger writes and puts online each week. Though Trump does not attend, he receives transcripts of the teachings and, according to Drollinger, often returns them with scrawled comments. "He's got this leaky Sharpie felt-tip pen that he writes all capital letters with. 'Way to go Ralph, really like this study, keep it up.' Stuff like that," Drollinger said.[53]

It's extraordinary access—and Drollinger also hosts Bible studies in the U.S. Senate and House of Representatives office buildings and in many state capitol buildings. Yet his teachings are often misleading or outright incorrect and out of touch with basic biblical scholarship standards, according to André Gagné, a former evangelical pastor turned critic and associate professor in the Department of Theological Studies at Concordia University in Montreal.[54]

There are other reasons for concern. In his 2013 book, *Rebuilding America: The Biblical Blueprint*, Drollinger claims that it is the state's "God-given responsibility to moralize a fallen world through the use of force." In an op-ed for the *New York Times,* Katherine Stewart describes Drollinger as believing that "social welfare programs 'have no basis in Scripture,' that Christians in government have an obligation to hire only Christians, and that women should not be allowed to teach grown men."[55] An early supporter of Trump, he once called on him to create a "benevolent dictatorship."[56] According to the Capitol Ministries website, "Drollinger's comments were made in passing reference to a divided Congress that fails to accomplish business. He was speaking of the nation's need for a strong leader with gifts of persuasion."[57] It may be worth noting that Drollinger has also been quoted as saying that Catholicism is the "world's largest false religion,"[58] that homosexuality is an "abomination," and that it is "a sin" for "women with children" to "serve in public office [or be] employed."[59]

OPUS DEI AND THE CATHOLIC RIGHT

Catholics and Protestants have been at odds, sometimes even open warfare, for hundreds of years. Even now the relationship can turn bitter, as Drollinger's comment suggests. A historic shift occurred in 2009—one year into the Obama presidency—when Catholic and Evangelical Christian Right leaders, along with a few leaders of the Eastern Orthodox Church, pledged to "join across historic lines of ecclesial differences" and affirm their commitment to defend three "truths"—"the sanctity of human life, the dignity of marriage as a union of husband and wife, and the freedom of conscience and religion." Contained in the manifesto, known as the Manhattan Declaration—which was signed by 150 leaders including fifty sitting bishops, archbishops, and cardinals—was a vow to defend the vision at all costs. "Through the centuries, Christianity has taught us that civil disobedience is not only permitted, but sometimes required," it declares.[60] According to Frederick Clarkson, the Declaration's three-part formula would serve as a kind of rallying cry for the Christian right. Its "integrated approach to abortion, marriage, and religious liberty, is designed to unite key leaders of major factions around common arguments and to function as a catalyst for political renewal,"[61] he writes.

A principal drafter of the Declaration—which at last count had over 550,000 signatures—was Princeton jurisprudence professor Robert P. George, a leading light among Catholic neo-Conservatives with deep ties to a network of conservative political and religious groups across the country. "If there really is a vast, right-wing conspiracy, its leaders probably meet in George's basement," writes Anne Morse, in an article for the conservative Catholic magazine *Crisis*.[62] Among those relationships—though George downplays it—is the secretive organization, Opus Dei. The organization has supported several of George's projects, most notably the James Madison Program in American Ideals and Institutions at Princeton, which, according to Max Blumenthal writing in *The Nation*, "serves as a testing ground for the right's effort to politicize college campuses." According to Blumenthal, "George's program is funded by a stable of right-wing foundations and a shadowy web of front groups for the Catholic cult known as Opus Dei."[63] (According to a 2005 article in *The Daily Princetonian*, the organization has funneled hundreds of thousands of dollars to Princeton campus projects—there is even an Opus Dei residence on campus—many of which included on their boards a man named Luis Tellez, who served for years as the director of Opus Dei in Princeton.)[64]

Translated as "The Work of God," Opus Dei came to widespread popular attention in Dan Brown's bestselling novel *The DaVinci Code*, which depicts a self-flagellating, murderous albino Opus Dei monk who carries out the orders of his cultlike and power-hungry organization. While Brown's depiction was fictional (Opus Dei does not have monks) and sensationalized, the organization is, by many accounts, highly demanding and ambitious. "It is a closed, disciplined group guided by an authoritarian ideology," writes Robert Hutchison in a 1997 *Guardian* piece, "The Vatican's Own Cult"—one that "labours silently and stealthily" to align government with its own policies. "Its primary goal is to return the Catholic Church to the center of society, as in medieval times," writes Hutchison, who is also author of a book about Opus Dei, *Their Kingdom Come*.[65]

Among the defining features of the group—which was founded in 1928 by the Spanish priest Josemaria Escriva de Balaguer and elevated in 1982 by Pope John Paul II to a "personal prelature" that answers directly to the pope—are a need for secrecy and obedience, which often entails "putting away one's scruples" to serve the organization. Members and associates are organized in an internal hierarchy made up of numeraries, who are unmarried, celibate, and often living with the group; supernumeraries, who may be married and work outside the group but turn over a portion of their earnings; and cooperators, who are sympathetic nonmembers. Numeraries, and even some supernumeraries, live under high-demand circumstances—often cut off from family members, as was the case with the daughter of Dianne DiNicola, a prominent critic of the group and founder of the Opus Dei Awareness Network (ODAN),[66] and with a number of former members whom I have counseled. They participate in secret initiation rites, swear obedience, and submit to "formative norms," which Hutchinson describes as a form of "mind-conditioning," including reporting weekly to a director who oversees all activities, personal and professional, and confessing once a week. "Celibates must regularly wear a cilis—a spiked thigh chain used by religious communities in the middle ages," he writes, and practice self-flagellation.

Membership is small—only 3,000 in the United States and 85,000 worldwide. Only some of these are priests. Most are lay members. But as with the Family, the focus is on "quality, not quantity." As Frank L. Cocozzelli, a Catholic writer, attorney, and stem cell research advocate, writes, "They seek out the elite and the wealthy."[67] In Washington, D.C., Opus Dei operates out of the Catholic Information Center (CIC), in a building located two blocks from the White House that houses offices, a bookstore, and a chapel, where daily mass is held (and where Robert George blogged that he attended the Catholic conversion ceremony of a formerly Jewish colleague[68]). For years, the center was under the direction of Reverend C. John McCloskey—a brash and charismatic leader who in 2002 was accused of groping a young woman and was relocated the following year. (Opus Dei later settled the suit for $977,000.)[69] During his heyday at the Catholic Information Center, McCloskey attracted a who's who of Washington luminaries to Catholicism, including then-Senators Rick Santorum and Sam Brownback[70] (who converted from mainline Protestant Presbyterianism); Lawrence Kudlow, a financial analyst and, since 2018, director of the National Economic Council; and former Speaker of the House Newt Gingrich.[71]

Though McCloskey is long gone, the Catholic Information Center[72] still maintains a strong presence in Washington, D.C. The center's board continues to include Leonard Leo, conservative legal activist and vice president of the Federalist Society, which has worked for decades to organize the right wing takeover of the Supreme Court.[73] Leo helped to block Obama's nomination of Merrick Garland and campaigned to put conservative (Catholic) judges Samuel Alito, John Roberts, Neil Gorsuch, and Brett Kavanaugh on the Supreme Court—the very same justices who, along with fellow Catholic Clarence Thomas, are considered mostly likely to overturn the landmark Supreme Court ruling *Roe v. Wade*, which declared that restricting access to abortion is unconstitutional. Aiding those judicial campaigns was a nonprofit organization that Leo helped to found, the Judicial

Crisis Network, which according to *The Guardian*, spent $17 million to quash the Garland nomination and elevate Gorsuch[74]—and which was originally run out of the home of Ann Corkery, an avowed member of Opus Dei.

According to *The Washington Post*, Opus Dei's small Washington center continues to have "an outsize impact on policy and politics."[75] It is not clear if Leo—who has Trump's ear[76]—played a role in nominating William Barr for the position of attorney general. But Pat Cipollone—who also served as a Catholic Information Center board member—probably did. He was brought on as White House Counsel[77] two months before Barr's nomination in December 2019. (Cipollone was an assistant to Barr when he was attorney general to George H. W. Bush.) It turns out, Barr was himself a member of the eight-member Catholic Information Center board of directors. As part of his confirmation process before the Senate Judiciary Committee, Barr completed a questionnaire which reveals that between 2014 and 2017, he served as a director of the Catholic Information Center—a period overlapping the tenures of Leo and Cipollone, according to the Catholic Information Center website.[78] Barr's connection to Opus Dei goes back further. From 1992 to 1993, an Opus Dei numerary, John Wauck, who later became a priest, served as Barr's speech writer.[79]

In his article, "Did Opus Dei Teach A.G. Barr to 'Put Away his Scruples,'" Cocozzelli describes Barr's presentation of the Mueller Report to Congress. "When questioned about his famous four page memo and repeated mischaracterization of the Mueller Report, time and again, Barr obstructed, bobbed and weaved—all while refusing to answer basic questions put forth by the Democratic Senators," Cocozzelli writes. "We also know that Barr gave misleading testimony before the House Appropriations committee,"[80] claiming that he had not heard any criticism from Mueller, who had sent Barr a letter precisely to that effect two days after Barr made his memo public. According to Cocozzelli, Barr's obfuscation and obstruction may be part of his Opus Dei "put scruples aside, ends justifies the means" mindset.

As to what those ends might be, Opus Dei is an extremely wealthy group, with assets of nearly $2.8 billion—the organization owns a building in Rome and a $42 million building in New York City. But its riches are a means to furthering a theocratic goal: to return the Catholic Church to the center of society. Barr made his own theocratic views known as early as 1992, in a speech to the Catholic League for Religious and Civil Rights, when he called for the "imposition of God's law in America."[81] Barr let Trump off the hook with regard to the Mueller Report, despite the weight of evidence showing that the president attempted to obstruct justice by trying to interfere with the Mueller investigation. Though many have speculated about Barr's motives, it is possible that he holds Trump above the law because he believes that the president could serve a higher purpose. Certainly, for Opus Dei, the desired payoff would be not just overturning *Roe v. Wade*, but overturning secular democracy itself by elevating conservative Catholics to key positions in government and public life, including and especially the judiciary. By replacing two conservative Catholic Supreme Court justices, Antonin Scalia and Anthony Kennedy, with two new ones, Gorsuch and Kavanaugh—and by placing conservative judges in federal courts across the country—Trump is already delivering.

HEART OF DARKNESS: THE ALT-RIGHT[82]

Trump has encouraged all kinds of erroneous and pernicious thinking, nowhere more dangerously than in his dealings with the "alt-right." Short for "alternative right," the term refers to a set of ideologies, groups, and individuals that, according to the Anti-Defamation League, "reject mainstream conservatism in favor of forms of conservatism that embrace implicit racism or white supremacy."[83] These include white nationalists, Confederate apologists, Klansmen, neo-Nazis, John Birchers, anti-Semites, isolationists, and antiglobalists. White supremacist leader Richard Spencer claims to have coined the term alt-right, which has been described as a euphemism for racist, neo-fascist, and neo-Nazi beliefs. At the heart of the mindset is the idea that "white identity" is being attacked—by Jews, Blacks, Muslims, gays, Communists, and other multicultural forces—under the banner of "political correctness" and "social justice."[84] "The Alt-right is a pushback against our ethnic dispossession," wrote an alt-right Reddit user, quoted in a *Medium* article. "It's an attempt to jumpstart white people into fighting for their ethnic interests the same way other races do, because our current policies are a net detriment to whites."[85]

Portraying the white majority as an oppressed insurgency, struggling against the globalist left, the alt-right is taking a storyline right out of Lind and Weyrich's fourth-generation warfare playbook. One of the tactics advocated by Weyrich and Lind is "an unrelenting barrage of criticism" against the left and other opponents. While the alt-right uses propaganda and other fourth-generation techniques, it has also taken the struggle into the streets. Fighting is something the alt-right has become known for, both through their growing—often inflammatory and hate-filled—online presence and in real life. Trump has done little to stop it—indeed the opposite. As shown by the white nationalist march on Charlottesville, where a white supremacist killed a young woman and injured many others, and by attacks in South Carolina, Pittsburgh, and New Zealand, there has been a rise in hate crimes and hate-inspired violence since Trump took office.[86]

There is reason to believe that it is not a coincidence. After the Charlottesville tragedy, Trump referred to "the egregious display of hatred, bigotry and violence on many sides, on many sides." Though he walked his comments back in a prepared statement, condemning racism and calling out alt-right groups by name, he later doubled back down, equating the actions of the counterprotesters with the white supremacists, saying that both sides were responsible. (It was Steve Bannon, Trump's former advisor and a supporter of the alt-right, who helped craft this "both sides" rhetoric.)[87] Then there was Trump's reaction to the murder of fifty people in two mosques in Christchurch, New Zealand, which was carried out by a white supremacist who referred to Trump as "a symbol of renewed white identity." While Trump can't directly be blamed for the reference, his response to the shootings was to deny that white nationalism is a rising global threat. Trump has also retweeted the meme #WhiteGenocide from four white supremacy accounts that were later suspended.[88] Remarkably, the Trump administration has restructured and marginalized the unit of the Department of Homeland Security responsible for domestic terrorism.

Hate groups have been emboldened by Trump's use and growing mastery of the cult playbook—his use of loaded language, incitements to violence, us-versus-them thinking, his sowing confusion and his tough-guy persona, his lies, distortions, and veiled threats—like this one, reported in *The New York Times*. "I can tell you I have the support of the police, the support of the military, the support of Bikers for Trump. I have the tough people, but they don't play it tough—until they go to a certain point and then it would be very bad, very bad."[89] From the moment he stepped into the White House, advised by alt-right sympathizer Steve Bannon and others, Trump has violated so many of the norms of moral decency expected of a U.S. president.

People come to their hate-filled views in various ways—through their upbringing and life experiences and, increasingly, by immersing themselves in the more shadowy precincts of the internet. University of Pittsburgh sociologist Kathleen M. Blee found that middle- and upper-middle-class men are being drawn from the mainstream into deeper and darker corners of the internet, where they are being radicalized through fearmongering and other influence tactics.[90] Their online recruitment is actively paved not just by white supremacist media like the alt-right website *The Daily Stormer* and Breitbart but also by outside forces like Russia, which is seeking to divide America through psychological manipulation. They could not have picked a better flashpoint. "The cynical brilliance of Vladimir Putin's propaganda campaign is that it exploited America's foundational commitment to white supremacy," writes Spencer Ackerman in *The Daily Beast*. "The term itself is so raw and so hideous that it inspires an allergy to its usage within mainstream political discourse. But no other term—racism, white privilege, etc.—better captures the dynamic at issue."[91]

THE RIGHT-LIBERTARIANS AND AYN RAND

One group who seeks to diminish, if not delegitimize, government is the libertarian movement. Inspired in part by the writings of the novelist and philosopher Ayn Rand—who, in books like *The Fountainhead* and *Atlas Shrugged,* promoted a ruggedly individualistic, survival-of-the-fittest, elitist ideology—they have a clear agenda: to shrink government, cut taxes and regulations, and do away with social safety nets. They include billionaires like the Koch brothers and PayPal founder Peter Thiel, who have contributed heavily to Trump's campaign and whose influence may be felt in Trump's corporate tax cuts, judicial appointments, deregulation of business, and defense of the fossil fuel industry.

While they defend the constitutional rights of individuals to pursue health, happiness, and liberty, there is an antidemocratic strand running through the libertarian movement, at least among elites like the Kochs, Thiel, former Speaker of the House Paul Ryan, Trump advisor Stephen Moore, and politicians Ron and Rand Paul. In an article in *New York* magazine, Jonathan Chait describes how "many of them see democracy as a process that enables the majority to gang up on the rich minority and carry out legalized theft through redistribution. Their highest notion of liberty entails the protection of property rights from the democratic process, and they have historically been open to authoritarian leaders who will protect their policy agenda."[92] Their main concern, as Chait observes, is to protect the makers from the takers, which appears to be right in line with Trump's own philosophy of winning—and his penchant for authoritarianism.

THE WEB OF INFLUENCE

The Christian right, Russia, and the alt-right share the goal of destabilizing democratic institutions to achieve their own ends. Yet this attack upon democracy—using anger, fear, and panic to destabilize and disrupt—has been happening from within our institutions. James Scaminaci III sees its early political applications in the late 1980s, when Newt Gingrich became Speaker of the House and began actively sowing division between the political parties through his use of inflammatory rhetoric, ushering in a kind of us versus them, good versus evil style of political discourse.[93] According to Scaminaci, the rise of the Tea Party, which gained power by mobilizing populist hatred of government, can be traced back to Gingrich.

This subversive approach to politics is all too familiar to me. When I was in the Moonies, I was told that democracy—like communism—was satanic, yet Moon spent much of his time worming his way into democratic institutions, cultivating senators, congressmen, presidents, religious leaders, businessmen—anyone who had influence and power. He shared many of the same theocratic goals as the Christian right—to take over the American government—and colluded with them for decades.[94] Moon recruited members under the guise of being a messiah, the leader of a religious organization that wanted to bring about the kingdom of heaven on earth, but he was in fact the leader of a complex organization with a highly political agenda. Though Moon started the group in the 1950s, the South Korean CIA (KCIA) would later turn it into a front group to combat what they claimed was the rising tide of communism. Of course I did not know this when I joined the group. Nor did I know that Moon had forged links with Japanese organized crime.

When Moon came to the United States in the 1960s, it was with the express aim of forging links with influential people.[95] He attended Abram Vereide's National Prayer Breakfast several times. In the early 1970s he would throw the support of the Moon organization behind the reelection of Richard Nixon, a man I'd previously despised. As Moonies, we were taught that God was using Nixon—he was God's choice. I would join my fellow members in a fast on the steps of the Capitol to show support for Nixon during the Watergate scandal. We looked like young, idealistic, and enthusiastic Americans who—under the leadership of our religious leader—had spontaneously assembled there to show support for the president. We were actually there as a result of a more complicated and entangling set of events and circumstances.

The same may be said of Trump's followers. They are caught in a web of influence that is much larger and more complex than one man saying, "I alone can fix it."

CHAPTER EIGHT

Trump's Followers

Donald Trump took the stage in Fort Wayne, Indiana, on November 5, 2018, greeting the cheering throngs with waving arms, the occasional pumped fist, and many mouthed thank-yous. He opened by pointing to the "thousands and thousands" who were still outside, wishing they could get in. "You got lucky," he told the audience, who had filled the 13,000 seats of the arena and were spilling onto the stadium floor. If they hadn't already felt blessed to be in his presence, they most likely did as he reeled off his accomplishments. "Jobs are soaring, wages are rising, optimism is skyrocketing," he said. We have created "the single best economy in the history of our great country" and "the hottest job market on the planet earth." And then he lowered the boom. But—a big but—"everything we have achieved is at stake tomorrow." It could all come crashing down at the hands of the "radical Democrats"—"they can take it apart just as fast as we built it."

There is always a villain—and a hero—at a Trump rally, and that's exactly what his audience expects—along with his insults, boasts, and takedowns of liberals and other enemies. He makes them feel heroic by association, and they adore him for it. "Trump supporters remain as enthusiastic as ever, standing for hours in hot sun or driving rain," wrote Jill Colvin, reporting on the 2018 midterms for *Business Insider*.[1] Lines to get into these rallies would wind around buildings and twist through alleys. "Look at this," said Brenda MacDonald of Woodbury, Minnesota, gesturing at the thousands waiting with her on a line that reached more than a mile. "I think it's amazing what he's doing, I really do," said Tami Gusching, at the Fort Wayne rally. "I love the aggression that he has and the power behind him."[2] "I think the fact he's still turning out these crowds of people, two years in, it's absolutely amazing," said Richard Eichhorn, seventy-two, of Stockholm, Wisconsin. "I think it's huge."[3] "I'm just totally, madly in love with him," said Peggy Saar, sixty-four, of Rochester, Minnesota.[4]

Millions of Trump supporters echo Peggy's sentiments—to the astonishment of Trump's critics. Who are these people, they wonder, and why do they support and even adore Trump after he has lied, cheated, bullied, and betrayed the country by believing the Russian president rather than his own intelligence agencies? Clearly, there is no simple answer. Trump supporters—63 million strong—are a patchwork of diverse yet distinct groups, each with varying levels of allegiance.[5] They range from fervent followers on the Christian and alt-right, who see Trump as a change agent who can forward their agenda, to traditional Republicans who vote the party line, to pro-lifers, NRA members, and the poor and out of work. They include older, white Americans who were persuaded, in part, by Trump's angry and fearful rhetoric. Finally, there are independents who voted for Trump simply because he was not Hillary Clinton.

Some had their own agendas, motivations, and allegiances, as we have seen. But Trump's campaign was an aggressive recruiting machine, using many of the black-and-white, us-versus-them techniques used by cults—along with rousing fourth-generation warfare "government versus the people" rhetoric. "Our movement is about replacing a failed and corrupted political establishment, with a new government controlled by you, the American people," began a 2016 Trump campaign ad. "The only people brave enough to vote out this corrupt establishment is you, the American people. I am doing this for the people and for the movement, and we will take back this country for you, and we will make America great again."[6]

The flamboyant New Yorker spoke to disaffected people everywhere in 2016. More than two years later, most of them are still behind him, maybe even more so. Trump has kept his base the same way he attracted them, by drawing upon his grandiosity, exaggeration, and ability to manipulate and lie, and also upon the techniques of a cult leader—distracting, overloading, and lying; framing issues using simplistic good-versus-evil, us-versus-them narratives; promoting fear and phobias.

That said, it is important to underscore that not every Trump supporter is a fervent follower. And not every fervent follower is necessarily a member of the Cult of Trump. If we think of Trump's followers as comprising a pyramid structure, with circles radiating from its base, most would occupy the outermost circles. Forming the bottom of the pyramid—literally, the base—would be Trump's most

The Cult of Trump

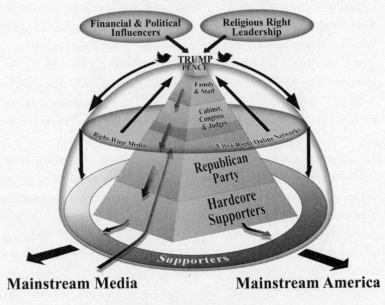

graphic: Karen Spike Robinson

loyal followers, including members of the Christian right, alt-right, listeners of Fox News and right-wing media, dyed-in-the-wool Republicans, and others. Above the base, in ascending tiers, would be business, political, and religious leaders who support and promote Trump, often to satisfy their own agendas. Closest to Trump—and atop the pyramid—would be his family and staff.

In the last chapter, we looked at how leaders and prominent people associated with movements like the Christian right and alt-right have influenced Trump. They occupy the middle tiers of the pyramid. In this chapter we will take a closer look at the top and bottom tiers—the people who are closest to Trump, his inner circle, as well as the supporters that constitute his base. Many in this bottom tier are members of other groups, some of them high-demand and cultlike. In general, those most at risk for being drawn into a cult have often had prior experience with other high-demand relationships or groups, especially those with authoritarian figures who promote a similar message. Some of Trump's most zealous followers are members of high-demand groups on the Christian right whose leaders have helped shape Trump's message of religious freedom. Members of such groups were ready—indeed, primed—for a leader like Trump.

THE TOP OF THE PYRAMID: TRUMP'S INNER CIRCLE

The Trump White House is a porous place—people come and go with their various political, religious, and economic agendas, as they do at Trump's Florida resort, Mar-a-Lago. Members of Congress and cabinet secretaries may put on sycophantic displays—as we have seen in an earlier chapter—but they typically spend only a few hours in Trump's presence. There is a core group of White House staffers, some of whom are family members, who are in regular contact with Trump. This is typically true of cults—there is a coterie of aides who are loyal and subservient to the leader, carrying out directives and doctrine. Sun Myung Moon's inner circle comprised Korean and Japanese aides who would then direct other Moonies to carry out his commands. When Trump arrived at the White House, he was surrounded by people who were not entirely of his own choosing. Steve Bannon, who was White House chief strategist, had essentially been assigned to him by billionaire Robert Mercer. Though Trump eventually bonded with him, Bannon lasted only seven months. Trump's chief of staff was Reince Priebus, who had publicly criticized Trump early in his campaign and, as the immediate past chairman of the national Republican Party, was seen by some as a party plant. He lasted about six months. His successor, retired U.S. Marine Corps general John Kelly, who was viewed as a disciplining influence and reportedly called Trump an "idiot," was fired nearly a year and a half later. Trump's current chief of staff is Mick Mulvaney, who is widely seen as a "yes man," and who lets Trump be Trump.

Trump has long been obsessed with loyalty. He has always tried to surround himself with an inner circle of loyalists and devoted staff—and family. Trump's oldest son, Don Jr., and daughter, Ivanka, worked closely with their father at the Trump Organization. Ivanka and her husband, Jared Kushner, were given important White House roles—and security clearances—despite a complete lack of governmental and political experience. Interestingly, L. Ron Hubbard Jr. helped run Scientology, but defected because he couldn't feed his family. Moon saw his sons as direct heirs to his divine lineage. When he died, an internecine struggle broke out, with each of them competing for power, and rebelling against Moon's surviving wife, known as "True Mother."

Many hoped that, with their more liberal politics, Ivanka and Jared would be moderating influences on Trump—championing issues such as climate change and, in the case of Ivanka, women's issues. There is little evidence that has happened. According to Omarosa Manigault Newman, "Trump's children never criticized him to his face—they're afraid of him, they don't have the boldness. To each other, in a supportive way, they would be like, 'Oh my God, can you believe he did this?' Jared, from a policy point of view, would make suggestions but would never disagree."[7] According to investigative journalist David Cay Johnston, who has written two books on Trump, the relationship with Ivanka may be largely transactional. Johnston believes that

Trump would throw any of his family members under the bus to save himself, including Ivanka.[8]

As head of the Trump Organization, Trump's narcissism was apparently on full display. He was known to be mercurial, and demanded absolute loyalty from employees. Similarly, among Moon's inner circle, there was no tolerance for people talking back or not succeeding in what they were told to do. There was also a lot of blaming, shaming, and competition—pitting people against each other, supposedly to get the most out of them. Manigault Newman, who has known Trump for more than fourteen years, first as a contestant on *The Apprentice*, then as a political aide, describes a similar situation: Trump would often pit his employees against one another, as he did on *The Apprentice*. In her memoir, *Unhinged*, she describes how he relished conflict and confusion. His face lit up when people argued or fought, and when they ably defended themselves. She adapted her behavior accordingly, modeling herself on Trump—even eating the same fast food—and looking to him for positive reinforcement. When she criticized someone, he would smile in approval. She learned to read him. Former lawyer Michael Cohen described, in his testimony before Congress, how Trump never directly ordered him to lie but instead made his wishes clear by speaking in "code" that was understood by anyone who worked with him. "He doesn't give you questions, he doesn't give you orders, he speaks in a code, and I understand the code, because I've been around him for a decade," Cohen said.

During his testimony, Cohen described how he would have taken a bullet for Trump, despite the fact that Trump often treated him poorly—praising him as a great lawyer one moment, then humiliating him the next. Alternating praise and criticism is a common technique in cults. Trump would also control his employees' behavior more directly, making them eat the same thing—mostly fast food like McDonald's—and disturbing their sleep with constant late-night emergencies. During his campaign, he would insist that all the women dress the same. When they went on vacation, it was always to Mar-a-Lago or Trump's Bedminster, New Jersey, golf resort, "where we knew we'd be safe and not condemned or criticized," Manigault Newman said.

For her and for Cohen, leaving Trump's orbit felt like escaping a cult—"the cult of Trumpworld," as she put it. One person who appears still to be in Trump's thrall is former White House press secretary Sean Spicer. Known for his combative and blustery defense of his boss, he would cover up and obfuscate his way through daily press briefings, repeating or defending demonstrably false assertions—most notoriously about the crowd size at the inauguration. Though he resigned after only six months, in his 2018 book, *The Briefing: Politics, the Press, and the President,* Spicer showers his former boss with praise: "I don't think we will ever again see a candidate like Donald Trump. His high-wire act is one that few could ever follow. He is a unicorn, riding a unicorn over a rainbow. His verbal bluntness involves risks that few candidates would dare take. His ability to pivot from a seemingly career-ending moment to a furious assault on his opponents is a talent few politicians can muster."

According to Spicer's replacement, Sarah Huckabee Sanders, it may be a God-given talent. Sanders, who is an evangelical Christian, was an even more devoted spokesperson for Trump, deflecting, stonewalling, and lying with a completely straight, almost emotionless, face. She spoke with the conviction of a true believer, which she apparently is. *The New Yorker* called her "Trump's Battering Ram."[9] Then there is presidential aide Kellyanne Conway, who, like Bannon, was appointed to Trump's campaign by the Mercers. A longtime Republican strategist and expert in spin, she famously coined the term "alternative facts." During the 2016 campaign, she defended Trump on national TV, sometimes with a slightly less straight face than Sanders. She appears now to be a Trump true believer, despite the fact that her husband, attorney George T. Conway, is a vocal critic of Trump. Like good soldiers, they fall in line, and even mirror him.

One of Trump's most trusted aides was former White House communications director Hope Hicks, who was plucked from a Trump Organization PR firm. The former model, who became a gatekeeper of information flow to and from Trump, seemed to have a sixth sense about how and when to break news to him. She resigned in March 2018 after her subpoenaed appearance before the House Intelligence Committee, where she admitted to telling "white lies" on Trump's behalf.[10] She was made an executive vice president and chief communications director at Fox News.[11] While Trump has surrounded himself with loyalists, some White House aides have apparently felt a greater allegiance to the country. Indeed, much to the president's frustration and distress, Trump's White House is one of the leakiest in American history. Yet his aides may have helped Trump's presidency. The Mueller Report found that Trump's efforts to obstruct the special counsel "were mostly unsuccessful, but that is largely because the persons who surrounded the President declined to carry out orders or accede to his requests."[12]

TRUMP'S BASE
The Christian Right

More than 80 percent of white evangelicals voted for Trump and yet it's important not to paint them with too broad a brush. In 2018, as migrant children were being separated from their parents, the National Association of Evangelicals, representing most of the major evangelical denominations, wrote a protest letter to Trump: "The Bible says that families came first, and government later."[13] Of Trump's followers, those who attend church are generally more favorable to minorities than nonchurchgoing Trump supporters, according to Emily Ekins, director of polling and research fellow at the Cato Institute. "It seems church teachings can curb tribalistic impulses by regularly reminding worshipers that we are all God's children," Ekins writes, though such goodwill does not necessarily extend to the LGBTQ community.[14]

And yet those tribalistic impulses have been fanned by some churches, especially those of the New Apostolic Reformation, who want to turn America into a Christian nation, and who claim a religious-freedom justification to deny constitutional rights to customers, clients, or patients. We have already seen how leaders of the NAR appropriated Trump, casting him as a figure of deliverance. They are not the only ones to do so. According to a Fox News poll, nearly half of Republicans believe Trump was chosen by God to be president.[15] But the NAR is especially effective at turning their members into true and active believers of Trump.

New Apostolic Reformation

With its network of "apostles" and "prophets," each of whom claims to receive direct revelations from God, the NAR is a sophisticated movement using business strategies and complex systems approaches.[16] NAR ministers tend to operate in a top-down, authoritarian, cultlike fashion, but they also communicate with one another and have their own hierarchical leadership structure. They all preach that the world is in the Last Days and that Judgment will be coming, and that behaving faithfully is essential.

Their followers number over 10 million in America, and 300 million around the world.[17] Many have been recruited through high-energy megachurches, as well as small ministries, Bible study groups, spiritual retreats, and an active online effort. Their meetings are carried out in a highly emotional, immersive, and experiential way. One might see demon possession, spiritual deliverance, faith healing, people acting "drunk in the Spirit," and speaking in tongues, or glossolalia, in which believers think they are speaking ancient languages. Linguists who have analyzed the utterances say they are simply combining phonemes in a fluid way. In addition, there would be intense, emotion-driven chanting, singing, and praying, and the use of hypnotic visualizations. "It's all about adrenaline. Music and preaching that is very emotively based—it's all about getting people to experience what is said to be the Spirit," said John Weaver, author of *The New Apostolic Reformation: History of a Modern Charismatic Movement.*[18]

The spirit world and supernatural beings play a big role in the NAR. According to Rachel Tabachnick, a former fellow at Political Research Associates, NAR is "an aggressively political movement within Christianity, [that] blames literal demonic beings for the world's ills and stresses." To combat these demons, and to deliver the world from darkness, followers are commanded to undertake a kind of spiritual warfare—to become spiritual warriors. In reality, they are being used to "advance a right-wing social and economic agenda," Tabachnik writes.[19]

Inspired by their apostolic leaders, some of whom met with Trump at Trump Tower, followers of NAR would direct their energy toward getting Trump elected. They would spend hours doing intercessory prayers, making calls, electioneering, donating money, telling friends, and recruiting them to his cause. One follower, Mary Colbert, claimed to have heard from her husband about a firefighter, Mark Taylor, who had a vision in 2011 that God had chosen Trump to be president. To make the prophecy come true, she organized a prayer chain that grew into a worldwide movement, giving rise to a book and a film, *The Trump Prophecy*, produced by Liberty University, an evangelical school founded by televangelist and early Christian right leader Jerry Falwell.[20] It is now the largest Christian university in the world. (Falwell's son, Jerry Falwell, Jr., is a major figure in the Cult of Trump.)[21] Promotional materials for *The Trump Prophecy* describe how God used this "team of passionate individuals to lead the nation into a fervent prayer chain that would accomplish one of the most incredible miracles our country has ever seen."[22]

NAR members are among Trump's most passionate and energetic believers, yet their spirit, savvy, and enthusiasm belies a darker reality. Many NAR ministries are high-demand groups that, according to former members and academics who study them, seem to fit the BITE model of recruitment and indoctrination. Members are conditioned to be dependent and obedient to the leader, who is said to give them "covering"—protection from evil spirits. Children and young adults are taught to mold themselves in the leader's image. In many cults, members are taught to revere the group's doctrine above all else. In NAR, a member's first commitment is to the prophet or apostle, who is seen as a conduit to God, and so can set the group's beliefs. The leader's teachings often come in the form of experiences—with the spirit world, faith healings, hypnotic trances. If a follower doubts or questions their experience, they are told that it is the work of demons, evil spirits, or Satan, or a lack of commitment on their part. They are told they must renew their commitment to be spiritual warriors to "win the world"—take it back from Satan and pave the way for the resurgence of a new Christian nation and world, in keeping with the Dominionist vision.

In much of NAR, as in most cults, complex realities are reduced to binary opposites: black versus white; good versus evil; spirit world versus physical world. Satan and demons are everywhere, tempting and trying to influence us. Demons are thought to possess outsiders or anyone who is critical of the group—parents, friends, ex-members, and reporters. Parishioners and followers are told they are "chosen" by God to carry out a mission. They are the special elite corps of humankind who will be rewarded by God for their efforts. Supporting and recruiting followers of Donald Trump is now a central feature of that mission.

This mission is shared between parent and child—and the NAR movement is careful about how they educate their children. Homeschooling is preferred. In fact, children from Christian backgrounds account for about 75 percent of American homeschooled children.[23] From 2003 to 2007, the percentage of students homeschooled to "provide religious or moral instruction" rose from 72 percent to 83 percent.[24] In this isolated environment, children are taught to be true believers, as shown in the documentary *Jesus Camp*. They are taught that homosexuality is abhorrent to God, science and secular history are illegitimate, and climate change is a hoax. As the film further shows, children are also often trained in political action, such as militant antiabortion activism, as a direct outgrowth of their religious teachings.[25]

The NAR mission is also shared between members, through discipling—essentially learning from one another by sharing experiences with God, telling one another what Christ has done for them personally. They basically indoctrinate one another. They are told that happiness comes through discipleship and that if they do what they are told, they will be loved—by Jesus and by everyone in the group. Members' behavior is additionally controlled through a system of punishments and rewards. Competitions are used to inspire and shame members to be more productive. If things aren't going well for the group—if recruitment is down, or people have left, or there is unfavorable media coverage—it is always individual members' fault. They haven't worked or prayed hard enough. Or it is due to their demons. To NAR believers, demons are real—they lie in wait, can drive people insane, or can even kill them. If a believer does become "possessed," an exorcism is performed.

NAR followers come to live within a narrow corridor of fear, guilt, and shame. Unlike healthy organizations, which recognize a person's right to choose to leave, this group tells members that people who leave are weak, sinful, gave into temptation, or the devil got to them. Phobia programming is a major mind control technique of any destructive cult, and NAR members are especially vulnerable. They are told that if they ever leave, terrible things will happen to them, their family, and humanity. If they do leave, they are shunned. Other members will be told that the person was possessed by the devil and to stay away from them. For those who grew up in one of these extreme groups, this means that all their family and friends will no longer speak or interact with them. As one might imagine, that alone is strong incentive to stay in the group.

Riddled with demons, doubt, and fear, NAR members are especially susceptible to Trump, a candidate who himself practiced a form of shunning, ejecting protesters and reporters from rallies; who emphasizes power and authority; who shames and bullies nonbelievers; and who uses fear and sees enemies lurking everywhere.

The Working Class

J. D. Vance grew up in the rust belt city of Middletown, Ohio, and the Appalachian town of Jackson, Kentucky—areas where the economy, and the chance for upward mobility, fell off in the 1970s and never fully recovered. In his book, *Hillbilly Elegy,* he writes simply and eloquently about the forgotten American working class. It is a class that includes people who have been marginalized by automation and other technological change and boxed in by systemic poverty. They are concerned about keeping their jobs, getting a paycheck, putting food on the table. They don't have the luxury of thinking about second mortgages, college funds, or 401(k)s. Vance talks about the lack of agency felt by his neighbors—"a feeling that you have little control over your life and a willingness to blame everyone but yourself."[26]

Trump cultivated such disengaged, disenfranchised Americans while Hillary Clinton largely ignored them. They would be key to his win in 2016. Someone else with so much wealth, say, Mitt Romney or John Kerry, might have been seen as out of touch. Trump flaunted his wealth in a way that endeared him to them, claiming to have made his fortune with hard work, savvy negotiating skills, and by beating the "establishment" at its own game. During the first presidential debate, Trump bragged that avoiding federal taxes made him smart.[27] He cast himself as an outsider, an underdog who understood the working-class malaise and would "drain the swamp" of political elites and bring change for the common man.

Trump read his audience and learned to speak their language. He saw their vulnerabilities—their alienation and distrust of government—and played to them. At rallies and in ads, he would utilize a kind of fourth-generation warfare strategy, blaming their situation on "global elites" who have "robbed our working class and stripped our country of its wealth and put that money into the pockets of a handful of large corporations and political entities."[28] Trump spoke about saving the coal industry, using its decline as a metaphor for a dying way of life and promised to restore it, rather than help people move into twenty-first-century occupations. He spoke about rolling back climate change initiatives and stopping manufacturing jobs from being outsourced. He was going to lower their taxes, repeal Obamacare—which actually benefited many working-class people— and build a wall to keep migrants from stealing their jobs. He used all the influence techniques in his arsenal—inflaming resentments and anger, drumming up fear, exaggerating his accomplishments, insulting and demonizing the "other." He also gave them a good story—a vision of a new America that looked a lot like the old one and pro-viding assurance that he would "fix it." He also put on a good show. They would come to love him for it.

The Republican Party

When Trump defeated a long list of Republican primary contenders, including Senators Marco Rubio and Ted Cruz, to win the nomination for president, most of the Republican Party fell in line. Even Senator Lindsey Graham—who called Trump a "kook," a "jackass," and "unfit for office" before the election—would become one of his staunchest supporters.[29]

Though many wondered if he was the right man for the job, Trump—who had earlier staked out a more liberal platform, saying he would preserve and defend social security, renegotiate NAFTA, pull back on Iraq and Afghanistan, and support LGBTQ rights—would reverse himself, pushing a pro-life, pro-gun, anti-immigration, anti-globalist, and anti-climate-change agenda. He was also boastful, self-confident, attention-getting, and emphatically anti-Clinton and Obama. That would help to persuade many of the rank and file, as well as politicians—congressional leaders, governors, mayors—to support him. Many Republican business and political leaders had enduring ties with the conservative Christian movement through their participation in such events as prayer breakfasts and Bible study groups sponsored by the Family and Ralph Drollinger's Capitol Ministries. They would hold their nose and vote the ticket to get a Republican elected. With one or more Supreme Court seats at stake, it was imperative to stop Hillary Clinton.

The Republican Party is now widely seen as the party of Trump, to a large extent due to the same web of influence—spun by the media, religious, and populist groups—that helped Trump win the presidency. Trump's approval rating with Republicans has never gone below 77 percent, according to Gallup.[30] At the end of February 2019, it was 87 percent.[31]

Some of this can be explained by party loyalty. According to social science research, when it comes to voting, party affiliation matters greatly. Most people stay with their party.[32] This tends to be truer of Republicans than Democrats. When a candidate or elected official disappoints them, people will adjust their views of the candidate, or rationalize or justify their actions, rather than question the decision. Cult leader Lyndon LaRouche went from the extreme left, politically, to the extreme right, and yet most members remained loyal to him, believing that only he could save the world from ruin. It's confirmation bias at work, and it has been working overtime for some Republicans. Trump's core supporters—numbering about two in five of all voters, polls suggest—have stayed with him, despite his campaign violations, revelations of financial and sexual impropriety, disappointing midterm elections, and the longest government shutdown in history.[33]

In 2016, 42 percent of women voted for Trump. College-educated white women gave Trump 45 percent of their vote, and non-college-educated white women gave him 64 percent of their vote.[34] Many have wondered how any woman, educated or not, could vote for a man who had cheated on all three of his wives and claimed to grab women's genitals—especially in the #MeToo era. In their book, *Nasty Women and Bad Hombres: Gender and Race in the 2016 US Presidential Election*, Christine A. Kray, Hinda Mandell, and Tamar Carroll set out to answer this question. "Republican women will mainly stand firm in their party affiliation. They are loyal to the party, even if political moderates and those who identify as the progressive Left have concluded that the GOP does not respect women's voices and bodies," they write.[35] They found that while "Republicanism encompasses different visions of womenhood"—and Republicans like Iowa Senator Joni Ernst and New York Representative Claudia Tenney are providing new images of women who assert their power while staying true to the party—in general married women tend to vote in concert with their husbands.

They are also loyal to their sons—a point that Trump played upon during the 2018 Supreme Court confirmation hearings of Brett Kavanaugh when he offered an "out" to Republican women who may have worried about being seen as betraying female survivors of sexual assault. Trump reframed the dilemma by constructing an "imaginary choice, urging Americans to protect their sons against 'false accusations' by women. Pretending to be a wrongly accused son about to lose his job, [Trump] said, plaintively, 'Mom, what do I do? What do I do?'"

Then there are those Republican women who, for one reason or another, admire—and even adore—Trump. Amy Kremer, a Tea Party activist and co-founder of Women for Trump, said she and the other women in her Atlanta-area social circle "love" Trump, adding, "We like when somebody promises to do something and they follow through on it."

The Jewish Right

Jews make up a fraction of this country's population—about 1.8 percent or 5 to 6 million people. While the vast majority—nearly eight in ten Americans—disapprove of Trump, there is a powerful minority of mostly Orthodox or ultra-Orthodox voters who support Trump. Most of them are allied with Israel's right-wing Likud party of Benjamin Netanyahu, and also with the Orthodox and ultra-Orthodox communities in Israel. The Orthodox and ultra-Orthodox tend to be closed groups who live in accordance with what they believe to be traditional Jewish values. They practice a rigorous tradition-oriented and highly proscriptive way of life. The rabbi is like a guru, interpreting the tradition along with the beliefs, attitudes, and practices. In some groups, women are encouraged not to work, have as many children as they can, run the household, and care for their husbands and family. Children are sometimes homeschooled or sent to yeshivas where they receive both secular as well as religious education. In some ultra-Orthodox groups they are mostly taught the Torah, as opposed to American or world history, science, and literature. Many do not speak English in the home. They tend to be intolerant of homosexuality, are against abortion, and do not question what they are told to believe or do. Some of the insular groups practice shunning against those who question or who do not abide with the strict code of behavior. Shunning is a common feature of high-demand groups and cults. Organizations like Footsteps have sprung up to help those who wish to leave.[36]

Some communities, especially those in Israel, have tried to define what is considered true and legitimate Judaism, just as some Christian groups profess to speak for all Christianity. They claim that people practicing reform, conservative, reconstructionist, humanistic, and renewal forms of Judaism are not "real" Jews. These distinctions have generated rifts both in Israel and among American Jews like myself, who support Israel but see the ultra-Orthodoxy's rejection of any but their own version of Judaism as a kind of anti-Semitism. While many in these traditionalist communities want to see a peaceful, workable solution to the conflict between Israel and the Palestinians, they often take a more authoritarian perspective, such as the one-state solution proposed by Prime Minister Netanyahu. They are comfortable that the Chief Rabbinate and Orthodox Jews in the Knesset seem to prevail in most disputes. (The Israeli legal system is sometimes more powerful, such as with its decision that all Israelis must serve in the military. Ultra-Orthodox Jews are fighting this recent ruling.)

Though Netanyahu (like Trump) has faced charges of corruption and scandal, he was reelected in 2019—in fact, he has been supported by Trump, who soon after becoming president, moved the U.S. embassy to Jerusalem. Many on the Jewish right—and even on the left—joined Netanyahu in touting it as a Cyrus-like act of deliverance. Though Trump does not appear to have strong sympathies with Jews, and has made anti-Semitic statements since coming to office, he appears to be influenced by powerful donors like Sheldon Adelson, a billionaire with strong ties to Israel.

Trump is also undoubtedly influenced by his family. His son-in-law Jared Kushner and daughter Ivanka are active members of the Orthodox Jewish organization Chabad (also called Lubavitch), which is a sect of Hasidism. Often referred to as "a spiritual revivalist movement,"[37] Hasidism arose in Eastern Europe during the eighteenth century and draws heavily on Jewish mystical tradition, seeking direct experience of God through ecstatic prayer and other rituals, conducted under the spiritual direction of the charismatic figure of the rebbe, or rabbi.[38] In these and other respects, the movement mirrors practices of the New Apostolic Reformation. Chabad grew to be one of the most widespread Hasidic movements under the leadership of Rabbi Menachem Mendel Schneerson, historically the seventh leader of this sect, who was revered as a Jewish messiah[39] by many members. Ivanka Trump and Kushner visited Schneerson's grave in Brooklyn, New York, three days before the 2016 presidential election, presumably to pray for Trump to win.[40] Chabad has outposts across the United States and the world, including Russia. In fact, Putin welcomed Chabad rabbi Berel Lazar to practice in Russia. Lazar, who is now the chief rabbi of Russia, is considered to be a close friend of the Russian leader and is sometimes referred to as "Putin's rabbi."[41] Putin has other connections to Israel through the large network of Russian emigres who now make up about 10 percent of the population and who occupy powerful positions in business and government.[42]

Chabad aggressively seeks to convert Jews to their form of orthodoxy—they do not recruit Christians, Muslims, or other non-Jews. They use what I consider to be high-pressure tactics, though they often appear deceptively friendly and accepting, both in their recruitment and indoctrination campaigns. The organization is viewed by many Jews as messianic, elitist, and cultish. In fact, it currently appears to be forming alliances with messianic groups on the Christian right. In an article in *The Forward,* Jay Michaelson describes how the codirector of the Utah Chabad was scheduled to give the invocation at the World Congress of Families, an annual convention of evangelical, Catholic, Mormon, and other religious factions and interest groups—including an "extreme fringe that opposes human rights and in some cases, the foundations of secular democracy itself," Michaelson writes. "Indeed, some of them—Christian Reconstructionists, Dominionists and others—seek to do away with the secular law altogether, one day replacing the United States as we know it with an explicitly Christian nation."[43]

When prominent evangelical Vice President Mike Pence gave a speech at the Israeli Knesset, on the occasion of the opening of the U.S. embassy in Jerusalem, he appeared to be offering support and solidarity with Israel. Yet, like many on the Christian right, Pence does not believe that Jews can be saved without accepting Jesus. The Christian right agenda is to make the world safe for Christianity—and for some evangelicals, to prepare the world for the coming of Christ—not to recognize Judaism as a legitimate religion or to make Israel safe for the Jewish people. In his talk, Pence cited a passage from Torah in a way that appeared to appropriate the biblical figure of Abraham as the father of Christians, not Jews, and to make Jewish history appear as a mere stepping-stone to the main event, the coming of Christ.[44] As Amit Gvaryahu wrote in *Haaretz,* he "used texts that insinuated that any redemption would come to the Jews was but a harbinger of final and real redemption for the world under Christ as king and messiah."[45] Few in the audience appeared to notice the discrepancy, except perhaps the evangelicals. By moving the U.S. embassy to Jerusalem, Trump was killing two birds with one stone. He was satisfying his Jewish right base while playing to the much larger audience, the Christian right.

White Power: Alt-Right

Of all the factions in Trump's base, the alt-right may be the most dangerous. They are responsible for the tragedies in Charleston, Charlottesville, Pittsburgh, and Christchurch, New Zealand. Though the perpetrators appear to have acted alone, they are increasingly connected to one another through online websites, often on the dark web, according to a report in *The New York Times*. In a manifesto published online, the perpetrator of the New Zealand attack on two mosques, which killed fifty people, said that he drew inspiration from white extremist terrorism attacks in the United States, Sweden, Norway, Italy, and the United Kingdom. "His references to those attacks placed him in an informal global network of white extremists whose violent attacks are occurring with greater frequency in the West," write Weiyi Cai and Simone Landon in *The New York Times*.[46] They found that, since 2011, a third of extremists were inspired by others who carried out similar attacks.

White supremacist and nationalistic thinking has existed for centuries in the United States but Trump's words and deeds—his America First sloganeering; his apparent excusing of, or failure to acknowledge, the violence; his racist remarks; his own bullying—have given it a legitimacy that hadn't existed before, according to Mark Potok, former senior fellow at the Southern Poverty Law Center. According to Potok, the number of hate groups has grown to its highest number ever. The FBI hate crime statistics back up this point.[47]

Arno Michaelis was a founding member of the racist skinhead band the Centurion. He is now an activist and an outspoken critic of white nationalism.[48] He told me that white supremacists, "across the board, were delighted to vote for Donald Trump." He described how hate groups like the Ku Klux Klan actively campaigned for him, organizing and paying for robocalls for Trump and other right-wing politicians. "As much as [Trump] may deny an affiliation with the ideology, or as much as he may grudgingly condemn it, the fact is that his rhetoric and his policy is exactly what these guys want to hear," Michaelis said. "His rhetoric of building walls, of monitoring Muslims, of casting people of color as inherently dangerous saying that, 'Mexicans are rapists'— Donald Trump is using the language of genocide. It's a language that dehumanizes people." Michaelis compares it to the rhetoric used in Nazi Germany, where Jews were compared to rats, and during the genocide of the Tutsi people by the Hutus in Rwanda in 1994, where Tutsis were labeled cockroaches and snakes. David Neiwert's book *The Eliminationists* goes into the history of this kind of hate influence and how right wing talk radio has carried this forward.[49]

"Today, we have a sitting president of the United States who refers to people crossing the border as an infestation of our country. He has called them animals. Of course, this genocidal language strikes a chord with hate groups because it's the language they're familiar with. That's how they talk about people who they're afraid of, people that are different than them. They hear the president of the United States using that language from a position of power, that's really unparalleled, it's an incredible concern," said Michaelis. "It's also an incredible kind of uplift to people in hate groups, who felt for a very long time that they were on the margins of society, and now, here's the President of the United States speaking their language."[50]

QAnon

During the summer of 2018, people wearing the letter Q emblazoned on T-shirts and signs made an attention-getting appearance at a Trump rally in Florida. It was a surprising, even shocking, display. The symbol is associated with a right-wing conspiracy cult, called QAnon, which started in 2016, soon after the Pizzagate hoax, which promoted the outrageous idea that Hillary Clinton was running a pedophilia ring out of the basement of a pizza parlor. A year later, more conspiracy ravings about Clinton appeared on a website called 4chan. They were signed by a person who identified himself as "Q Clearance Patriot," "Q Clearance" being a designation for top-secret security access to materials concerning nuclear weapons. Over the following months, the mystery poster would offer up a series of ever more cryptic posts—for example, "Your president needs your help"—which looked like clues to a grand conspiracy by the deep state and global elites to remove Trump from office. They would gain a life of their own in alt-right and other groups, as people assembled and interpreted the clues, known as "crumbs," and "baked" them into explanatory diagrams and word collages that would be circulated online.

Though some speculated that the original Q was a military intelligence officer and even Trump himself, what came to be known as QAnon turned out to be the brainchild of three men—a YouTube video creator and two moderators of 4chan. They developed and used the whole conspiracy mythology as a way to make money by selling T-shirts and other QAnon paraphernalia. Trump did nothing to dispel the conspiracy theory and even had his photo taken in the Oval Office with Michael "Lionel" Lebron, a TV and radio host and active promoter of the QAnon conspiracy theory. In some ways, the theory is just an extension of the fourth-generation warfare scenarios Trump spun on the campaign trail—of a global elite headed by Hillary Clinton and the radical Democrats.

Though fringe at first, the QAnon movement has gained ground through its circulation on alt-right websites and Reddit, YouTube,[51] and other sites. Celebrities like Roseanne Barr referred to it, giving it a bigger platform. QAnon believers are not just showing up at rallies; some are becoming dangerous. In June 2018, a QAnon supporter named Matthew Wright drove his armored vehicle onto a bridge near Hoover Dam, blocking traffic for hours, and engaging in a standoff with police. He had a rifle and a handgun when he was taken into custody. His motive was not clear, but he had sent letters to Trump and other officials that included the phrase "For where we go one, we go all"—a line popular among followers of QAnon.[52] While on the bridge, he held a sign that said "Release the OIG Report," which apparently referred to the Justice Department's Office of Inspector General's internal report on the department's handling of the Clinton email probe.[53] It is not clear what his psychological state was—and it is the case that some of the white terrorist tragedies that have taken place over the past two years were carried out by psychologically disturbed men, armed with angry rhetoric and guns.

Dilbert cartoonist Scott Adams has tried to debunk QAnon using logic and social psychology.[54] Logic rarely works to disarm a conspiracy movement with passionate followers. Meanwhile, people are making money. In March 2019, a book written by twelve "citizen journalists," called *QAnon: An Invitation to the Great Awakening*, reached bestselling status on Amazon.[55] That same month, at a Trump rally in Grand Rapids, Michigan, thousands of Q supporters filled the audience.[56]

NRA Members and Gun Owners

In a 2017 Gallup poll, 42 percent of American households reported owning guns—that's 50 million households with 393 million guns.[57] NRA Americans take the Second Amendment seriously. The NRA claims five million members.[58] They operate an online video network, whose home page features stories like "The Left is Unrelenting in Painting a Picture of How Horrible Gun Owners Are," and how Representative Eric Swalwell (D-CA) "Wants to Rob You of Your Guns," and "Imprison all Pro-Gun Americans."[59] In a banner at the top, it announces Trump's appearance at the upcoming annual NRA meetings in Indianapolis. Trump campaigned on a broad pro-gun agenda, which he maintained even after the mass shooting at the Marjory Stoneman Douglas High School in Parkland, Florida, where seventeen students and teachers were killed, and the massacre in Las Vegas, which killed fifty-eight people and wounded hundreds more—not to mention the several white-supremacist-inspired massacres. In the spring of 2018, Trump spoke to a rapt audience at the annual NRA convention in Dallas: "Thanks to your activism and dedication, you have an administration fighting to protect your Second Amendment and we will protect your Second Amendment. Your Second Amendment rights are under siege, but they will never ever be under siege as long as I am your President."

Trump would both soothe and incite his audience's fears with his repetition of the word "siege"—it's all part of his influence formula: repetition, us versus them, and fearmongering. Not that the NRA needs any help. Not all gun owners are Republicans. Nor are they all in favor of military assault rifles, machine guns, or bump stocks, which can be used to kill many people very quickly. Many think they should be banned.[60] But the gun industry, and their main lobbying organization, the NRA, feed the fears of many Americans who do not feel safe in their own homes and also of members of conspiracy groups who believe an armed revolution is coming. Gun culture is deeply ingrained in American society and the liberal "Hollywood elite" that Trump and other Republicans rail against has done little to dampen it, producing gun-glamorizing movies, video games, and TV shows.

As with other issues, Trump held different views until he began to consider running for president as a Republican. "I oppose gun control, but I support the ban on assault weapons and I support a slightly longer waiting period to purchase a gun," he wrote in his 2000 book, *The America We Deserve*.[61] Unsurprisingly, he experienced what political observers call a "campaign conversion," adjusting his views to match the voters he was seeking.[62] This was also part of a larger strategy based on promoting fear, danger, and enemies at every turn—and a tough guy to make America safe again.

ALL TOGETHER NOW

For Trump and his followers, the safest place may be at one of his rallies. "Outside the world is a cruel and ugly place. Here, inside, they are safe," writes Ed Pilkington in *The Guardian*. In 2018, Pilkington attended five Trump rallies in eight days and talked to scores of Trump supporters. He asked them what America would be like in 2050 if Hillary Clinton had been elected president. Among the most common refrain he heard was that America would become socialist. "Taxes and unemployment would go through the roof, the economy would collapse, there would be riots for food and water." "People are going to get killed," said Rick Novak, fifty-seven, a retired building foreman. "Gang wars. We are going to get gang wars between white and black, whites and Mexicans. We could have our own little Vietnam right here."

Trump fans their fears and they love him for it. "He says what I'm thinking," many followers said. Pilkington described how the rallies were a place where they could commune, a kind of love fest of hate. They are also critical for keeping Trump stoked. "The rally is his charging station, the place he goes to refuel his ego and his zealotry," Pilkington writes. They are massive indoctrination sessions for both him and his followers in the Cult of Trump. Some of them are so fervent that there is nothing they wouldn't do to maintain their membership. One such member, Steve Spaeth, told Pilkington a story about how far he would go. "The other day he talked to his sister who is liberal and votes Democratic," Pilkington writes. "He said to her: 'If there is a civil war in this country and you were on the wrong side, I would have no problem shooting you in the face.' You must be joking, I say. 'No I am not. I love my sister, we get on great. But she has to know how passionate I am about our president.' "[63]

How to Undo Mind Control

Michael Cohen—Trump's former personal attorney and back-room fixer—appeared before the House Oversight and Reform Committee on February 27, 2019, looking tired, chastened, and bewildered. He had lied, cheated, threatened, and bullied; he had committed fraud and perjury—all on behalf of his former boss. Now he was going to prison. "Sitting here today, it seems unbelievable that I was so mesmerized by Donald Trump that I was willing to do things for him that I knew were absolutely wrong," Cohen said. Though some questioned Cohen's motives in coming clean, arguing that he was spilling dirt on Trump, or even making up stories, to save his own skin, I saw it differently. He reminded me of myself after I left the Moonies—and of countless other former members of high-demand groups and relationships who had to grapple with the reality of their involvement. Cohen would later refer to his relationship with Trump as "something akin to a cult."[1]

It is a devastating moment to realize that you have given your life to a false leader, prophet, or messiah. For me, that moment came on the fifth day of my deprogramming, when I was shown a speech that Moon had delivered to a room of politicians in 1974. The media at the time had been filled with reports that the Moonies brainwashed people. In the speech, Moon talked about how much he respected Americans and thought they were much too smart to be brainwashed. And yet, while I was in the cult, I had heard Moon talk endlessly about how Americans' brains were dirty and needed "heavenly brainwashing," and how he had no respect for Americans. Koreans were God's chosen people. I had my first conscious negative thought in more than two years: Moon was a liar. If he had lied, then he could not possibly be trustworthy, let alone be the messiah. My Moonie mindset split open—I had a snapping (sudden awakening) experience and my mind flooded with suppressed doubts. I realized that my deprogrammers, who told me I had been brainwashed by Moon, were right. I realized that I had been mind-controlled by a right-wing authoritarian cult that wanted to take over the world, and that I myself had become a fascist who would have obeyed any order from my superiors, including breaking the law.

It was a long road back to my old self after that. As I've written, the goal of the indoctrination process is to suppress a person's authentic self with a pseudo- or cult self, one that is dependent on and obedient to the leader. Even after my realization, my cult identity kept fighting my real self. Add to that the embarrassment and shame that I felt for having betrayed my family, religion, and country. I had to do a lot of researching and processing. Talking with ex-members of other destructive cults like Scientology, the Children of God, and the Hare Krishnas helped a lot as I could see so many parallels in the psychology of undue influence.

On the face of it, the situation with the Cult of Trump might seem easier. The evidence of Trump's lies is all around us. Yet they are being countered, covered up, and completely turned around by Trump and those who surround him, including the former White House press secretary, the Republican leadership, the right wing media apparatus, and a huge Christian right propaganda machine that excuses Trump's habit of lying as the foible of a man chosen to carry out God's plan.

Given the contours of Trump's world—where scientific evidence is often discounted and alternative facts are taken seriously—the question arises: How can anyone wake up from the Cult of Trump? The

situation might seem hopeless at first—that is often the reaction when
it comes to the prospect of freeing a cult member. I have worked
with hundreds of families seeking to rescue a loved one from a group.
None of them are easy—many are incredibly difficult. There are always huge challenges to helping a person wake up. With a political
leader like Trump, who has the support of a huge web of powerful
organizations, people, and resources, that is especially true.

One of the first steps in helping someone break free is to separate
them from the abusive group or person. I had a broken leg, which allowed my parents to sequester me; Michael Cohen was in New York
City, separated from Trump and spending time with his family, including his father, a Holocaust survivor and an important influence.
Frank Senko, the subject of the documentary *The Brainwashing of My
Dad*, was bed-ridden, which allowed his family to remove his access
to right-wing TV and radio. In my practice, I've helped to creatively
engineer all kinds of physical separations—bringing a cult member
home for a holiday, family celebration, or even a funeral. It might
seem manipulative, but it is a critical first step to helping a person
free themselves from the clutches of a cult—one that has become
increasingly difficult with 24/7 access to the internet through smartphones. In the case of Trump, there are also the continual tweets
and right-wing and Christian right programming through radio and
television. The relentless programming streaming from both ends of
the political spectrum is pushing supporters ever deeper into Trump
country.

This brings me to an important point and a key aspect of my
approach. By attacking or belittling Trump's followers, political opponents and traditional media may be helping Trump to maintain his
influence over his base. In my experience, telling a person that they
are brainwashed, that they are in a cult, or that they are following
a false god, is doomed to fail. It puts them immediately on the defensive, confirms you are a threat, possibly an enemy, and reinforces
their indoctrination. It closes their mind to other perspectives. I've
seen this happen over and over again. It happened to me when I was
in the Moon group. It immediately triggers a person's mind control

programming—including thought stopping and us-versus-them thinking, with you being the "them."

A guiding principle of my approach is to act with respect, warmth, and integrity. I want the person I work with to feel that I genuinely care about them, and I do. That is first and foremost. After getting to know them better, I share my story of how I got interested in the subject of brainwashing, mind control, and cults. I then share stories of other situations and groups. I ask questions with a "curious, yet concerned" tone, allowing for long silences afterward. I want to encourage the person to think and hopefully draw comparisons to other high-demand groups. When presented with the bizarre beliefs and practices of a group like the Moonies, who believe that an overweight Korean billionaire arms dealer is the messiah, and Scientologists, who believe that humans are inhabited by extraterrestrial creatures, or body "thetans," most people will agree that they are outlandish. When people learn that members are willing to commit their lives to these groups and to cut off from family and friends, and even do illegal acts, they usually shake their heads.

It is a step-by-step process. I help people realize the big picture and hopefully the parallels with their own group or situation will stand out for them. When the person is engaged in thinking it through, the cognitive dissonance or discrepancy becomes that much greater—they find it harder to maintain the weird beliefs that their group tells them are true.

I cannot overstate the impact of the digital world on the whole area of undue influence and mind control. People no longer need to be physically isolated to be indoctrinated by destructive cults. Digital technology has provided access and a powerful set of tools for destructive groups and individuals to indoctrinate, control, and monitor believers day and night. When cult members go home for family visits, they are often receiving multiple texts every hour to keep them connected and faithful. Social media and tech platforms like Google, Facebook, Amazon, and Apple are collecting massive amounts of data on people. Much of this data is vulnerable to hacking or selling on the dark web—including to cults. Libertarian Trump supporter Peter

Thiel owns a company named Palantir that has lucrative government intelligence contracts to do deep data mining on people. Law enforcement also uses their programs to dig up valuable information about private citizens who are of interest.[2]

When governments use high-tech companies to spy on their own people, they can find themselves on a slippery slope—running the risk of becoming like Russia or China. The flip side is that if a citizen becomes curious, there are many places to go for critical information—websites, Facebook pages, and Reddit groups. Of course, not all of these portals are reliable. Some may promote dangerously biased views. Critical thinking is vital.

My approach to helping people has had to evolve along with these new developments. Over the past decades, I have developed a customized, step-by-step ethical counterinfluence method that family or friends can use to help a loved one—including a member of the Cult of Trump. Here I will say that if a person is involved with NAR or an alt-right group, I would first focus on the mind control techniques used by that group before addressing the Cult of Trump. Here I might discuss Chinese thought reform programs currently operating to ensure loyalty to the dominant Han Chinese ideology.

The candidacy and election of Trump have deeply affected and even divided families and friends. Relationships with siblings, parents, children, aunts, uncles, best friends, and colleagues have been affected. The country as a whole has rarely been more polarized. If we are to heal these relationships, perhaps the best place to begin is with ourselves.

HOW WOULD YOU KNOW
IF YOU WERE UNDER MIND CONTROL?

Cult members believe that they are completely in control of their own thoughts, feelings, and actions. That's true of most, if not all, of us—we believe that we are in possession of our faculties, that we make our own decisions and choose our own path. Yet, as we have seen, we are all continually being influenced by our parents, friends, bosses, colleagues, government, and the media, both traditional and online. We all have an illusion of control. It's part of being human. This raises the question: how would any of us—Trump supporters or critics—know if we were being unduly influenced? Here is a five-step formula for answering that question, one that requires an investment of time and energy, but that is quite powerful. I have geared this five-step experiment to a Trump supporter but anyone could benefit from it, no matter their political affiliation or group involvement.

Reality test: The first step is to take a break from your situation—disconnect from all sources of influence that could reinforce your current point of view. It might mean turning off your cell phone and laptop and unplugging from social media, television, and radio. People are often addicted to their phones and social media, so this is not an easy thing to suggest. If you are in a questionable group or relationship, you might take several days away from people in the group. If you are not in a formal group, take a time-out from those who share your ideology as well as from ideology-promoting texts, tapes, and videos. You need to make sure you are getting enough sleep—seven to nine hours, so you wake up refreshed and energized. (Some people need less sleep, others more—the point is waking up energized.) Exercise daily, including activities that increase your heart rate and flexibility, and eat healthily. Go for long walks in nature and find other ways to reset, restore, and rebalance yourself, independent of external influence. The goal is to be in touch with your authentic self by being in your body and connecting to an internal locus of control. Listen to your own thoughts, feelings, hopes, and dreams about what is important to you and what you want to do with your life.

Educate yourself: Read about social psychology, in particular mind control, and the models created by Robert Jay Lifton, Margaret Singer, along with my BITE model. Educate yourself about social influence techniques, propaganda, and logical fallacies. Libraries are great places. Hopefully this book has given you a good start. You also might contact responsible, ethical mental health professionals to help you.

Listen to critics and former believers: Seek out highly respected, credentialed, or experienced experts who hold views that differ from your own. Look for verifiable facts. The Mueller Report, though a daunting 448 pages long, is an important read, especially since Trump and Barr have stated their biased conclusions. Robert Mueller gave a brief but definitive statement before resigning from the Department of Justice, which is worth listening to or reading. If you are a Trump supporter and think Trump is a great leader, or even God-chosen, seek out the views of critics and evaluate dispassionately what they have to say. Listen to your inner voice as well as your conscience. When you hear trigger words like "fake news," "deep state," or "radical Democrats," adopt a neutral attitude and use your critical abilities to sort through sources, check credentials, and look for supporting factual evidence. Ask probing questions like "Why is that?" or "Is that plausible?" Listen to what others have to say and reach your own conclusions based on research and evidence. Read books, newspapers, blogs, and magazines that run the gamut of political orientation, remembering always that facts do matter. When a leader or group makes extraordinary claims, demand extraordinary proof. The burden of proof is always on the leader or group to prove their claims. It's not on us to disprove them. If Trump claims that he knows more than anyone else on a subject, fact-check his assertions. I have quoted several resources in this book including books written by David Cay Johnston, Bob Woodward, Malcolm Nance, and James Comey, to name just a few.

Self-reflect: Once you have taken a time-out, learned about mind control, and exposed yourself to opposing points of view, it is time to honestly self-reflect. Go back in time to before you came to adopt your current belief system. When was the first time you ever heard of Trump? Was it through tabloids or his reality TV show *The Apprentice*? What did you think of him then? How long did you watch—was it more than one season? Did you come to believe the persona portrayed on that show—that Trump was a successful billionaire businessman, an authority figure that people should learn from and emulate? Have you listened to former insiders who worked on the show who have talked about how they were told—through their acting, directing, and especially editing—to make Trump look good? Consider what they report. Were you influenced by a religious figure you respect who told you God wants Trump to be president? Are you on social media that promotes the notion that God is working with Trump?

Then, from a more neutral or objective perspective, trace step by step how you came to arrive at your current point of view. Be honest with yourself. What captured your attention and made you take Trump seriously? Were you captivated by the fantasies, both positive—Make America Great Again—and negative, that America is being invaded? Did the swamp really get drained or was it filled by billionaires with agendas? What other claims and promises in ads or campaign rallies influenced you? Was the information distorted or withheld? Have you listened to Tony Schwartz, Trump's ghost-writer on *The Art of the Deal,* speak about how he regrets fabricating Trump's image as a successful businessman?[3] I recommend Omarosa Manigault Newman's book, *Unhinged,* which describes her waking up from the Cult of Trumpworld.

Ask questions: Would you knowingly give up your power to choose and blindly follow someone who demonstrably lies numerous times a day? If you could go back in time knowing what you now know, would you support a person with a documented history of false and exaggerated claims, lies, and scandals? Did you support Trump because you disliked Hillary Clinton? Was it because she wasn't a Republican? Were there people who were persuasive or were there movies or ads that made you decide Clinton was unworthy, corrupt, unqualified, or even evil? Even if you know that you would never have voted for Clinton, knowing what you know now, would you still vote for Trump? Do you feel empowered to disagree with Trump in your own mind? With others in person? Online? Do you believe Trump's claims that America will be overrun by terrorists and crimi-nals if a wall is not built? Are your fears rational?

In a piece for *The Forward,* army veteran and former Trump supporter David Weissman describes how he was influenced to hate Clinton and support Trump. "I did not even think to research any of Clinton's accomplishments as First Lady, Senator, or Secretary of State—like most conservatives, I just focused on her seemingly never ending 'scandals.' I was part of the 'LOCK HER UP' chorus, even though she was thoroughly investigated and cleared by the FBI. I did, and perhaps still do, feel Clinton's leadership was lacking during and after the [2012] Benghazi attack, but many among the MAGA crowd blamed her personally for the resultant deaths, and I joined in," Weissman writes. "Trump, on the other hand, was hailed as a friend of Israel and the Jewish people. Yet, unlike with Clinton, I looked only at Trump's accomplishments, ignored his failures, and defended or even celebrated his bad behavior. Consequently, I put all my efforts into helping elect him."[4]

Though my focus has been on Trump supporters, anyone could benefit from thorough self-reflection. Usually it's the family and friends of cult members who go through the long, laborious process of helping someone undo the effects of mind control. By the time they come for help, they are highly motivated. When a loved one is recruited into a cult, the entire family system is affected. We have seen the polarization that the Trump presidency has caused—it has split apart families and communities and divided the country. Some of those fractures may have begun long before. As we have seen, many followers were members of other high-demand groups before pledging their allegiance to Trump. As the fractures grow deeper, there is a tendency to retreat into separate camps, and into hopelessness. We continue to blame and demonize the other side, sometimes to the point that we do not see them as human. Some Democrats have said that anyone who voted for Trump must be uneducated, stupid, or crazy. Trump supporters believe that Trump critics have been brainwashed by the liberal media. A recent study showed that 42 percent of people regard their political opponents as "downright evil." Twenty percent believe that they "lack the traits to be considered fully human."[5]

Labeling large groups of people on either side of the Trump divide is a mistake. It tends to inflame and incite others, as we have seen, widening and deepening already seemingly irreconcilable divisions. It is also a psychological error. In chapter 4, we looked at the fundamental attribution error, which describes how we tend to attribute another person's actions to inherent personality characteristics or qualities: if they do something bad, they must be bad. Yet we explain and excuse our own mistakes as a function of circumstance or environment.

We also looked at confirmation bias—how our minds filter and select information that confirms our own point of view, and dismiss information that does not fit in or negates it. And confirmation bias is certainly not limited to cults. We basically see and hear what we want to, whether we realize it or not, and rationalize away what does not fit our preconceptions and predictions. We find it hard to accept or agree with even well-argued or supported views when they are expressed by a member of the other side. We speak to—and find affirmation from—those of our own political persuasion, but the level of passion is so high that often we do not, or cannot, talk to those across the divide. When all of one's actions are seen in light of their support or antipathy for Trump, it can be hard to understand another's point of view and how they are making sense of information. We may find community and comfort on social media or TV, which can keep us in an ideological silo and further inflame interpersonal tensions.

At those moments, it's important to remember that it was a process of influence that pushed people into their separate silos and it's a process of influence—one based on rapport and trust-building—that will get them out. My step-by-step approach, which I call the Strategic Interactive Approach, is based on a fundamental presupposition—that respect, trust-building, and love are stronger than fear, hate, and mind control. It's hard to hate someone who is genuinely warm, friendly, and nice—at least that's the case for all but the psychopaths among us.

HOW CAN YOU HELP YOUR FRIEND OR LOVED ONE?

The first step is knowledge. Eleanor Roosevelt wrote in 1960, "It is not only important but mentally invigorating to discuss political matters with people whose opinions differ radically from one's own. . . . Find out what people are saying, what they are thinking, what they believe. This is an invaluable check to your own ideas. Are you right in what you think or is there a different approach . . . ?"[6] A Trump critic may watch MSNBC's Rachel Maddow and CNN's Anderson Cooper regularly while their pro-Trump family member is glued to Fox News, Breitbart, or Trinity Broadcasting. Step into the other person's media world—as painful as that may be. Find out what they are listening to or watching. Do it little by little. I do not recommend spending many hours at a time. Take breaks. Write down notes. When I research a controlling group, I limit my exposure so I can remain more objective. They may use powerful influence techniques and I don't want in any way to be susceptible. Just showing you care enough to watch can be a big step. You will learn a lot and better understand how your loved one believes what they do. Also, you will be able to talk with them about what they are listening to or watching—though it's best not to come on too strong.

Cults use a whole array of techniques to recruit and indoctrinate members—they control behavior, information, thoughts, and emotions. The same is true for the Cult of Trump. In addition, they use loaded language and play upon other psychological mechanisms—the fundamental attribution error, cognitive dissonance, confirmation bias—to render people dependent and obedient. If the person demonstrated a radical personality change, assume the real identity is still there, just submerged. It's important to remember that while mind control creates a cult self, the authentic self is still there, suppressed by the cult identity. The goal is to reach and reconnect with the authentic self to help empower people to think critically and do a reality test.

I should say at the outset, do not ever go for a win-lose scenario where you think you will be able to rationally argue a Trump follower out of their worldview. Facts matter, but respect, context, and your communication delivery are key. Your most potent weapon is a good, thoughtful question: Tell me—how did you come to feel so strongly about Donald Trump? What was it that attracted you? What is it about him that makes you think he is fit to be president? Be patient and listen for an answer. When I have asked people this question, I have frequently been told how much they hated Hillary Clinton, how they distrusted her, how corrupt she is. How she would be a continuation of Obama policies. I say to them, "I hear you. I can see how emotional you are about this. But she lost the election and that was years ago. What about today? And going forward?"

It's about building rapport and trust, finding common ground, having positive experiences and not getting into arguments. Avoid a win-lose, all-or-nothing, I'm-right-you're-wrong frame of mind. Definitely reject name calling, even though Trump does it. Learn to identify ad hominem attacks whenever they occur. These are attacks on the person rather than focusing on the substance of the issue. Trump and his supporters use this logical fallacy all the time, but so do Trump critics. It just doesn't work if we want to build bridges and heal our country.

HELP PEOPLE GET IN
TOUCH WITH THEIR AUTHENTIC SELF

Deep down, people want to know the truth. They do not like to be lied to, exploited, abused, or taken advantage of, especially by narcissists who are incapable of empathy and love, or who appear to care, but only if you do as they say. Cult leaders practice conditional love—they express love only to those who do what is asked and never question the leader, doctrine, or policy. When Trump cries out at his rallies—"I love you, Indiana!"—it is clear that, even as president, he is reserving his "love" only for those who support him. In my experience, people want to know that the love and acceptance they receive is authentic, and not conditionally offered.

With true believers, whose very personalities seem to have altered since supporting Trump—or since joining one of the cults within the Cult of Trump—it may help to remind them of who they were before their involvement. Reminiscing, going through photos and old videos, reminding a person of loving family and friendships, can be a powerful way to reactivate a person's authentic self. Once you have established that rapport, the key is to build upon it, and to educate. Attacking a person's beliefs, group, or leader, in this case, Trump, does not work, as I have said. Instead, my approach is to talk with the person about other groups or leaders who have lied, cheated, or covered up improprieties and have manipulated their followers—for example, Moon, Hubbard, or LaRouche. I ask them what they think about these people.

In helping this person return to their authentic self, it's easy to make mistakes. If you respond in an emotionally balanced way, the chances are much better that you will succeed. Focus on areas that you can agree on. You want to open yourself up by saying, "Teach me—share with me why I should change my beliefs to be more like yours." Once the person has revealed their point of view, you might ask them to listen to yours. You might say, "I want to get your feedback and share another perspective."

You are basically walking people through a psycho-educational set of experiences based on your respecting them, being thoughtful and kind, listening to them, and looking for, and sharing, things you have in common. The goal is to let them tell you what else needs to happen for them to wake up. That might include talking with people—former Trump supporters—who once believed as they do and can tell them why they left.

The best way to counteract resistance as well as outright thought stopping—and in the case of some NAR groups, singing, praying, and speaking in tongues—is to avoid triggering them in the first place. Thought stopping is a defense mechanism that is triggered in direct response to what are perceived as negative comments. Again, be careful not to make remarks that are critical of the leader, the group, or the doctrine, such as "Trump is crazy" or "Trump supporters are stupid." Develop strategies, such as taking deep breaths if you feel like you are getting triggered and becoming angry. Self-control is vital.

WORK ON DEVELOPING A GOOD RELATIONSHIP

Maybe you had a good relationship with a certain friend or family member in the past but since the election you have stopped talking about politics. Maybe you have stopped talking altogether. The key is to open up communication in an honest, respectful manner.

In his *Forward* piece, David Weissman describes how he was a self-proclaimed troll for Trump until a conversation started, in a series of tweets, with comedian Sarah Silverman.[7] In his tweets, Weissman accused Silverman and all liberals of caring more about undocumented immigrants than about military veterans. To his surprise, Silverman responded—and in a way that was respectful and inviting. What followed was a months-long dialogue about issues such as immigration, gun reform, and abortion. "Not only did I learn from her, but I learned from her followers who showed me why they fight for these rights. I discovered sources with journalistic integrity, which debunked the lies and generalizations that conservative media often report. I slowly began reevaluating my principles," Weissman said.[8] He no longer identifies as a Trump supporter. Weissman described leaving the fold as a kind of waking up—the whole experience was like being in a trance. When he started publicly questioning and researching the issues, he was hacked and shunned by Trump's supporters.[9] This is often the case for ex-members—they are often treated like a traitor or enemy. But it usually just confirms to them that their involvement was cultlike.[10]

Silverman has done even more to heal the divisiveness of this country. She invited Trump supporters on her Hulu TV show, *I Love You America,* to have an open dialogue—no fighting, no name calling. "When you're one-on-one with someone who doesn't agree with you, or whose ideology is different than yours, when you're face to face, your porcupine needles go down," Silverman would later say in an interview with *New York* magazine's Frank Rich. To her great surprise, "I fell in love with them. I had a great time with them and I felt comfortable." "I'm trying to be open," she explained. "I'm finding if I do engage with someone who is angry at me, or angry, and I'm a place where they can put that anger . . . it's almost always a good experience, because more than anything, all of us, what we have in common is, we want to feel seen. We want to feel like we exist."[11]

Silverman is a role model for us all, no matter our political affiliation. She exemplifies the approach I've been advocating. As a famous comedian, she has a lot of power to influence people to engage with her. Bill Maher, Trevor Noah, Jimmy Fallon, John Oliver, and other television hosts do a huge service to bring on people who support Trump, act respectfully, and ask good questions. It will likely get Trump folks to watch their shows, perhaps for the first time.

Rapport and trust building are absolutely key to working with any member of a high-demand group, as I have said. Even if a true Trump believer holds on to their views, the avenues of communication have been opened. The healthier your precult relationship, and the stronger the member's sense of identity prior to being in the cult, the easier it will be to reconnect and get the person to open up.

Reestablishing regular positive contact, even if you haven't talked or seen each other in a long while, is very important. I spoke to a man who bet his brother five dollars that Hillary would win the 2016 election. After the election, he told me that he made out a five-dollar check, wrote the words "Fuck you" on it, and mailed it. He has not spoken to his brother for more than a year. Please do not follow this example. If you have done something similar, please apologize and ask for forgiveness and a redo. Be nice. Tell your loved one that you miss them and that you want to find common ground where you can respect each other's point of view. Once you reconnect, avoid falling into destructive patterns, like trying to prove your position is right. On the other hand, avoiding interacting about substantive issues is not enough. The other's involvement—with the Cult of Trump or another group—will not likely get better on its own.

The goal is to talk in a way that helps cast doubt on their involvement without berating them or making them feel stupid. People hate to admit they are wrong; let them come to their own realizations.[12] A 2011 study by the RAND Corporation concluded that "factors associated with leaving street gangs, religious cults, right-wing extremist groups, and organized crime groups" include positive social ties and an organic disillusionment with the group's beliefs or ideology. Close relationships are critical in helping people get out of groups and stay out.

Actress Leah Remini left Scientology after being a dedicated and high-profile member for more than thirty-five years. She has since produced and starred with Mike Rinder, a former forty-six-year

Scientology member and leader, in an Emmy Award–winning series on A&E called *Scientology and its Aftermath*. (I was pleased to be on an episode.) She decided to leave the group after experiencing troubling things when she spoke out about her friend Shelly Miscavige, wife of Scientology leader David Miscavige. Shelly Miscavige has not engaged in normal social contact for a long period. "I believe that people should be able to question things. I believe that people should value family, and value friendships, and hold those things sacrosanct," Remini said in an interview in 2013, soon after she left the group. "That for me, that's what I'm about. It wouldn't matter what it was, simply because no one is going to tell me how I need to think, no one is going to tell me who I can, and cannot, talk to."[13]

HELP THEM SEE FROM DIFFERENT PERSPECTIVES

One remedy for blind faith is to see the world from different perspectives. If your loved one is stuck in their beliefs—about Trump or anything concerning—try a role-switching exercise with them. Begin by asking them to teach you how to see Trump or his policies through their eyes. Tell them you really want to understand them. Ask them to teach you so well that you could step into their shoes and talk from their perspective. Do it and have them critique your performance. Keep refining it until they say you have it right.

Then invite them to reciprocate and do the same exercise. Ask them if they are willing to step into your shoes and talk from your perspective. Be prepared for a long silence. Long silences are very important to empowering people to think for themselves. You do not want to rush people you are interacting with. You want them to think and reflect. If you make a big effort to understand them, they will be more likely to reciprocate, providing a great opportunity. Make sure you have your points well formulated ahead of time. This book is filled with specific points about Trump's use of influence tactics. Show them Trump through your eyes and then let them mirror your perspective. Stepping out of our own shoes and seeing things from another's perspective is incredibly powerful.

My father did a version of this technique with me early in my deprogramming in 1976. The intervention started out involuntarily—he took away the crutches I was using after my van accident and would not let me call the group. "How would you feel if it was your son who met a controversial group, dropped out of college, quit his job, donated his bank account, and you didn't see him for over a year? How would you feel?" he asked me, with tears in his eyes. I had never seen him cry before. It forced me to put myself in his shoes, as a parent. After reflecting on it, I told him that I would probably be doing exactly what he was doing. I then asked him what he wanted from me. He asked me to commit to listening, with an open mind, to what the ex-members wanted to share for five days. I made him promise to let me go back to the group if I wanted to, fully intending to do exactly that. Fortunately, on the final day I had my wake-up moment about Moon being a liar. But it began with my father's genuine caring—and a strategic switch-perspective intervention.

HELP UNDO THEIR PHOBIAS

The world is a scary place for Trump's true believers—filled with migrant invaders, Muslim terrorists, the deep state, and a cabal of global elites, not to mention radical Democrats, liberal socialists, and people like Hillary Clinton and the philanthropist George Soros who want to take down our country. Fearmongering and phobia indoctrination are among Trump's main tools for recruiting and rallying his base. He issues threatening messages at rallies and in his tweets. On April 12, 2019, he tweeted out a video of Minnesota Democratic representative Ilhan Omar speaking to the Council on American-Islamic Relations (CAIR) about how Muslims had been losing access to civil liberties since 9/11. In the Trump tweet, Omar's comments were intercut with images of the twin towers falling and the caption "We Will Never Forget." Trump's tweet was almost tame compared to some of the images and videos attacking Omar put out by alt-right and Christian right websites. In his phobia- and fearmongering, Trump has a great deal of help—from Fox News, Christian right groups like NAR, and the Russian propaganda machine, who are all spinning out their own frightening imagery and rhetoric.

Legitimate fears warn us of real dangers. Phobias occur when fears persist in a conditioned and irrational way, detached from any real danger. They can be triggered by a cue that initiates a cycle of fearful images, thoughts, and feelings. The cue can be an internal or external stimulus, such as a thought, image, word, smell, taste, feeling, or behavior. Fear of public speaking, heights, snakes, and airplane travel are common phobias. An estimated 19 million Americans suffer from phobias. Though many arise spontaneously, cult leaders use them intentionally, implanting phobias that often target their members' underlying anxieties—in the case of Trump, fear of jobs being taken away by immigrants or the supposed white Christian way of life disappearing.

In a destructive cult, phobia indoctrination is the single most powerful technique for keeping people dependent and obedient. I have encountered many people who had long ago stopped believing in the leader but are psychologically paralyzed with deliberately implanted phobias, which are often unconscious.

Phobias are so integral to the cult mindset that I consider undoing them to be a high priority when working with a cult member. Fortunately, phobias can be treated. You can help others by following my three-step approach.[14] If you have a phobia yourself, you first cure yourself, or fix the problem with professional help. Then you can use yourself as a kind of success story, sharing what you learned with the cult member. It makes the intervention more personal and effective. If you do not have a phobia, use someone you know who has one. If you do not know anyone, you can use examples provided here.

I advise people not to do all three steps at once. Nor is it wise to spread them out over many weeks. Timing the steps so they occur within a few days to a week is most effective. The goal is to empower the person to self-reflect, analyze, and cure their phobia.

STEP ONE

Explain what a phobia is—how irrational fears are different from rational, legitimate fears. Using examples of different phobias, describe how a cure is possible. Usually when a person has a phobia, they simply make excuses to avoid the stimuli. They take stairs if they have an elevator phobia, claiming it is healthier, which it often is. I agree with that logic, but I want people to be able to choose to take an elevator.

Typically, a phobia has a structure to it. First, there is a negative image or movie in one's head, along with negative self-talk or hearing the leader's voice reinforcing the phobia. It provokes a physiological response, such as holding one's breath or breathing quickly and shallowly. The three things create a chain reaction that results in extreme fear. In the case of an elevator phobia, people may see themselves plummeting and crashing (they might have seen this in a movie), or being trapped between floors for eternity. They not only visualize it; they hear themselves screaming. Their heart races and either they hold their breath or their breathing quickens.

For someone with an elevator phobia, just imagining riding safely and comfortably from floor to floor, possibly even humming along the way, and exiting with a normal heart rate and breathing pattern, seems all but impossible. But that, in a nutshell, is the goal of a successful intervention. The first step is to provide facts and data: You explain to them that modern elevators are equipped with emergency brakes that make freefall impossible, and with phones. If they get stuck, they can call for help. Even if it takes a while to be rescued, they will survive. You help them realize that they are not in danger.

Next, ask the person to visualize themselves in the future having been cured of the phobia, getting into an elevator and riding comfortably until they get to their floor and exit. They might imagine doing soothing self-talk while in the elevator—commenting to themselves about the colors of the elevator, the people in it, or something else altogether, all the while breathing normally. They do that over and over. The last step in the process, which is known as systemic desensitization, is to get into a real elevator and ride it, repeating some of the same soothing behaviors they practiced in their minds. Successfully carrying out this last behavioral step often convinces the person the phobia is a thing of the past.

STEP TWO

The next step is to explain how other destructive groups or people deliberately install phobias to control their members. For example, the Jehovah's Witnesses tell followers that receiving a blood transfusion goes against the Bible and will result in eternal damnation—and their being shunned by the group. Many followers have refused blood transfusions for themselves or their children, with consequences far more real and tragic than the threat of damnation or expulsion. Of course, no Jew, Christian, or Muslim who studies the Bible would ever interpret the kosher laws to mean letting someone die by refusing a blood transfusion. Life is always sacred in the Abrahamic faiths. But the fear of shunning is real and can be powerful. As a Moonie, I was brought to see the movie *The Exorcist* and was told by Moon that God made the movie as a prophecy of what would happen if anyone left the Unification Church. Crazy, but I totally believed it and became fearful of demonic possession.

Domestic violence survivors often talk about their abusers convincing them that they will never be loved by anyone else or have a healthy relationship. Lyndon LaRouche filled his members with conspiracy theories, which in the group were elevated to phobias about the world coming to an end if they didn't follow him. Once a person has engaged with such scenarios, they will often agree with you that people in *those* groups have phobias. They would never fall for that kind of programming—they would get the blood transfusion or leave the Moon or LaRouche cult.

STEP THREE

Millions of Trump's true believers are convinced that he has been chosen by God to build a Christian kingdom on earth—a prophecy that he must complete, otherwise terrible things will happen to our country and our planet.

The last step is to help the believer connect the dots between their positive visualizations—in the case of Trump, one in which the world won't come to an end without him, where Christians can live with people from different races, cultures, and religions in harmony—and their newfound knowledge that phobias can be deliberately implanted, but also removed and cured. Might they agree to speak to former Trump supporters who have left the fold, or to consider circumstances under which they would no longer trust Trump and might even want a different leader? Do they believe it is possible that they might ever change their mind? If not, why? Do they fear something bad will happen if they change their mind or speak with a critic? In my experience, once a person sees how much they have been controlled by deliberately installed phobias, they are often well on their way out of a destructive group or relationship.

HOW TO PROTECT YOURSELF FROM UNDUE INFLUENCE

Sometimes the most intelligent and well-educated people can get locked into ideologically rigid mindsets that prevent them from changing their views, despite overwhelming evidence. How can we avoid blinkered thinking and bias—not just with regard to a specific political figure or party, but in general?

Be discriminating about your sources of information and how much you consume in twenty-four hours. Do you tune in to only one TV channel or talk radio show, or do you expose yourself to other perspectives? It's good to get news from multiple places across the political spectrum. Give yourself time to digest the information. Figure out who is credible and who is not. The internet and social media have made it so easy to click and share. Read the full article and check out the sources before you pass it on. If someone else shares something, do your due diligence and see if you can corroborate the story with another source.

Remember to check yourself on confirmation bias—people unconsciously filter out information that does not confirm their preexisting viewpoint. Everyone is subject to this—it's much easier to sustain a false belief than to admit a mistake. I described earlier a switching process, which is called counter-attitudinal argumentation. This involves taking the opposite position, learning it thoroughly, and arguing it as if it were your own. Doing this helps give you a social perspective completely opposite to your own. It helps you see that others have profoundly different and perhaps even legitimate beliefs. When I was in the Moon cult, I was 100 percent sure that I was right and that everyone who was a critic dwelled in the darkness of Satan. After my wake-up moment, I realized that I was the one who was in the dark—and in need of help.

Be wary of people, organizations, or companies that use undue influence to promote their own interests—often financial. Oil and gas companies often suppress information about climate change. It's not uncommon for corporations—even those we might have once viewed as ethically sound, like Facebook and Google—to seek out and hire so-called experts who will support and promote their views so they remain profitable. Many also hire lobbyists to get their causes championed by political officials and gain even more support by making donations to political candidates.

Peer pressure heavily contributes to the formation of beliefs. If the people you love and trust hold a certain view, you are more likely to also hold that view. Though most of those in our social circles don't intentionally try to misinform us, it is quite common for friends, colleagues, and associates to play a big role in shaping our beliefs. We need to examine the source of everything we read, even if it is shared with us by someone we trust. We must seek out multiple credible sources in order to be more informed citizens.

TODAY'S WORLD

Another way to stay well-rounded is to look at the world from many perspectives. Some people worry that taking another point of view—especially one we find reprehensible—will compromise their integrity. Perhaps they are irrationally concerned that they might become convinced and switch perspectives. If something is true, it will stand up to scrutiny. Be willing to consider how you might alter your point of view if the evidence is convincing, testable, and reliable. A fact does not become any less true because we assume other viewpoints. By examining what the opposition has to say, we better understand the issues, and why we believe what we believe. Not only do we become better informed, we are better able to explain why we hold certain beliefs. On the other hand, if a belief cannot withstand criticism or research, then it may not be worth holding.

Beliefs should never be held as if they are the truth. The more strongly someone claims to have the truth, the more evidence we need to accept it. Certitude is not evidence of truth. Nor does repetition make it true. If anything, repetition should make you suspicious. Truth always stands up to scrutiny on its merits.

Allow yourself the flexibility to change your beliefs when presented with new evidence and perspectives. There are large gaps in our knowledge. Acknowledging where those gaps are does not make us weak. It makes us intelligent consumers of information. We don't usually know what we don't know. Yet we live in a world where it's more important than ever to be an informed citizen. The beliefs that we form affect not only how we live our lives, but also which causes and public figures we support. In order to keep our freedom of mind, we all need to continually examine our beliefs, carefully consider the information we are presented, and engage with a world that is larger than ourselves. We also need to listen to people who have left mind control cults and are speaking out about their experiences. They are courageous and have important stories to share. I believe they can play a critical part in helping to heal our fractured country. They are role models who show us how to move on after life inside a cult or destructive relationship, whether it be personal, political, or religious— or all wrapped up in one. So many former members have gone on to become highly successful people, on many different levels. Their personal stories, combined with our knowledge about how undue influence and mind control works, can help others. There are many different types of mind control groups, and while a cult member might be reluctant, if not unwilling, to hear stories about their own group, they will likely be willing to hear and discuss people's experiences with other groups. Especially now, when human trafficking, terrorist, and other extremist groups have become so prevalent, we need to pay attention to former members who have lifesaving stories to tell. Let's seek them out and hear their stories.

The Future

Jim Jones's voice came across the loudspeaker, summoning his followers to the central pavilion of Jonestown, a sprawling outpost in the jungles of Guyana, on an overcast afternoon in November 1978. As he sat on stage, his voice still bellowing over the PA system, Jones exhorted his followers to pour cyanide-laced fruit punch down their children's throats, and then drink the fatal potion themselves. When the Guyanese authorities arrived hours later, they found 912 bodies lying mostly facedown. More than 300 were children. Jones died by a bullet to his head, not self-inflicted. A courageous congressman, Leo J. Ryan, who had been visiting Jonestown with his aides to investigate allegations of people being held against their will, was assassinated on a nearby airstrip, along with four others.

The images coming out of the Peoples Temple compound in Jonestown shocked the world—indeed, they are seared into the minds of many Americans, though many young people may have never seen them, or even heard of Jonestown. Among the images, there is one that stands out to me. Hanging above the stage where Jones sat, issuing his murderous commands, was a sign: "Those who do not remember the past are condemned to repeat it."

I've puzzled over the meaning of those words. The phrase is at-tributed to the Spanish-born philosopher George Santayana, but why did Jones hang it there? Was it a self-fulfilling prophecy? A malig-nant narcissist, Jones saw himself as a modern-day Jesus and often talked about the government coming to "crucify" him for preaching the truth. In his last ravings, he would describe the massacre as "an act of revolutionary suicide to protest the conditions of an inhumane world." Maybe he saw the sign as linking him to Jesus and other prophets who, through the ages, would be killed for preaching the "truth."

But the sign holds another meaning, almost a taunt: forget what happened here at Jonestown and you may find it happening again. Jones's followers were diverse but most of them were good, idealistic Americans who fell under the sway of a pathological authoritarian leader who used threats, intimidation, and black-and-white, us versus them thinking as well as phobias and other mind control techniques to recruit and indoctrinate them.

It may seem to be a leap to mention Jonestown when writing about the Cult of Trump. As we have seen, cults differ in their identity and the consequences of their activities. But the takeaway is this—mind control exists and it is a potent threat to our lives—our families, communities, institutions, and nation. We live in an age of digital in-fluence, where people have access to one another anytime and any-where, and where people can be deeply influenced and radicalized as never before. In an essay for *The Washington Post*, Terrence McCoy describes a young man who underwent a radical personality change after spending hours online, visiting white nationalist websites and viewing white supremacist rallies. He had one persona online and another with his family. "I don't know how you got this way," said his liberal mother, after he finally came out to her as a neo-Nazi.[1] This young man was twenty-one, but children of thirteen, fourteen, and fifteen years of age are becoming radicalized through video games, websites, and online communities. Young gunmen can broadcast hate crimes in real time, as happened with the twenty-eight-year-old New Zealand shooter, and gain a platform, as well as a following. As

B. J. Fogg of the Stanford Persuasive Tech Lab observed, the overlap between our digital experiences and persuasion is growing. "Persuasion is part of human existence, but now that computers can persuade, the landscape has changed," he said.[2]

Adding to the stress are potentially enormous environmental changes—droughts, floods, hurricanes, and fierce storms—that could, in turn, bring about mass immigration, social upheaval, and possibly wars, among other life-as-we-know-it changes. What is especially troubling is that, according to climate scientists, the next ten years are critical in the battle against global warming. And yet we have a president who willfully ignores the threat.

Eventually Trump will be gone, but his presidency will have left us a deeply divided nation. How do we restore a sense of trust and civility to government and society? How do we encourage the media to dampen rather than inflame internal divisions? How do we protect ourselves from future authoritarian-leaning leaders who may draw us even further into a world of conflicting loyalties, allegiances, and ideologies?

These are huge and difficult questions. In the last chapter, I described the importance of listening to and benefiting from the experiences of former cult members. We need to hear from others who have lived under authoritarian regimes—people like Madeleine Albright, former secretary of state, who as a child fled Hitler's Germany and later communist Czechoslovakia. In her book *Fascism*, published shortly after Trump was elected, she describes how American isolationism led to the rise of fascism in the early twentieth century, and might do so again. "I fear a return to the international climate that prevailed in the 1920s and '30s, when the United States withdrew from the global stage and countries everywhere pursued what they perceived to be their own interests without regard to larger and more enduring goals," she writes.[3]

The late Italian writer and Holocaust survivor Primo Levi described how fascism arises not just by military force or police intimidation but by "denying and distorting information, by undermining systems of justice, by paralyzing the education system, and by spreading in myriad subtle ways nostalgia for a world where order reigned."⁴ Levi wrote those words in 1974, but they sound all too prophetic in this era of Make America Great Again.

"History does not repeat, but it does instruct," writes Yale professor Timothy Snyder in his book *On Tyranny*. He shows how the framers of the constitution turned to the ancient Greeks—Aristotle, who warned that inequality brings instability; and Plato, who warned that demagogues would exploit free speech to install themselves as tyrants. "Americans today are no wiser than the Europeans who saw democracy yield to fascism, Nazism, or communism in the twentieth century. Our one advantage is that we might learn from their experience," he writes.⁵

In their book, *How Democracies Die*, Steven Levitsky and Daniel Ziblatt, both professors of government at Harvard, show us how democratically elected leaders can gradually undermine democratic norms, and set the stage for authoritarian regimes.⁶

Experts in social influence such as Robert Jay Lifton, Philip Zimbardo, Margaret Singer, Kathleen Taylor, Robert Cialdini, and Anthony Pratkanis have revealed our susceptibility to influence and authority. Daniel Kahneman and Amos Tversky showed that though we often rationalize, we are often not rational creatures and that the unconscious mind works off heuristics, which are subject to error and bias. Neuroscientists and psychologists since then have made great headway in the scientific study of the mind. Influence is inevitable—it's part of the human condition—but we can distinguish between ethical and unethical forms. The more we understand how influence works, the better able we will be to inoculate ourselves—as well as our families, communities, institutions, and country—against undue forms and sense when we are being duped, controlled, deceived, or coerced by individuals, organizations, and governments.

European countries, including Germany, France, and Belgium, have recently recognized the dangers posed by undue influence, and in particular mind control cults, and have created task forces to investigate them. There has been no such visible effort in any part of the U.S. government, despite the threat that terrorist and hate organizations have posed to our national safety. The U.S. government actively pursued a program of mind control research for decades and yet there has been no official government statement on the existence—let alone the dangers—of mind control.

PRESIDENTIAL MENTAL HEALTH

The federal goverment was founded on the concept of a separation of powers, one that uses operational checks and balances between the executive, judicial, and legislative branches to ensure that policies are made with due consideration and to prevent any trend toward tyranny. Those checks and balances have been disrupted by President Trump, who appears to view these branches as extensions of—and answerable to—the White House. Also, while Congress and the judiciary are comprised of hundreds of people, many with significant power, the focus of the executive branch is a single person. It is all the more imperative that the person filling that office be of sound mind. Going forward, we need to have standards and legal mechanisms that safeguard our democracy from psychologically unstable leaders and would-be authoritarians. In their book, *The Dangerous Case of Donald Trump*, Bandy X. Lee and her colleagues argue that anyone who runs for the office of the president should be required to have a full neuropsychiatric, forensic evaluation by a bipartisan—or apolitical—committee of professionals to establish a baseline of mental competence. That person should then also undergo routine follow-ups. The World Mental Health Coalition has been set up as a nonprofit to work toward creating practical solutions to having fit leadership.[7]

THE LEGAL SYSTEM

After many years of helping those under mind control, I have come to realize how much more could be done if the legal system's definition of undue influence were updated to take into account scientific advances in understanding how the mind works. As it now stands, destructive cults, especially if they have IRS designation as a religion, are often not held accountable for violating their members' rights. Nor are websites—or the media—held responsible for inciting people to violence. Part of the problem is the lack of a clear, scientifically supported legal definition of undue influence. Santa Clara University emeritus law professor Alan Scheflin has proposed a theoretically grounded framework to evaluate undue influence in courts of law.[8] According to his Social Influence Model, there are three aspects of undue influence—the influencer, the influencee, and the motives, goals, and methods used to influence. Each of these could be evaluated by an expert; together they would constitute a kind of forensic analysis. The framework could be applied on a case-by-case basis. It would ultimately be up to a judge or a jury to decide if a particular case involved undue influence and to what extent. It's a start, but clearly we have a long way to go to create the legal tools we need to keep up with the needs of the twenty-first century.

Part of the challenge is that our legal system needs to get a better grip on how undue influence operates on the internet. We could learn from Germany and other European governments in this regard. In 2017, Germany implemented a law requiring the biggest social media networks—those with more than two million users—to take down blatantly illegal hate speech within twenty-four hours of its being reported.[9] China, one of the most authoritarian societies, monitors, controls, and collects data on all internet activity. Programs of data collection now include facial recognition of people as well. Of course, we do not want totalitarian surveillance. On the other hand, the internet should not be a "wild, wild west," where companies can do whatever they want to draw in users and make money, with virtually no legal or moral accountability. Companies like Facebook and Google should move out of a business model of selling data to third parties— laws to that effect should be written and enforced. Data firms, like the now-disgraced and defunct Cambridge Analytica—which gained access to more than 87 million Facebook users for the purpose of targeting them with political ads—need to be held accountable.[10] Across the board, social media and app companies need to be vetted and responsible standards established to protect citizens' private information.

RELIGIOUS FREEDOM

Freedom of religion is called the "first freedom" for several reasons. It is the first part of the First Amendment to the Constitution—it precedes freedom of speech and freedom of the press. In order for people to be able to speak and publish freely, they must be able to think freely—to believe differently from the government and powerful religious institutions. Freedom of religion is not just about religion— it's about the right to think for ourselves, to change our minds in a way that is neither an advantage nor a disadvantage to our status as citizens. While the Constitution protects beliefs, it does not necessarily protect all actions and behaviors stemming from those beliefs. Human sacrifice to the gods may be part of a person's religious belief system, as it was in earlier times, but if carried out anywhere in the United States today, it is homicide. Courts have routinely banned snake-handling rituals, because of the many deaths that have resulted from that practice. It has famously been said that "Your right to swing your arms ends just where the other man's nose begins."

In his 1997 book, *Eternal Hostility: The Struggle Between Theocracy and Democracy,* Frederick Clarkson shows how the men who shaped our nation's approach to religious freedom tried to make clear its limitations. And yet as we have seen in chapter 7, factions on the Christian right have interpreted religious freedom to mean that they may violate the Constitution if it is in keeping with their religious, and ultimately theocratic, beliefs or practices. They are pushing state-level legislation that would carve out religious exemptions to civil rights and labor laws under the banner of Project Blitz—which Trump has supported. It is a slippery slope from proposals that would allow heath care providers to deny services to LGBTQ people, which is bad enough. The Trump administration is now allowing state and federally funded adoption and foster care agencies to refuse prospective parents who are single, divorced, LGBTQ, Jewish, or belong to other religions. If these policies are upheld in court, it may become open season for forms of discrimination that a few years ago, many would not have thought possible.

According to Clarkson, religious freedom is one of the central issues of our time. He is not alone. There is a movement of civil rights groups and religious and nonreligious organizations, from American Atheists to the National Council of Churches, that is rising to confront the challenge posed by these theocratic movements. "It has taken time, but organized opposition is mounting," Clarkson said.[11] Americans United for Separation of Church and State and a broad coalition of forty-three prominent religious, civil rights, secular, LGBTQ, and reproductive freedom organizations have issued a joint national statement warning about Project Blitz.[12] An overlapping coalition of a dozen groups has created a website called BlitzWatch to monitor the campaign and provide resources for opponents.[13]

Putting these efforts to advance theocratic ideas under the rubric of religious freedom aside, the underlying issue of mind control ought to be a religious freedom issue of concern to everyone. If there are laws that protect people from being conned out of their property, there should be laws that protect people from being conned out of their opinions, thoughts, and beliefs. At the point that the Moonie recruiters lied to me, telling me they were college students, not a religious group, and failed to disclose that they worshipped a Korean billionaire they thought was the messiah—and that they were members of a group that used deception and mind control techniques—they were infringing on my religious freedom as a young Jewish man. My point is not to diminish or disparage a particular religion, but instead to ensure that the rights of others to believe or not believe as they choose, without undue influence or coercion, are upheld. "Respect for religious freedom means respect for the integrity of the conscience of the individual," Clarkson writes.

A final note on the subject of religion: I believe that tax-exempt status should not be granted to just any group that says they are a religious organization. I would like to see a governmental body set up that acts as a consumer clearinghouse, linked to the FBI and the IRS, that has the power to investigate and prosecute any tax-exempt group or entity that systematically violates people's rights. If such an entity is found to be deceptively recruiting, thereby violating people's civil and religious rights; or to be using high-pressure methods of mind control to keep them from seeking the health care or education they need; or to be preventing them from being able to meet with people outside the group, the entity should lose its tax-exempt status. Any group whose aim is to subvert the Constitution or commit crimes should be held accountable.

THE MENTAL HEALTH PROFESSION

Buried deep inside the *Diagnostic and Statistical Manual of Mental Disorders, Fifth Edition* (*DSM-5*) is a special designation for victims of cult brainwashing and undue influence. It is labeled Other Specified Dissociative Disorder 300.15 (F44.9). It is defined as an identity disturbance "due to prolonged and intense coercive persuasion. Individuals who have been subjected to intense coercive persuasion (e.g., brainwashing, thought reform, indoctrination while captive, torture, long-term political imprisonment, recruitment by sects/cults or by terror organizations) may present with prolonged changes in, or conscious questioning of, their identity." Though the *DSM-5* is used by clinicians, researchers, drug companies, health insurance companies, the courts, and policy makers, very few have learned about this category, or about the clinical tool known as the Structured Clinical Interview for DSM-V for Dissociative Disorders (SCIDV-D), which is considered the gold standard for assessing dissociative disorders.

TRAINING HEALTH PROFESSIONALS

I wish I could say that most mental health professionals were even aware of the DSM category that pertains to brainwashing and mind control. In fact, only a small percentage of psychiatrists, therapists, and other practitioners have received any training in working with this population. Most are largely unaware that an assessment of mind control can be made and are unfamiliar with the specialized approaches that have been developed to address it. Meanwhile, they may have patients in their practice who continue to suffer as a result of their cult involvement. Curricula that explain undue influence and mind control, and show practitioners what to look for in patients, need to be developed and incorporated into all mental health training programs.

MENTAL HEALTH AND PUBLIC HEALTH RESEARCH

Millions of people are born or brought into cults of all sorts—religious, political, sex trafficking. Often they are haunted by undiagnosed mental and emotional scars that can lead to addiction, depression, even suicide as a result of their cult involvement. They may undergo multiple medical evaluations and treatments, with little benefit and often at great expense. A starting place to help these people—and our health care system—would be to conduct an epidemiological study to determine the public health risks and the costs of treating such patients using traditional approaches—drug and alcohol addiction programs, psychotherapy, medications, and hospitalizations. Getting to the root problem, the cult involvement, can be a much more effective, and less expensive approach.

A few years ago, I worked with a woman who had walked out of a destructive discipling Bible group, the International Churches of Christ, after a thirteen-year involvement. She was misdiagnosed, given a laundry list of medications, and hospitalized several times over eleven years, and she still had self-harm and suicidal impulses. She read my book *Combating Cult Mind Control* and contacted me for help. I worked with her intensively over several days, at the end of which she felt dramatically better. She had a much better understanding of why she was suffering and how to help herself. She returned to her psychiatrist, who helped wean her off her medications entirely. I put her in touch with a local therapist, who was properly trained for follow-up. She went on to fully reclaim her life, received a Ph.D., and is in a fulfilling relationship. We made a presentation together in Harvard Medical School psychiatrist Judith Herman's seminar on Victims of Violence Trauma where she taught about all of the errors made in her treatment.

The diagnosis—and treatment—could also extend to people who have been recruited by human trafficking and extremist terrorist organizations. Many former terrorists are ostracized and thrown in jail and yet in most cases they are the victims of coercive mind control recruiting and indoctrination. I have long believed that counseling such people—helping them understand what happened to them—and then having them teach others would be a great deterrent to future terrorist recruitment efforts.

Jennifer Panning, a contributor to *The Dangerous Case of Donald Trump*, coined the name for a new type of anxiety disorder—Trump Anxiety Disorder—which pinpoints symptoms "specific to the election of Trump and the resultant unpredictable sociopolitical climate." In an interview with *Politico Magazine*, Panning said the disorder is marked by "increased worry, obsessive thought patterns, muscle tension and obsessive preoccupation with the news."[14] It also includes feelings of loss of control and helplessness, and even excessive time spent on social media.[15]

According to a 2018 survey by the American Psychiatric Association, 39 percent of people said their anxiety level had risen over the previous year. Fifty-six percent were extremely anxious or somewhat anxious about "the impact of politics on daily life." A 2017 APA study found that two-thirds of Americans see the nation's future as a "very or somewhat significant source of stress."[16]

THE MEDIA

In their book, *Network Propaganda*, Yochai Benkler, Robert Faris, and Hal Roberts suggest that an independent apparatus be set up to independently verify sources and perform fact checks of the news—especially in the face of the overwhelming amount of disinformation and propaganda being circulated, especially by the right-wing media. There are lots of good ideas out there, though it remains to be seen which will gain traction. The point is there are serious conversations going on among scholars, journalists, and legislators to try to find solutions. Let's hope they find some soon.

Whatever solutions may be found, we need to be resolute in our insistence that we also need to protect journalists who report on governments and powerful interests everywhere, including dictators and authoritarian regimes. They help maintain our country's commitment to combating coercive and destructive regimes around the world. At the same time, their reports—about crackdowns on freedom of the press or the abrogation of civil liberties—can provide a basis for comparison to see if there are ways that our own country veers into such territory. Yet investigative journalists have been kidnapped or killed in shocking numbers.[17] Most recently and horribly, *The Washington Post*'s Jamal Khashoggi was killed by agents in the Saudi Arabian government and yet no American sanction was levied against its leadership.

In 1969, the philanthropist Philip M. Stern established the Fund for Investigative Journalism, which gave its first grant—of $250—to journalist Seymour Hersh, who used it to begin investigating a tip about a U.S. Army massacre at the Vietnamese village of My Lai. The story turned into a huge exposé of Army wrong-doing. The Fund for Investigative Journalism has since awarded grants totaling $1.5 million to scores of investigative journalists, resulting in over 700 stories and some fifty books.[18] There are similar organizations, including the Center for Investigative Reporting and ProPublica, whose mission is to "expose abuses of power and betrayals of public trust by government, business, and other institutions."[19] If every American holding a driver's license were to donate a dollar a year, we could fund important centers like these to the tune of $225 million annually.[20]

INTERNET AND TECHNOLOGY

Whatever has the power to help has the power to hurt. That has been abundantly clear with the internet, and especially platforms like Facebook and Twitter. It was through these social media platforms that Russia entered the fray of the 2016 presidential elections and may seek to do so in the future, along with Iran, China, and other nations that have historically sought to influence American elections. How can we ensure that future innovations—like artificial intelligence—adhere to ethical standards? After the 2019 New Zealand massacre, prime minister Jacinda Ardern immediately banned the circulation of the video that the gunman made. Social media platforms need to find ways to prevent such videos and other hate-filled and inflammatory materials from being circulated in the first place. YouTube took a step in this direction when, in January 2019, it announced that it was changing its algorithms for recommending videos in a way that would reduce the spread of "borderline content and content that could misinform users in harmful ways." It was very specific about what that content would include—"videos promoting a phony miracle cure for a serious illness, claiming the earth is flat or making blatantly false claims about historic events like 9/11."[21] Facebook has also promised to be more accountable, in part as a face-saving gesture for having played a role in spreading false information during the 2016 election season.[22] They announced in March 2019 they were banning content that glorifies white nationalism and separatism.[23]

Future efforts to protect our citizens might take advantage of what is known about undue influence and mind control and might even consider using the BITE model when devising algorithms to detect coercive and unethical forms of influence. When it comes to the future world of AI, we need to make sure that compassion and kindness are included in the wiring of any robots. Maybe the single most important AI algorithm would be the most ancient—the Golden Rule: treat others as you would have them treat you.

COMMUNITY

Once at a plenary lecture I gave at a conference on Complex Systems, a woman from China asked me, "There's a lot of emphasis on the individual's freedom and individuality in America, but what about the collective self?" Good question! We need to cultivate a greater sense of responsibility—not just to our family and friends but to our local communities, our country, and to all who share the planet. We hit our brakes when coming at a stop sign. It's the law, of course. But we know it is going to make all of us safer. People consensually abide by rules for the common good. That is also true of our social behavior—the Ten Commandments were established thousands of years ago as a mechanism for helping people get along in groups. They were also established as a form of social control, with their focus on worshipping the "one God." What we may need now are commandments that guide our ethical behavior as citizens, regardless of race, creed, ethnicity, or sexual or religious preference.

Humans are intrinsically social creatures. We seek connection, though it is often with people we view as similar to us. If we are to heal the current rift between parties and ideologies, we need to talk with people who are different, which can be a tall order. And yet, struggling with and resolving our differences is at the heart of the best of what the American experiment has been all about. Learning to cope with and navigate those differences will let us flourish as individuals and as a society going forward—if we commit ourselves to the process.

When I'm counseling people and describing healthy versus unhealthy functioning, I use the image of a funnel. If you believe that you have the truth with a capital *T,* you are going from the wide end of the funnel toward the narrow end. Your view of the world grows limited because you're only looking for confirmation of your existing beliefs. When you are growing and expanding, you realize how little you know and how much knowledge and understanding you have yet to discover. You are looking from the narrow end toward the ever-widening one.

Healing the rift requires education—teaching people about influence techniques, propaganda and persuasion, fantasies versus facts, as well as the warning signs of destructive groups and leaders. We might turn the internet into a tool for reconnection and reconciliation by creating an online resource that teaches everyone—politicians, law enforcement, businesspeople, artists, doctors, children—about the issues and information contained in this book and others focusing on similar themes. It could provide resources, videos, and courses for more detailed study. One of my mentors, Philip Zimbardo, developed

the Heroic Imagination Project, which uses videos to teach about social psychology and how to stand up and do the right thing.[24] This
should be a standard curriculum item in middle and high schools.

Civic meetings could be organized in communities focusing on
themes of reconciliation and trust building. When people meet across
belief systems and share their personal stories, understanding and
tolerance often follow. We should especially concentrate on teaching
children how to know the difference between ethical and unethical
influence, and how to protect themselves. We need to educate them
about citizenship and the importance of expressing their voice—and
their vote. We are all responsible for creating and sustaining institutions in which civil democracy flourishes.

Part of this means teaching our children that the current
situation—in which a president actively sows discord and division—is
not what the founding fathers envisioned. It is not normal, and it is
certainly not what we envision as leading to a better future for them
and for all of us.

LEST HISTORY REPEAT ITSELF

Meanwhile, there is evidence that Trump's behavior is becoming more
unbalanced. Though the Mueller Report found no criminal conspiracy between his election campaign and Russia, Trump has continued
to argue that the FBI and the Democrats are "treasonous" people who
have done "very evil things" and should themselves be investigated.
Trump's paranoia and desire for vengeance would be disturbing in an
ordinary citizen, but in a president, they are dangerous. Of course, the
fact remains that Trump had a fair amount to hide from the publishing
of the report, not least his reaction when he heard that Mueller was
assigned to the investigation: "Oh my God. This is terrible. This is
the end of my Presidency. I'm fucked."[25] Tony Schwartz, ghostwriter
for *The Art of the Deal*, tried to warn the electorate about candidate
Trump. But in the wake of the Mueller Report, he commented that
the reason Trump does not want his tax and other financial records
made available to Congress and federal prosecutors, or allow his aides

to testify before Congress, is that "they will all reveal he is a stone cold felon."[26]

Jim Jones also had a lot to hide—he was running a cult that was denying civil liberties to its members. I said earlier that comparing Jones with Trump might seem like a leap but the parallels are too important to ignore. Jones was a malignant narcissist with a strong paranoid streak. He believed that ultimately, he would be attacked—by the government, the media, even his own devotees—and intended to bring them with him. The massacre of his followers did not come out of the blue. He had them conduct suicide drills, so-called "white nights," to prepare for such a catastrophe. Congressman Leo Ryan had visited Jonestown in 1978 because he had received information that people were being held against their will and even tortured there. During his visit, several people passed him notes saying that they wanted to leave. Jones heard about this and had a psychotic implosion at the thought that his own followers had been disloyal. The rest was tragic history.

Is Trump that fragile? At a meeting on March 19, 2019, in Washington, D.C., experts from the World Mental Health Coalition gathered to express their grave concerns about Donald Trump's fitness for leadership. One of the most chilling moments came during a talk by Scott Ritter, former Marine intelligence officer who served as chief weapons inspector for the United Nations in Iraq from 1991 to 1998, and who is the author of several books. Ritter described how he voted for Trump but came to regret his decision out of fear that the president might start a nuclear war with North Korea or Iran. Ritter further stated that he did not think that any one person, including the president, should have the power to press the nuclear button, especially to carry out a preemptive nuclear strike.[27]

According to Bandy X. Lee, the situation with Trump may get worse. "The problem is, we as a nation have enabled it, allowing him to put in place individuals and structures that echo his distorted views, such as the new attorney general," Lee said. "Pathology coopts normal structures to destructive ends, not the other way around."[28]

Cult leaders do not relinquish power. If Trump runs again and is not reelected in 2020, he might claim that the election was rigged. Who knows what he might call on his followers to do in that case? The lives of the 917 people who were murdered by Jim Jones may seem like a distant lesson from a faraway time. And yet as someone who has lived a version of their experience, I know that the dangers of mind control are no less real today than they were forty years ago, in the remote jungles of Guyana.

In my work with clients, I have seen miracles happen. I have seen people throw off the mental and emotional shackles of many years—even a lifetime—of cult indoctrination. I believe that love is stronger than fear and that truth is stronger than mind control. But I also believe that the dangers of mind control are greater now than ever. We ignore the lessons of history—of Jonestown and other destructive groups—at our own peril.

ACKNOWLEDGMENTS

Each day brings new information and stories—often disturbing and sometimes shocking—demonstrating the reality of the Cult of Trump. This book needed to be finalized, but I trust there will be many more revelations coming out about the Trump White House before it appears in bookstores. While it applies the psychology of destructive cults to illuminate the dark corners of the Trump presidency, I hope that it will shed light on any leader or group with authoritarian behaviors. This book is a beginning—it offers what I hope is a new perspective in the ongoing struggle to uphold human rights, justice, and the democratic principles on which this country is founded.

Writing such an encompassing book in a very short period of time has been one of the most challenging but rewarding projects of my life. It was first conceived in the summer of 2018, when I met with Steve Troha, my literary agent at Folio, who proposed I write a book called *The Cult of Trump*. Steve believed in my expertise and in the importance of this project. He graciously advised and encouraged me every step of the way. My editor Natasha Simons at Simon & Schuster knew she wanted this book and made it happen. Natasha had edited Omarosa Manigault Newman's book *Unhinged,* as well as Catherine Oxenberg's book *Captive,* about the destructive group NXIVM, and so her interest in cults was whetted. Natasha arranged an interview for me with Omarosa, whom I also thank. Thank you, Steve and Natasha.

This book could not have happened without Misia Landau—anthropologist, science writer, artist, photographer, and my loving wife, who has been strong enough to deal with all the stresses of life with me and my difficult work. Thank you for all your incredible support on many levels. For more than two decades, you have helped me write, strategize, and cope. You have been my number one. Special thanks for putting aside your own writing projects and art classes to write your heart out to get this book into its best form for publication. You are an amazing writer. You are my most trusted and valued advisor. Thank you in ways far more than words could ever communicate. Also, to our son, Matthew. Thank you for dealing with the extra stress of having both your parents working on this book—and your willingness to take Uber one too many times!

Special thanks to Frederick Clarkson, who first interviewed me many decades ago, to find out about my experiences as a former Moon cult member and leader. Frederick has been writing articles to expose right-wing unethical activity, especially in regard to religious freedom. Frederick has been an amazing advisor and editor on this project and introduced me to many of the people I interviewed in researching this book. Frederick, your knowledge, guidance, and wisdom have made this a much stronger book. Thank you so much.

Months of writing and researching was supplied by Kathy Huck, with support from science writer Daniel Klein. Turning around a book on a four-month deadline is simply crazy. Thank you so much, Kathy. You helped to structure and shape the book and contributed a lot. Thank you, Daniel, for your contributions.

I would like to acknowledge people who have had a tremendous impact on my life, and taught, guided, and supported me for many decades. When I reached out to them to tell them about this book project, they each gave me lengthy interviews. Thank you, Robert Jay Lifton, M.D.; Dr. Philip Zimbardo; and law professor emeritus Alan Scheflin. I wish to recognize the late scholars Dr. Margaret Singer, Dr. Louis Jolyon West, and Dr. John Clark for their courageous work speaking out about destructive cults. I also wish to thank extraordinary social psychologists Dr. Anthony Pratkanis and Dr. Robert Cialdini.

Thank you to my colleagues, who are each considered cult experts and contributed to this book's research: Dr. Steve Eichel, president of the International Cultic Studies Association; Dr. Dennis Tourish; Dr. Alexandra Stein; Daniel Shaw, LCSW; Dr. Stephen Kent; and Dr. Janja Lalich. Enduring thanks to Open Minds founding director, Jon Atack, for our many stimulating conversations over the years. There are many other cult experts who have been doing interviews and articles discussing the Cult of Trump. Most are former members of cults themselves who have become professors, mental health professionals, or lay scholars.

Yale forensic psychiatrist Bandy X. Lee, M.D., edited the groundbreaking volume *The Dangerous Case of Donald Trump: 37 Psychiatrists and Mental Health Experts Assess a President*. This was an extremely important book for me. I am indebted to Bandy and her world-class colleagues. Their book, and also my many discussions with Bandy, taught me about the duty to warn and explained the politics of the Goldwater rule. To its shame, the American Psychiatric Association has incorrectly and unethically tried to silence many internationally renowned experts whose life work it is to identify people, including in this case a president, who are a threat to themselves and others.

An enormous amount of research was undertaken to complete this book. I am grateful to the creators of the many books, articles, interviews, podcasts, and videos that helped me better comprehend the Cult of Trump. Thank you for sharing, directly, your knowledge, expertise, and time with me: David Cay Johnston (who has been writing about Trump for fifty years), James Moore, Dr. André Gagné, Frank Cocozzelli, Yves Messer, Dennis King, Chip Berlet, Jeffrey Sharlet, Dr. James Scaminaci III, Dr. Warren Throckmorton, Dr. John Weaver, Dr. Christopher Stroop, Dr. John Dehlin, David Weissman, Arno Michaelis, Scott Adams, Allen Tate Wood, Jefferson Hawkins, Michele (Chele) Roland, Taryn Southern, Spanky Taylor, Tory Christman, Hoyt Richards, Rabbi Terry Ross Bard, Stephane Acel-Green, Cell

Whitman, and Larry Zilliox. Special thank you to Karin Spike Robinson for research, copyediting, and graphics assistance. Thank you to Rebecca Johnston for your support. Thanks to Kimmy O'Donnell and Jane at the Freedom of Mind Resource Center.

I wish to thank my mentors at Harvard's forensic think tank, The Program in Psychiatry and Law, and especially its founders, Dr. Thomas Gutheil, Dr. Harold Bursztajn, and Archie Brodsky. Special thanks to my mentor, Dr. Michael Commons, who runs the research arm of the Program. He told me that if I was serious about wishing to help update the legal definition of undue influence—and become a respected expert witness—I needed to get a doctorate, do quantitative research, and publish articles in peer review. He directed me to the doctoral program at Fielding Graduate University, and introduced me to my faculty mentor, Dr. Judy Stevens-Long, who has been so helpful, along with my dissertation committee members, Dr. Keith Melville and Dr. John Austin. Dr. Commons became my external faculty member and is supervising my research. He encouraged me to set up Freedom from Undue Influence, a research arm under his nonprofit, Dare Association. My research assistant, Mansi Shah, helped me to execute my first quantitative study and to ready my first peer review journal article for Elsevier, "The anatomy of undue influence used by terrorist cults and traffickers, so creating false identities" [*Ethics, Medicine and Public Health* (2019) 8, 97–107].

A special thanks to Eric Rayman. As my attorney, he has provided, over many years, legal support and advice for getting my work to the broader public.

Thanks so much to long-time friend, advisor, and all-around mentor Hank Greenberg. Ellen Krause-Grosman, of Make Your Vision Real, has been my business coach for several years. She advised me through many difficult moments with her characteristic pragmatism, creativity, and insight. She encouraged me to embark on a doctoral program, become an expert witness, and generally has done so much to support and help me get my work more broadly known. I am very grateful to you, Ellen.

This book could never have been written without my deprogramming from the Moonies in 1976, thanks to my dear sister Thea and her husband, Doug Luba, and my parents, Milton and Estelle Hassan. Thanks to those who did my deprogramming and who have helped encourage and support my efforts. Thanks again, to my colleague, ex-Scientologist Jon Atack, who is the leading authority on Hubbard and Scientology and a wonderful writer and editor. Jon, you have been much more than a colleague—you are a very dear friend and a source of enormous encouragement and inspiration always.

Last, but most importantly, thanks to my extended family and good friends, my community at Temple Beth Zion in Brookline, Massachusetts, and the tens of thousands of people I have met all over the world in this forty-three-year journey of activism. I have had a most astounding life and pray that this book helps to bring light to people everywhere.

NOTES

Introduction

1 Nicholas Confessore and Karen Yourish, "$2 Billion Worth of Free Media for Donald Trump," *The New York Times,* March 15, 2016, https://www.nytimes.com/2016/03/16/upshot/measuring-donald -trumps-mammoth-advantage-in-free-media.html.

2 "The Guy Who thought Up 'the Wall' Says Trump Should Shut Government to Fund It," *Bloomberg.com*, accessed April 14, 2019, https://www.bloomberg.com/news/articles/2018-12-20/the-guy-who -thought-up-the-wall-says-trump-should-shut-government-to-fund-it.

3 Stuart Anderson, "Where the Idea for Donald Trump's Wall Came From," *Forbes,* January 10, 2019, https://www.forbes.com/sites/stuart anderson/2019/01/04/where-the-idea-for-donald-trumps-wall-came -from/#16fe3ebe4415.

4 Editorial Board, "The Cult of Trump," *The New York Times*, June 7, 2018, https://www.nytimes.com/2018/06/07/opinion/trump-republi can-party.html.

5 Tess Bonn, "Dem Lawmaker Compares GOP to 'Religious Cult,'" *The Hill,* March 6, 2019, https://thehill.com/hilltv/rising /432834-dem-lawmaker-compares-republican-party-to-religious-cult.

CHAPTER ONE: What Is a Cult?

1 Nathaniel Rakich, "Two Years In, Turnover in Trump's Cabinet Is Still Historically High," *FiveThirtyEight*, January 8, 2019, https://

fivethirtyeight.com/features/two-years-in-turnover-in-trumps-cabinet
-is-still-historically-high/.

2 John Eligon, "Hate Crimes Increase for the Third Consecutive Year,
   F.B.I. Reports," *The New York Times,* November 13, 2018, https://
   www.nytimes.com/2018/11/13/us/hate-crimes-fbi-2017.html.

3 "How Scott Adams Got Hypnotized by Trump," *Bloomberg.com*,
   accessed April 13, 2019, https://www.bloomberg.com/news/features
   /2017-03-22/how-dilbert-s-scott-adams-got-hypnotized-by-trump.

4 Charles M. Blow, "The Commander of Fear." *The New York Times*,
   August 29, 2018, https://www.nytimes.com/2018/08/29/opinion
   /trump-fear.html.

5 "Trade Regulation Rule on Disclosure Requirements and Prohibitions
   Concerning Franchising and Business Opportunity Ventures—16
   CFR Part 436," *Federal Trade Commission*, July 5, 2013, https://
   www.ftc.gov/policy/federal-register-notices/trade-regulation-rule
   -disclosure-requirements-and-prohibitions.

6 Tony Ortega, "NXIVM: Actress Allison Mack Pleads Guilty—'I Was
   Lost and Wanted a Community,'" *The Underground Bunker*, April 8,
   2019, https://tonyortega.org/2019/04/08/nxivm-actress-allison-mack
   -pleads-guilty-i-was-lost-and-wanted-a-community/.

7 Pratkanis, A. R., and E. Aronson, *Age of Propaganda: The Everyday
   Use and Abuse of Persuasion* (New York: W. H. Freeman and Company, 1991), pp. 240–249.

CHAPTER TWO: The Making of a Cult Leader

1 Michelle Ye Hee Lee, "Donald Trump's False Comments Connecting
   Mexican Immigrants and Crime," *The Washington Post,* July 8, 2015,
   https://www.washingtonpost.com/news/fact-checker/wp/2015/07
   /08/donald-trumps-false-comments-connecting-mexican-immigrants
   -and-crime/?utm_term=.7a64fb2cd9b7.

2 Michael Kranish and Marc Fisher. *Trump Revealed: The Definitive
   Biography of the 45th President* (New York: Scribner, 2017).

3 Ibid., p. 32.

4 Caroline Mortimer, "Donald Trump's Mother Asked: 'What Kind
   of Son Have I Created?'" *Independent,* November 4, 2017, https://
   www.independent.co.uk/news/world/americas/us-politics/donald

-trump-mother-mary-relationship-what-have-i-created-psychology
-macleod-fred-trump-a8037181.html.

5 Michael Kruse, "The Mystery of Mary Trump," *Politico Magazine*,
   accessed April 14, 2019, https://www.politico.com/magazine/story
   /2017/11/03/mary-macleod-trump-donald-trump-mother-biography
   -mom-immigrant-scotland-215779.

6 Ibid.

7 Shane Snow, "Trump Insights: Appearance," *Hatch Institute*, April 27,
   2017, https://thehatchinstitute.org/all-stories/2017/5/1/trump-tales-vol-1.

8 Harry Hurt, *The Lost Tycoon: The Many Lives of Donald J. Trump*
   (New York: Norton, 1993).

9 Kruse, "The Mystery of Mary Trump."

10 Donald J. Trump and Tony Schwartz, *The Art of the Deal* (New York:
   Ballantine Books, 1987).

11 James Walsh, "Shoko Asahara: The Making of a Messiah," *Time*, April 3,
   1995, http://content.time.com/time/subscriber/article/0,33009,982749
   -1,00.html.

12 Ailsa Chang, "This Is Where Donald Trump Played by the Rules
   and Learned to Beat the Game," NPR, November 10, 2015, https://
   www.npr.org/2015/11/10/455331251/this-is-where-donald-trump
   -played-by-the-rules-and-learned-to-beat-the-game.

13 Paul Schwartzman and Michael E. Miller, "Confident. Incorrigible. Bully: Little Donny Was a Lot like Candidate Donald Trump,"
   The Washington Post, June 22, 2016, https://www.washingtonpost
   .com/lifestyle/style/young-donald-trump-military-school/2016/06/22
   /f0b3b164-317c-11e6-8758-d58e76e11b12_story.html?utm_term=
   .d14578a0ff49.

14 Paul Matzko, "The Pastor Who Helps Explain Donald Trump," *The
   Gospel Coalition*, January 14, 2019, https://www.thegospelcoalition
   .org/reviews/surge-piety-norman-vincent-peale/.

15 "Does Trump Display the Stereotypical Profile of a Cult Leader?"
   Freedom of Mind Resource Center, December 13, 2018, https://free
   domofmind.com/does-trump-display-the-stereotypical-profile-of-a
   -cult-leader/.

16 "Charles Manson: Master Manipulator, Even as a Child," NPR, August 4, 2013, https://www.npr.org/2013/08/04/206652873/charles
   -manson-master-manipulator-even-as-a-child.

17 Susan Brinkmann, "What's Wrong with Norman Vincent Peale?" *Women of Grace* (blog), February 2, 2016, https://www.womenof grace.com/blog/?p=47645.

18 Robert L. Park, *Superstition: Belief in the Age of Science* (Princeton, NJ: Princeton University Press, 2010).

19 Gwenda Blair, Adam Wren, David Fontana, and Renato Mariotti, "How Norman Vincent Peale Taught Donald Trump to Worship Himself," *Politico Magazine,* October 6, 2015, https://www.politico.com /magazine/story/2015/10/donald-trump-2016-norman-vincent-peale -213220#ixzz4Mt5Se1uO%C2%A0.

20 Ibid.

21 Ibid.

22 Eugene Scott, "Donald Trump Is Not an Active Member, Church Says—CNNPolitics," CNN, August 28, 2015, https://www.cnn.com /2015/08/28/politics/donald-trump-church-member/index.html.

23 Kranish and Fisher, *Trump Revealed.*

24 Paul Schwartzman and Michael E. Miller, "Confident. Incorrigible. Bully: Little Donny Was a Lot like Candidate Donald Trump," *The Washington Post,* June 22, 2016, https://www.washingtonpost .com/lifestyle/style/young-donald-trump-military-school/2016/06/22 /f0b3b164-317c-11e6-8758-d58e76e11b12_story.html.

25 Trump and Schwartz, *The Art of the Deal.*

26 Schwartzman and Miller, "Confident. Incorrigible."

27 David Shields, "Donald Trump's Father Is the Root of His Rage," *Salon.com,* October 7, 2018, https://www.salon.com/2018/10/06 donald-trumps-father-is-the-root-of-his-rage/.

28 Sophie Kozub, "Inside Trump's Days at Fordham," *The Observer,* January 26, 2017, https://fordhamobserver.com/30994/news/inside -trumps-days-at-fordham/.

29 William E. Geist, "The Expanding Empire of Donald Trump," *The New York Times Magazine,* April 8, 1984, https://www.nytimes.com /1984/04/08/magazine/the-expanding-empire-of-donald-trump.html ?scp=1&sq=%22THE%2BEXPANDING%2BEMPIRE%2BOF %2BDONALD%2BTRUMP%22&st=cse&pagewanted=all.

30 Philip Bump, "In 1927, Donald Trump's Father Was Arrested after a Klan Riot in Queens," *The Washington Post,* February 29, 2016, https://www.washingtonpost.com/news/the-fix/wp/2016/02/28

/in-1927-donald-trumps-father-was-arrested-after-a-klan-riot-in
-queens/?utm_term=.d797588a016a.

31 "1927 News Report: Donald Trump's Dad Arrested in KKK Brawl
with Cops," Boing Boing, August 6, 2018, https://boingboing.net
/2015/09/09/1927-news-report-donald-trump.html.

32 Will Kaufman, "Woody Guthrie, 'Old Man Trump' and a Real Estate
Empire's Racist Foundations," The Conversation, October 3, 2018,
https://theconversation.com/woody-guthrie-old-man-trump-and-a
-real-estate-empires-racist-foundations-53026.

33 Amanda Petrusich, "A Story About Fred Trump and Woody Guthrie for
the Midterm Elections," The New Yorker, November 6, 2018, https://
www.newyorker.com/culture/cultural-comment/a-story-about-fred
-trump-and-woody-guthrie-for-the-midterm-elections.

34 Thomas B. Edsall, "Trump Wants America to Revert to the Queens of
His Childhood," The New York Times, April 12, 2018, https://www
.nytimes.com/2018/04/12/opinion/trump-queens-childhood-america
.html.

35 Marie Brenner, "How Donald Trump and Roy Cohn's Ruthless Symbi-
osis Changed America," The Hive, Vanity Fair, June 30, 2017, https://
www.vanityfair.com/news/2017/06/donald-trump-roy-cohn-relation
ship.

36 Kranish and Fisher, Trump Revealed, p. 64.

37 David Von Drehle, "Trump's Résumé Is Rife with Mob Connections,"
The Washington Post, August 10, 2018, https://www.washingtonpost
.com/opinions/are-trumps-mob-connections-a-coincidence-fuhgedd
aboudit/2018/08/10/24b62e2c-9cad-11e8-843b-36e177f3081c_story
.html?utm_term=.3be54df843e6.

38 David Cay Johnston, The Making of Donald Trump (Brooklyn, N.Y.:
Melville House, 2017).

39 David Cay Johnston, Adam Wren, David Fontana, and Renato Mariotti, "Just What Were Donald Trump's Ties to the Mob?" Politico
Magazine, May 22, 2016, https://www.politico.com/magazine/story
/2016/05/donald-trump-2016-mob-organized-crime-213910.

40 David Smith, "Donald Trump: The Making of a Narcissist," The
Guardian, July 16, 2016, https://www.theguardian.com/us-news/2016
/jul/16/donald-trump-narcissist-profile.

41 Trump and Schwartz, The Art of the Deal.

42 Dan Alexander, "Why Is WWE Listed as the Trump Foundation's Biggest Donor?" *Forbes,* April 20, 2017, https://www.forbes.com/sites/danalexander/2017/04/20/why-is-wwe-listed-as-the-trump-foundations-biggest-donor/#3e57b3f85f90.

43 "Does WWE Explain Donald Trump's Rise to Power?" Spectator USA, July 5, 2018, https://spectator.us/does-wwe-explain-donald-trumps-rise-to-power/.

44 Russ Buettner and Susanne Craig, "Decade in the Red: Trump Tax Figures Show Over $1 Billion in Business Losses." *The New York Times,* May 7, 2019, https://www.nytimes.com/interactive/2019/05/07/us/politics/donald-trump-taxes.html.

45 Rupert Neate, "Trump and Atlantic City: The Lessons behind the Demise of His Casino Empire," *The Guardian,* September 2, 2016, https://www.theguardian.com/us-news/2016/sep/02/donald-trump-atlantic-city-casinos-taj-mahal-plaza-bankruptcy.

46 Patrick Radden Keefe, "How Mark Burnett Resurrected Donald Trump as an Icon of American Success," *The New Yorker,* February 28, 2019, https://www.newyorker.com/magazine/2019/01/07/how-mark-burnett-resurrected-donald-trump-as-an-icon-of-american-success.

47 Ibid.

48 Helaine Olen, "Trump, Carson, and Bush Have All Benefited from Get-Rich-Quick Companies That Prey on the Desperate," *Slate,* October 12, 2015, https://slate.com/business/2015/10/trump-carson-bush-all-benefited-from-multilevel-marketing-schemes.html.

49 Ike Swetlitz, "Donald Trump and the Vitamin Company That Went Bust," *STAT,* April 19, 2018, https://www.statnews.com/2016/03/02/donald-trump-vitamin-company/.

50 TrumpNetwork411, "The Trump Network—Donald Trump and Ideal Health Team Up," YouTube, December 6, 2009, https://www.youtube.com/watch?v=fK9AhOo3Fj0&feature=youtu.be&t=411.

51 Swetlitz, "Donald Trump and the Vitamin Company That Went Bust."

52 Ana Swanson, "The Trump Network Sought to Make People Rich, but Left behind Disappointment," *The Washington Post,* March 23, 2016, https://www.washingtonpost.com/news/wonk/wp/2016/03/23/the-trump-network-sought-to-make-people-rich-but-left-behind-disappointment/?utm_term=.b1985d499893.

53 Trump Network, "NBC's The Apprentice Leads Candidates to The

Trump Network," PR Newswire, June 30, 2018, https://www.prnews
wire.com/news-releases/nbcs-the-apprentice-leads-candidates-to-the
-trump-network-111679704.html.

54 Abby Haglage and Tim Mak, "Trump Vitamins Were Fortified with
B.S," *The Daily Beast,* May 25, 2016, https://www.thedailybeast.com
/trump-vitamins-were-fortified-with-bs.

55 Maria Dinzeo, "California High Court Rules Colleges Must Protect
Students," CNS, March 23, 2018, https://www.courthousenews.com
/california-high-court-rules-colleges-must-protect-students/.

CHAPTER THREE: The Cult Leader Profile

1 Raj Persaud, "Just How Narcissistic Are US Presidents? Does Ego
Rule?" *Psychology Today,* accessed April 14, 2019, https://www.psy
chologytoday.com/us/blog/slightly-blighty/201509/just-how-narcissis
tic-are-us-presidents-does-ego-rule.

2 Rich Morin, "The Most Narcissistic U.S. Presidents," *Pew Research
Center,* February 7, 2014, http://www.pewresearch.org/fact-tank
/2013/11/14/the-most-narcissistic-u-s-presidents/.

3 "The Double-Edged Sword of Grandiose Narcissism," *SAGE Journal,* accessed April 14, 2019, https://journals.sagepub.com/doi/abs
/10.1177/0956797613491970.

4 Mila Goldner-Vukov and Laurie-Jo Moore, "Malignant Narcissism:
From Fairy Tales to Harsh Reality," *Psychiatria Danubina,* U.S. National Library of Medicine, September 2010, https://www.ncbi.nlm
.nih.gov/pubmed/20856182.

5 Mark F. Lenzenweger, John F. Clarkin, Eve Caligor, Nicole M. Cain,
and Otto F. Kernberg, "Malignant Narcissism in Relation to Clinical
Change in Borderline Personality Disorder: An Exploratory Study,"
Psychopathology, U.S. National Library of Medicine, 2018, https://
www.ncbi.nlm.nih.gov/pubmed/30184541.

6 "Narcissistic Personality Disorder," HelpGuide.org, March 21, 2019,
https://www.helpguide.org/articles/mental-disorders/narcissistic
-personality-disorder.htm/.

7 Philip Zimbardo and Rosemary Sword, "Unbridled and Extreme
Present Hedonism," in Lee, Bandy X. *The Dangerous Case of Donald
Trump: 37 Psychiatrists and Mental Health Experts Assess a President:*

Updated and Expanded with New Essays {New York: Thomas Dunne Books, 2019).

8   *Master Speaks*, May 17, 1973 (a publication of Unification Church of transcribed speeches of Sun Myung Moon).

9   *Master Speaks*, March 24, 1974.

10 "Affidavit of Deborah Layton Blakey (Text)," Alternative Considerations of Jonestown Peoples Temple, accessed April 14, 2019, https://jonestown.sdsu.edu/?page_id=18599.

11 Aaron Blake, "19 Things Donald Trump Knows Better than Anyone Else, According to Donald Trump," *The Washington Post,* October 4, 2016, https://www.washingtonpost.com/news/the-fix/wp/2016/10/04/17-issues-that-donald-trump-knows-better-than-anyone-else-according-to-donald-trump/?noredirect=on&utm_term=.e1f1fe1e2498.

12 "Narcissistic Personality Disorder," HelpGuide.org, March 21, 2019, https://www.helpguide.org/articles/mental-disorders/narcissistic-personality-disorder.htm/.

13 Amy Zimmerman, "A Top NXIVM Sex Cult Recruiter Comes Forward, Says Founder 'Messed with the Wrong Person,'" *The Daily Beast,* May 27, 2018, https://www.thedailybeast.com/a-top-nxivm-sex-cult-recruiter-comes-forward-he-messed-with-the-wrong-person.

14 Jon Atack, personal interview, January 19, 2019.

15 Dominic Rushe, "'I'm Really Rich': Donald Trump Claims $9bn Fortune during Campaign Launch," *Guardian,* June 16, 2015, https://www.theguardian.com/us-news/2015/jun/16/donald-trump-reveals-net-worth-presidential-campaign-launch.

16 Ibid.

17 Leon F. Seltzer, "This Is What Really Makes Narcissists Tick," *Psychology Today*, accessed April 14, 2019, https://www.psychologytoday.com/us/blog/evolution-the-self/201507/is-what-really-makes-narcissists-tick.

18 "DSM-5: The Ten Personality Disorders: Cluster B," Mental Help DSM5: The Ten Personality Disorders Cluster B Comments, accessed April 14, 2019, https://www.mentalhelp.net/articles/dsm-5-the-ten-personality-disorders-cluster-b/.

19 Jodi M. Lane and Stephen Kent, "Malignant Narcissism, L. Ron Hubbard, and Scientology's Policies of Narcissistic Rage," Scientology Books and Media, June 18, 2014, *Scicrit*, https://scicrit.wordpress

.com/2014/06/18/malignant-narcissim-l-ron-hubbard-and-scientolo gys-policies-of-narcisstic-rage/.

20 "'Pawns of His Grandiosity': Molly Kronberg Tells How Lyndon LaRouche Controls His Cult," accessed April 14, 2019, http://www .lyndonlarouche.org/molly-kronberg.htm.

21 Lyndon LaRouche, *The Power of Reason*, self-published, 1988, p. 76.

22 Emily Jane Fox, "Michael Cohen Would Take a Bullet for Donald Trump," The Hive, *Vanity Fair,* September 6, 2017, https://www.vanity fair.com/news/2017/09/michael-cohen-interview-donald-trump.

23 Ian H. Robertson, "Personality and Potential Nuclear Confrontation," *Psychology Today,* accessed April 14, 2019, https://www.psychology today.com/us/blog/the-stress-test/201708/personality-and-potential -nuclear-confrontation.

24 Roxanne Roberts, "I Sat Next to Donald Trump at the Infamous 2011 White House Correspondents' Dinner," *The Washington Post,* April 28, 2016, https://www.washingtonpost.com/lifestyle/style/i-sat-next -to-donald-trump-at-the-infamous-2011-white-house-correspon dents-dinner/2016/04/27/5cf46b74-0bea-11e6-8ab8-9ad050f76d7d _story.html?utm_term=.91ec227df021.

25 Carolyn Banks, "Commentary: Why Trump Wants to Rid America of Any Trace of Obama," *Austin American-Statesman,* September 22, 2018, https://www.statesman.com/news/20171012/commentary -why-trump-wants-to-rid-america-of-any-trace-of-obama.

26 Jodi Lane and Stephen Kent, "Malignant Narcissism, L. Ron Hub- bard, and Scientology's Policies of Narcissistic Rage."

27 "Moon to Be Released From Danbury Prison," *The New York Times Archive,* July 3, 1985, https://www.nytimes.com/1985/07/03/nyregion /moon-to-be-released-from-danbury-prison.html.

28 Steve Reilly, "USA TODAY Exclusive: Hundreds Allege Donald Trump Doesn't Pay His Bills," *USA Today,* April 25, 2018, https:// www.usatoday.com/story/news/politics/elections/2016/06/09/donald -trump-unpaid-bills-republican-president-laswuits/85297274/.

29 Julie Bosman, Patricia Cohen, and Julie Turkewitz, "Federal Shut- down's Uneven Toll: Some Americans Are Devastated, Others Obliv- ious," *The New York Times,* January 11, 2019, https://www.nytimes .com/2019/01/11/business/federal-shutdown-divide.html.

30 Natasha Frost, "Trump's 'Jokes' About Blasey Ford Are an Attack,"

Quartz, October 3, 2018, https://qz.com/1411922/trumps-mockery
-of-christine-blasey-ford-is-a-strategic-attack/.

31 Tony Ortega, "Exclusive: The Rise and Fall of the 'Pope of
Scientology'—in His Own Words," *Underground Bunker*, June 5,
2018, https://tonyortega.org/2018/06/06/exclusive-the-rise-and-fall
-of-the-pope-of-scientology-in-his-own-words/.

32 "Trump's 'Dictator Envy' on Full Display in Latest Praise for Kim
Jong-Un," *South China Morning Post*, June 16, 2018, https://www
.scmp.com/news/world/united-states-canada/article/2151110/donald
-trumps-dictator-envy-full-display-latest.

33 Ian Schwartz, "Chuck Todd: Trump Has 'Elite Envy,'" *RealClear Politics*, accessed April 14, 2019. https://www.realclearpolitics.com/video
/2018/06/22/chuck_todd_trump_has_elite_envy.html.

34 Goldner-Vukov and Moore, "Malignant Narcissism."

35 Keith McMillan, "Trump Received 'Bone Spurs' Diagnosis as a 'Favor,'
Doctor's Daughters Allege," *The Washington Post*, December 26,
2018, https://www.washingtonpost.com/politics/2018/12/26/trump
-received-bone-spurs-diagnosis-favor-doctors-daughters-allege/?utm
_term=.39f13d7dad9f.

36 Angie Drobnic Holan, "Why Trump Is the Most Fact-Checked President," *Atlantic*, January 14, 2019, https://www.theatlantic.com
/politics/archive/2019/01/donald-trump-most-fact-checked-president
/579664/.

37 Paul Rosenberg, "Lies, Bulls**t and Gaslighting: A Field Guide to
Trump's Reality-Warping Mendacity," *Salon*, February 25, 2019,
https://www.salon.com/2019/02/24/lies-bullst-and-gaslighting-a
-field-guide-to-trumps-reality-warping-mendacity/.

38 Maggie Haberman and Benjamin Weiser, "Trump Persuaded Struggling People to Invest in Scams, Lawsuit Says," *The New York Times*,
October 29, 2018, https://www.nytimes.com/2018/10/29/nyregion
/trump-acn-lawsuit.html.

39 Dan Mangan, "New Lawsuit Accuses Trump and Three of His Children of Conning 'Thousands' of Americans in Marketing Ploy."
CNBC, October 29, 2018, https://www.cnbc.com/2018/10/29/trump
-accused-in-lawsuit-of-conning-thousands-of-americans.html.

40 Goldner-Vukov and Moore, "Malignant Narcissism."

41 David Corn, "If You Want to Understand Trump, Understand This:

Revenge Is What He Cares About Most," *Mother Jones,* January 30, 2018, https://www.motherjones.com/politics/2018/01/if-you-want-to -understand-trump-understand-this-revenge-is-what-he-cares-about -most/.

42 Chauncey DeVega, "Psychologist John Gartner on Trump's Behavior: 'It's a Coup That's Not Moving Slowly Anymore,'" *Salon,* June 13, 2018, https://www.salon.com/2018/06/13/psychologist-john-gartner -on-trumps-behavior-its-a-coup-thats-not-moving-slowly-anymore/.

43 Phil Mattingly and Eric Bradner, "Trump Picks Sessions for Attorney General," CNN, November 18, 2016, https://www.cnn.com /2016/11/17/politics/jeff-sessions-attorney-general-donald-trump -consideration/index.html.

44 ABC News, accessed April 14, 2019, https://abcnews.go.com/Politics /comey-opens-shocking-found-fired-trump/story?id=54486383.

45 Quint Forgey, Patrick Temple-West, and Caitlin Oprysko, "McCabe: 'I Was Fired Because I Opened a Case Against the President,'" *Politico Magazine,* February 18, 2019, https://www.politico.com/story/2019 /02/17/mccabe-fired-trump-fbi-1173596.

46 *United States District Court Central District Of California Rtc, .et al. Plaintiffs, vs. ROBIN SCOTT, et al., Defendants. RTC, et al. Plaintiffs, Vs. Larry Wollersheim, Defendants. (And Related Counter-Claims) No. Cv 85-711 Jmi (Bx) 1995.*

47 L. Ron Hubbard, "The Scientologist: A Manual on the Dissemination of Material," *Ability Magazine,* 1955.

48 Steve Cannane and Brigid Andersen, "How the Church of Scientology Tried to Bring Down Miss Lovely," ABC News, December 21, 2016, https://www.abc.net.au/news/2015-07-17/how-scientology-tried-to -bring-down-miss-lovely/6627782.

49 Nick Penzenstadler and Susan Page, "Exclusive: Trump's 3,500 Lawsuits Unprecedented for a Presidential Nominee." *USA Today,* October 23, 2017, https://www.usatoday.com/story/news/politics/elections /2016/06/01/donald-trump-lawsuits-legal-battles/84995854/.

50 Alexis Sachdev, "A Long List of Everyone Donald Trump Has Sued or Threatened to Sue." *Metro US,* March 23, 2017, https://www.metro .us/news/a-long-list-of-everyone-donald-trump-has-sued-or-threat ened-to-sue/zsJqcw—-MpxXnpvBtlilY.

51 Allan Tate Wood, "My Four and One Half Years with the Lord of

the Flies," accessed April 15, 2019, http://www.atwood7.com/essays/lordofflies.html.

52 Ibid.

53 Sarah Edmondson and Sarah Berman, "Why I Joined a Secret Society That Branded Me," *Vice,* November 3, 2017, https://www.vice.com/en_us/article/xwaaxd/why-i-joined-a-secret-society-that-branded-me.

54 Hava Dayan, "Sexual Abuse and Charismatic Cults," *Aggression and Violent Behavior*, Pergamon, April 21, 2018, https://www.sciencedirect.com/science/article/pii/S135917891730246X.

55 Steven Brocklehurst, "Children of God Cult Was 'Hell on Earth,'" BBC News, June 27, 2018, https://www.bbc.com/news/uk-scotland-44613932.

56 Butch Hayes, Robert Stahley, and Fritz Udiski, "View Miriam Hannon's Obituary on Citizensvoice.com and Share Memories," Miriam Hannon Obituary, Forty Fort, Pennsylvania, Citizens Voice, accessed April 15, 2019, http://www.legacy.com/obituaries/citizensvoice/obituary.aspx?pid=187603827.

57 Meg Kelly, "President Trump and Accusations of Sexual Misconduct: The Complete List," *Washington Post,* November 22, 2017, https://www.washingtonpost.com/news/fact-checker/wp/2017/11/22/president-trump-and-accusations-of-sexual-misconduct-the-complete-list/?utm_term=.3e46e518056b.

58 Jane Mayer, "Documenting Trump's Abuse of Women," *The New Yorker,* June 18, 2017, https://www.newyorker.com/magazine/2016/10/24/documenting-trumps-abuse-of-women.

59 Goldner-Vukov and Moore, "Malignant Narcissism."

60 Jamie Gangel and Dan Merica, "Bob Woodward's New Book Puts Readers 'Face to Face with Trump,'" CNN, July 30, 2018, https://www.cnn.com/2018/07/30/politics/woodward-new-book-trump/index.html.

61 Russell Miller, "Atlantic Crossing," *Bare-Faced Messiah*: Chapter 19, accessed April 15, 2019, https://www.cs.cmu.edu/~dst/Library/Shelf/miller/bfm19.htm.

62 Nina Burleigh, "In Newly Released Recordings, Trump Says He Groped Melania in Public and Ivanka Looks Down on Him," *Newsweek,* September 25, 2017, https://www.newsweek.com/trump-melania-ivanka-terrorists-howard-stern-670309.

63 Kate Taylor, "Trump Reportedly Loves McDonald's Because He Has a 'Longtime Fear' of Being Poisoned," *Business Insider,* June 25, 2018, https://www.businessinsider.com/trump-loves-mcdonalds-afraid-of-being-poisoned-2018-1.

64 Natasha Bach, "Trump Staff Turnover Hits 34%—a First Year Presidential Record," *Fortune,* accessed April 15, 2019, http://fortune.com/2017/12/28/trump-white-house-record-first-year-turnover-rate/.

65 Krysia Diverin Stuttgart, "Lost File Reveals Hitler's Paranoia," *The Guardian,* March 21, 2005, https://www.theguardian.com/world/2005/mar/21/books.secondworldwar.

66 Doug Peterson, "The Men Who Wouldn't Stop Clapping," History by the Slice, October 22, 2016, http://www.disappearingman.com/communism/men-wouldnt-stop-clapping/.

67 Tal Axelrod, "Former White House Aide Reveals Compiling of Trump 'Enemies List' in Memoir: Report." *The Hill,* January 18, 2019, https://thehill.com/homenews/administration/425978-former-white-house-aide-reveals-compiling-of-trump-enemies-list-in.

68 Bandy X. Lee, *The Dangerous Case of Donald Trump,* p. 60.

69 "Lyndon LaRouche, Perennial U.S. Presidential Candidate, Dies at 96," *Reuters,* February 14, 2019, https://www.reuters.com/article/us-people-larouche/lyndon-larouche-perennial-u-s-presidential-candidate-dies-at-96-idUSKCN1Q22Y5.

70 *The Washington Post,* accessed April 15, 2019, https://www.washingtonpost.com/wp-srv/national/longterm/cult/larouche/larou4.htm.

71 Hugh B. Urban, "Fair Game: Secrecy, Security, and the Church of Scientology in Cold War America," *Journal of the American Academy of Religion* 74, no. 2 (2006): 356–89, https://doi.org/10.1093/jaarel/lfj084.

72 Andreas Heldal-Lund, "Operation Clambake Present: The Scientology Fair Game Policy," accessed April 15, 2019, http://www.xenu.net/fairgame-e.html.

73 Clerk, "About SPDL," *Suppressive Person Defense League*, December 26, 1966, http://suppressiveperson.org/1966/12/26/hcopl-pts-sections-personnel-and-execs/.

74 "Statement of Angela Davis (Text)," Alternative Considerations of Jonestown Peoples Temple, accessed April 15, 2019, https://jonestown.sdsu.edu/?page_id=19027.

75　Goldner-Vukov and Moore, "Malignant Narcissism."

76　Ibid.

77　Tony Schwartz, "I Wrote 'The Art of the Deal' with Trump. His Self-Sabotage Is Rooted in His Past," *The Washington Post,* May 16, 2017, https://www.washingtonpost.com/posteverything/wp/2017/05/16 /i-wrote-the-art-of-the-deal-with-trump-his-self-sabotage-is-rooted -in-his-past/?utm_term=.01f6a548f115.

78　Sabrina Siddiqui, "Obama Speaks Out Against Trump and Attacks 'Politics of Fear and Resentment,'" *The Guardian,* September 7, 2018. https://www.theguardian.com/us-news/2018/sep/07/barack-obama -trump-illinois-dangerous-times.

CHAPTER FOUR: America: a Country Wired for Manipulation

1　Andrew Kragie, "The 7 Most Bewildering Moments From Trump's CPAC Speech," *The Atlantic,* March 3, 2019, https://www.theatlan tic.com/politics/archive/2019/03/president-trump-repeatedly-veered -off-script-cpac/584014/.

2　*Century of Self,* directed by Adam Curtis, BBC, 2002, YouTube, https://www.youtube.com/watch?v=eJ3RzGoQC4s.

3　"The Roar of a Bewildered Herd," *Historical Underbelly*, May 19, 2011, https://historicalunderbelly.wordpress.com/2011/05/19/the -roar-of-a-bewildered-herd/.

4　Edward L. Bernays, *Propaganda* (Brooklyn, N.Y.: Ig Publishing, 1928).

5　Theodor W. Adorno, *The Authoritarian Personality* (New York: Harper & Row, 1950).

6　Larry Tye, *The Father of Spin: Edward L. Bernays and the Birth of Public Relations* (New York: Henry Holt & Company, 1998).

7　Ynnor Mark, "Mind Control (ABC NEWS SPECIAL, 1979)," YouTube, January 2, 2013, https://www.youtube.com/watch?v=B6 5IgEjQie8.

8　Saul McLeod, "Saul McLeod," Asch Conformity Experiment, *Simply Psychology*, accessed April 15, 2019, https://www.simplypsychology .org/asch-conformity.html.

9　Daniel T. Gilbert and Patrick S. Malone, "The Correspondence Bias," *Psychological Bulletin* 117, no. 1 (1995): 21–38, https://doi.org /10.1037//0033-2909.117.1.21.

10 Leon Festinger, Henry W. Riecken, and Stanley Schachter, *When Prophecy Fails: A Social and Psychological Study of a Modern Group That Predicted the Destruction of the World* (Mansfield Centre, CT: Martino, 2012).

11 Linda Qiu, "The Many Ways Trump Has Said Mexico Will Pay for the Wall," *The New York Times*, January 11, 2019, https://www.nytimes .com/2019/01/11/us/politics/trump-mexico-pay-wall.html.

12 Omarosa Manigault Newman, personal communication, February 2, 2019.

13 Milton H. Erickson, M.D., and Ernest L. Rossi, Ph.D., "Varieties of Double Bind," *American Journal of Clinical Hypnosis* 17, no. 3 (1975): 143–57, doi: 10.1080/00029157.1975.10403733.

14 Holly Rosenkrantz, "DeSantis Says Trump Is a Role Model for Children Because He Keeps His Promises," CBS News, October 22, 2018, https://www.cbsnews.com/news/desantis-says-donald-trump-is-a -role-model-for-children-because-he-keeps-his-promises/.

15 Nancy Cook, Ben Schreckinger, and Nahal Toosi, "How Frank Luntz Went from Trump Enemy to White House Insider," *Politico Magazine*, March 27, 2019, https://www.politico.com/story/2019/03/27 /frank-luntz-trump-white-house-1238283.

16 "A Rigorous Scientific Look into The 'Fox News Effect,'" *Forbes*, July 21, 2016, https://www.forbes.com/sites/quora/2016/07/21/a-rigorous -scientific-look-into-the-fox-news-effect/#15374ed512ab.

17 Jon Simpson, "Finding Brand Success in the Digital World," *Forbes*, August 25, 2017, https://www.forbes.com/sites/forbesagencycouncil /2017/08/25/finding-brand-success-in-the-digital-world/#6f17a2036.

18 Gallup Inc., "In U.S., 40% Get Less Than Recommended Amount of Sleep," Gallup.com, December 19, 2013, https://news.gallup.com /poll/166553/less-recommended-amount-sleep.aspx.

19 Paul Alhola and Päivi Polo-Kantola, "Sleep Deprivation: Impact on Cognitive Performance," *Neuropsychiatric Disease and Treatment*, Dove Medical Press, October 2007, https://www.ncbi.nlm.nih.gov /pmc/articles/PMC2656292/.

20 Hilarie Cash, Cosette D. Rae, Ann H. Steel, and Alexander Winkler, "Internet Addiction: A Brief Summary of Research and Practice," *Current Psychiatry Reviews*, Bentham Science Publishers, November 2012, https://www.ncbi.nlm.nih.gov/pmc/articles/PMC3480687/.

21 Quentin Fottrell, "People Spend Most of Their Waking Hours Staring at Screens," *MarketWatch*, August 4, 2018, https://www.marketwatch .com/story/people-are-spending-most-of-their-waking-hours-staring -at-screens-2018-08-01.

22 "Facebook Addiction: An Emerging Problem," *American Journal of Psychiatry Residents' Journal*, accessed April 15, 2019, https://ajp.psy chiatryonline.org/doi/10.1176/appi.ajp-rj.2016.111203.

23 Mark Molloy, "Facebook Addiction 'Activates Same Part of the Brain as Cocaine,'" *The Telegraph*, February 17, 2016, https://www.telegraph .co.uk/news/12161461/Facebook-addiction-activates-same-part-of -the-brain-as-cocaine.html.

24 Cal Newport, "Is Email Making Professors Stupid?" chronicle .com, February 2, 2019, https://www.chronicle.com/interactives /is-email-making-professors-stupid.

25 Rob Price, "Apple CEO Tim Cook: I Don't Want My Nephew on a Social Network," *Business Insider*, January 19, 2018, https://www .businessinsider.com/apple-ceo-tim-cook-doesnt-let-nephew-use-so cial-media-2018-1.

26 Martin H. Teicher, "Wounds That Time Won't Heal: The Neurobiol- ogy of Child Abuse," *Cerebrum* 2, no. 4 (Fall 2000).

CHAPTER FIVE: The Persuasiveness of Trump

1 Scott Adams, "The Creator of Dilbert Explains Trump's Persuasion Style and Reminds Us Why People Stopped Caring About Facts," *Business Insider*, November 1, 2017, https://www.businessinsider.com /dilbert-creator-scott-adams-explains-trumps-persuasion-style-2017 -10.

2 Iain McGilchrist, *The Master and His Emissary: The Divided Brain and the Making of the Western World* (New Haven, CT: Yale Univer- sity Press, 2019).

3 Andre Bermont, "Trump's First Year Ends in Twice as Many Mass Shootings Than Obama's!" *Global Research*, February 21, 2018, https://www.globalresearch.ca/trumps-first-year-ends-in-twice-as -many-mass-shootings-than-obamas/5629856.

4 Melia Robinson and Skye Gould. "There Have Been 307 Mass Shoot- ings in the US so Far in 2018—Here's the Full List," *Business Insider*,

November 8, 2018, https://www.businessinsider.com/how-many
-mass-shootings-in-america-this-year-2018-2.

5 James H. Stewart, "Hypnosis in Contemporary Medicine," *Mayo
Clinic Proceedings* 80, no. 4 (April 2005): 511–24.

6 Tim Hains, "Full Replay: President Trump Holds 2020 Campaign Rally
in El Paso, Texas," *RealClear Politics*, accessed April 15, 2019, https://
www.realclearpolitics.com/video/2019/02/11/watch_live_president
_trump_holds_2020_campaign_rally_in_el_paso_texas.html#!.

7 Alayna Treene and Jonathan Swan, "One of Trump's Favorite Compliments Is Telling Powerful Men How Handsome They Are," *Axios*,
February 3, 2019, https://www.axios.com/trump-compliments-pow
erful-men-handsome-45fd6634-e97d-4a3f-9133-266efdf492be
.html.

8 Steven Hassan, *Combating Cult Mind Control,* 4th ed. (Newton, MA:
Freedom of Mind Press, 2018), p. 71.

9 Gabriel Thompson, "David Cay Johnston on the Trump We Don't
Know," *Capital & Main*, February 8, 2018, https://capitalandmain
.com/david-cay-johnston-on-the-trump-we-dont-know-0206.

10 "What Is NLP," accessed March 15, 2019, http://www.nlp.com
/whatisnlp.php.

11 Jon Atack, "'Never Believe a Hypnotist,'" Hubbard on Hypnosis, accessed April 15, 2019, http://home.snafu.de/tilman/j/hypnosis.html.

12 Jon Atack, *Let's Sell These People a Piece of Blue Sky: Hubbard, Dianetics and Scientology* (Colchester, Eng.: Richard Woods, 2013).

13 *Mind Control with Derren Brown*, Syfy Channel, 2007.

14 Derren Brown, "Derren Discusses the Assassin," September 16, 2012,
http://derrenbrown.co.uk/derren-discusses-assassin/.

15 "Coaching NLP Training," YouTube, accessed April 20, 2019, https://
www.youtube.com/user/coachingnlptraining/about.

16 Adrian Iacob, "Bill Clinton About Tony Robbins," YouTube, February
8, 2016. https://www.youtube.com/watch?v=jImh3dZ2k4A.

17 Marlow Stern, "Tony Robbins on the Key Differences Between His Pals
Hillary Clinton and Donald Trump," *The Daily Beast,* August 20, 2016,
https://www.thedailybeast.com/tony-robbins-on-the-key-differences
-between-his-pals-hillary-clinton-and-donald-trump.

18 TranceNet: TM Secret Teachings, accessed April 15, 2019, http://
minet.org/www.trancenet.net/secrets/index.shtml.

19   "Critically Examining Transcendental Meditation and the Programs
     Associated with Maharishi Mahesh Yogi," *Meditation Information
     Network*, accessed April 15, 2019, http://www.minet.org/Documents
     /shank-5.

20   Steve Phillips, "Trump Wants to Make America White Again," *The
     New York Times,* February 15, 2018, https://www.nytimes.com/2018
     /02/15/opinion/trump-wants-to-make-america-white-again.html.

21   Kayla Epstein, "Trump Responds to Megyn Kelly's Questions on
     Misogyny—with More Misogyny," *The Guardian*, August 7, 2015,
     https://www.theguardian.com/us-news/2015/aug/06/donald-trump
     -misogyny-republican-debate-megyn-kelly.

22   Ben Mathis-Lilley, "Trump Has Retweeted at Least Four White Nation-
     alist Accounts That Were Later Suspended," *Slate,* March 18, 2019,
     https://slate.com/news-and-politics/2019/03/trump-white-nationalist
     -accounts-suspended-retweets.html.

23   "Power of Donald Trump's Narrative Intuition & How He Beat Hil-
     lary Clinton," *Business of Story*, Storytelling Strategy, Workshops &
     Keynotes, accessed April 15, 2019, https://businessofstory.com/podcast
     /brander-chief-dr-randy-olson-explains-power-trumps-narrative-intuition/.

24   Chris Cillizza, "3 Theories on Why Donald Trump's Lies Don't Seem
     to Faze Him (or His Supporters)," CNN, April 3, 2019, https://www
     .cnn.com/2019/04/03/politics/donald-trump-lies-reasons/index.html.

25   "Danny Masterson Tells Us About His Life in the Church of Scientol-
     ogy," *Paper*, July 16, 2018, http://www.papermag.com/danny-master
     son-tells-us-about-his-life-in-the-church-of-scientology-1427506335
     .html.

26   Chris Baynes, "Trump Yanked around by Portuguese President during
     Vigorous Handshake," *The Independent,* June 29, 2018, https://www
     .independent.co.uk/news/world/americas/trump-handshake-portugal
     -president-rebelo-de-sousa-white-house-a8422741.html.

27   Charisma on Command, "Donald Trump's Debates: 5 Mental Tricks
     You Didn't Notice," YouTube, February 8, 2016, https://www.youtube
     .com/watch?v=9LR6EA91zLo.

28   Donald Trump, "Did Hillary Clinton Start the Obama Birther Move-
     ment?" *Politifact*, September 16, 2016, https://www.politifact.com
     /truth-o-meter/statements/2015/sep/23/donald-trump/hillary-clinton
     -obama-birther-fact-check/.

29   Peter Beinart, "Why Does Trump Accuse Others of the Things He Does Himself?" *The Atlantic,* July 14, 2017, https://www.theatlantic.com /politics/archive/2017/07/the-success-of-smoke-and-mirrors/533706/.

30   "The Projector in Chief," *Psychology Today,* accessed April 15, 2019, https://www.psychologytoday.com/us/blog/freud-lives/201807/the -projector-in-chief.

31   Gregory Krieg and Daniella Diaz, "Donald Trump vs. Hillary Clinton II: The Nastiest Lines," CNN, October 10, 2016, https://www.cnn .com/2016/10/10/politics/presidential-debate-donald-trump-hillary -clinton-quotes/index.html.

32   Richard Wolffe, "The Only Thing Trump Seems to Fear Is Running Out of Fear Itself," *The Guardian*, November 3, 2018, https://www .theguardian.com/commentisfree/2018/nov/03/donald-trump-mid terms-fear-immigration-fox-news.

33   "Remarks by President Trump at a California Sanctuary State Roundta- ble," White House, United States Government, accessed April 15, 2019, https://www.whitehouse.gov/briefings-statements/remarks-president -trump-california-sanctuary-state-roundtable/.

34   Richard E. Petty and John T. Cacioppo, "Source Factors and the Elab- oration Likelihood Model of Persuasion," in *Advances in Consumer Research,* vol. 11, ed. Thomas C. Kinnear (Provo, UT: Association for Consumer Research, 1984), pp. 668–72.

35   Sean Rossman, "Trump's Repetitive Rhetoric Is a Trick Used in Ad- vertising," *USA Today,* February 17, 2017, https://www.usatoday.com /story/news/politics/onpolitics/2017/02/16/mess-fake-news-disaster -trumps-repetition-advertising-tactic/98014444/.

36   ABC News, accessed April 15, 2019, https://abcnews.go.com/beta -story-container/Politics/president-trump-called-smart-six-times-be fore/story?id=52209712.

37   Nicole Ernst, Rinaldo Kühne, and Werner Wirth, "Effects of Message Repetition and Negativity on Credibility Judgments and Political At- titudes," *International Journal of Communication,* accessed April 15, 2019, https://ijoc.org/index.php/ijoc/article/view/6506.

38   Jason Hreha, "How Donald Trump Won," *Medium,* May 25, 2016, https://medium.com/@jhreha/trumpsuasion-the-donald-trump-per suasion-manual-9173129a7529.

39   Steven Hassan, *Combating Cult Mind Control,* p. 80.

40   Laurie Hanna, "Ohio Attorney Accused of Hypnotizing Female Clients to Perform Sex Acts Now Charged with Rape and Sexual Assault," *New York Daily News,* April 9, 2018, https://www.nydailynews.com /news/national/ohio-lawyer-hypnotized-women-charged-rape-article -1.2348477.

41   "Attorney to Pay Multi-Million Dollar Judgement after Hypnotizing Clients to Take Advantage of Them Sexually," *fox8.com*, October 13, 2018, https://fox8.com/2018/10/12/attorney-to-pay-multi-million-dollar-judge ment-after-hypnotizing-clients-to-take-advantage-of-them-sexually/.

42   Robin Goist, "Disbarred Sheffield Attorney to Pay Multimillion-Dollar Judgment after Hypnotizing Clients for Sexual Pleasure," *cleveland .com*, October 17, 2018, https://www.cleveland.com/crime/2018/10 /disbarred_avon_attorney_to_pay.html.

CHAPTER SIX: The Media

1   Katie Rogers and Ron Nixon, "A Border Patrol Agent (and Frequent Fox News Guest) Has Trump's Ear on Immigration," *The New York Times,* April 2, 2018, https://www.nytimes.com/2018/04/02/us/politics /border-patrol-trump-brandon-judd-fox.html.

2   Jane Mayer, "The Making of the Fox News White House," *The New Yorker,* March 20, 2019, https://www.newyorker.com/magazine/2019 /03/11/the-making-of-the-fox-news-white-house.

3   Jessica Estepa, "Report: President Trump and Sean Hannity Talk Nearly Every Weeknight," *USA Today,* May 14, 2018, https://www.usatoday .com/story/news/politics/onpolitics/2018/05/14/donald-trump-sean -hannity-speak-nearly-every-weeknight-report/607595002.

4   Marlow Stern, "Dan Rather: Fox News 'Closest We've Come to State-Run Media,'" *The Daily Beast,* March 22, 2019, https://www.the dailybeast.com/dan-rather-sounds-off-on-fox-news-the-closest-weve -come-to-state-run-media.

5   Collins, Eliza. "Les Moonves: Trump's Run Is 'Damn Good for CBS.'" *Politico Magazine*, February 29, 2016. https://www.politico .com/blogs/on-media/2016/02/les-moonves-trump-cbs-220001.

6   David Greenberg, "How Teddy Roosevelt Invented Spin," *The Atlantic,* January 24, 2016, https://www.theatlantic.com/politics/archive /2016/01/how-teddy-roosevelt-invented-spin/426699/.

7 Christopher B. Daly, "How Woodrow Wilson's Propaganda Machine Changed American Journalism," The Conversation, January 28, 2019, http://theconversation.com/how-woodrow-wilsons-propaganda-machine-changed-american-journalism-76270.

8 Ibid.

9 Jon Meacham, "Why Trump Is More Father Coughlin than Franklin Roosevelt," The New York Times, May 3, 2018, https://www.nytimes.com/2018/05/03/opinion/trump-father-coughlin-roosevelt.html.

10 Adrienne LaFrance, "Donald Trump Is Testing Twitter's Harassment Policy," The Atlantic, July 3, 2017, https://www.theatlantic.com/politics/archive/2017/07/the-president-of-the-united-states-is-testing-twitters-harassment-policy/532497/.

11 Alfred McClung Lee and Elizabeth Briant Lee. The Fine Art of Propaganda: A Study of Father Coughlin's Speeches (New York: Harcourt, Brace, 1939).

12 Federal Communications Commission. "FCC Reports, Volume 8, March 1, 1940 to August 1, 1941," Digital Library, U.S. Government Printing Office, August 18, 2013, https://digital.library.unt.edu/ark:/67531/metadc177289/m1/358/.

13 Thomas J. Houser, "Fairness Doctrine—An Historical Perspective," Notre Dame Law Review 42, no. 3, article 4. February 1, 1972.

14 "In the Matter of Editorializing by Broadcast Licensees 1949," Scribd, accessed April 15, 2019, https://www.scribd.com/document/385901903/In-the-Matter-of-Editorializing-by-Broadcast-Licensees-1949.

15 Penny Pagano, "Reagan's Veto Kills Fairness Doctrine Bill," Los Angeles Times, June 21, 1987, https://www.latimes.com/archives/la-xpm-1987-06-21-mn-8908-story.html.

16 Jonathan Mahler and Jim Rutenberg, "How Rupert Murdoch's Empire of Influence Remade the World," The New York Times, April 3, 2019, https://www.nytimes.com/interactive/2019/04/03/magazine/rupert-murdoch-fox-news-trump.html.

17 Pov, "Overview: The Rise of Talk Radio," POV, January 18, 2005, http://archive.pov.org/thefirenexttime/overview-the-rise-of-talk-radio/.

18 David Foster Wallace, "Host," Atlantic, March 15, 2019, https://www.theatlantic.com/magazine/archive/2005/04/host/303812/.

19   Michael D'Antonio and Peter Eisner, *The Shadow President: The Truth About Mike Pence* (New York: Thomas Dunne Books, 2018).

20   Keith Doherty, "Vice President Pence Talks to Rush About the Crisis at the Border," *The Rush Limbaugh Show,* January 9, 2019, https://www.rushlimbaugh.com/daily/2019/01/09/vice-president-pence-talks-to-rush-about-the-crisis-at-the-border/.

21   John MacArthur, "Unholy Trinity: Outraged at TBN's Brazen False Teaching," *Crosswalk.com*, February 24, 2010, https://www.crosswalk.com/faith/spiritual-life/unholy-trinity-outraged-at-tbns-brazen-false-teaching-11626683.html.

22   "FAQ," *TBN*, accessed April 15, 2019, https://www.tbn.org/about/faq.

23   Melanie McFarland, "Master Deceivers: When Roger Ailes Met Richard Nixon," *Salon,* May 19, 2017, https://www.salon.com/2017/05/18/master-deceivers-when-roger-ailes-met-richard-nixon/.

24   Ibid.

25   Gabriel Sherman, *The Loudest Voice in the Room: How the Brilliant, Bombastic Roger Ailes Built Fox News—and Divided a Country* (New York: Random House, 2017).

26   Dan Friedman et al., "Roger Stone Is Relying on a Debunked Conspiracy Theory to Fight His Criminal Case," *Mother Jones*, May 16, 2019. https://www.motherjones.com/politics/2019/05/roger-stone-is-relying-on-a-debunked-conspiracy-theory-to-fight-his-criminal-case/.

27   Tim Dickinson, "Roger Ailes' Keys to Campaign Success: 'Pictures, Mistakes and Attacks,'" *Rolling Stone,* June 25, 2018, https://www.rollingstone.com/politics/politics-news/roger-ailes-keys-to-campaign-success-pictures-mistakes-and-attacks-235990/.

28   Jeff Guo, "What Roger Ailes Did to America," *Vox*, May 19, 2017, https://www.vox.com/2017/5/19/15660888/roger-ailes-america-trump-television-fox-news.

29   Tim Dickinson, "How Roger Ailes Built the Fox News Fear Factory," *Rolling Stone,* June 25, 2018, https://www.rollingstone.com/politics/politics-news/how-roger-ailes-built-the-fox-news-fear-factory-244652/.

30   A. J. Katz, "2018 Ratings: Fox News Is the Most-Watched Network on Cable for the Third Straight Year," *TVNewser*, January 2, 2019, https://www.adweek.com/tvnewser/2018-ratings-fox-news-is-the-most-watched-network-on-cable-for-the-third-straight-year/387943.

31 Carolyn E. Schmitt, "'Network Propaganda' Takes a Closer Look at Media and American Politics," *The Harvard Gazette,* October 26, 2018, https://news.harvard.edu/gazette/story/2018/10/network-propaganda-takes-a-closer-look-at-media-and-american-politics/.

32 Jack Nicas, "Alex Jones Said Bans Would Strengthen Him. He Was Wrong," *The New York Times,* September 4, 2018, https://www.nytimes.com/2018/09/04/technology/alex-jones-infowars-bans-traffic.html.

33 Eric Killelea, "Alex Jones' Mis-Infowars: 7 Bat-Sh*t Conspiracy Theories," *Rolling Stone,* June 25, 2018, https://www.rollingstone.com/culture/culture-lists/alex-jones-mis-infowars-7-bat-sht-conspiracy-theories-195468/.

34 Aja Romano, "Apple's Infowars Ban Altered an Industry Overnight—and Dealt a Blow Against Fake News," *Vox,* August 6, 2018, https://www.vox.com/policy-and-politics/2018/8/6/17655516/infowars-ban-apple-youtube-facebook-spotify.

35 Killelea, "Alex Jones' Mis-Infowars."

36 Elizabeth Williamson, "How Alex Jones and Infowars Helped a Florida Man Torment Sandy Hook Families," *The New York Times,* March 29, 2019, https://www.nytimes.com/2019/03/29/us/politics/alex-jones-infowars-sandy-hook.html.

37 Michael Gold and Tyler Pager, "Sandy Hook Victim's Father Dies in Apparent Suicide in Newtown," *The New York Times,* March 25, 2019, https://www.nytimes.com/2019/03/25/nyregion/sandy-hook-father.html.

38 Sarah Posner, Kevin Drum, Hannah Levintova, Oliver Milman, James West, and Rosa Furneaux, "How Donald Trump's Campaign Chief Created an Online Haven for White Nationalists," *Mother Jones,* June 23, 2017, https://www.motherjones.com/politics/2016/08/stephen-bannon-donald-trump-alt-right-breitbart-news/.

39 Timothy B. Lee, "This Video of Ronald Reagan Shows How Much the Republican Party Has Changed on Immigration," *Vox,* January 29, 2017, https://www.vox.com/2017/1/29/14429368/reagan-bush-immigration-attitude.

40 Mark Achbar, *Manufacturing Consent: Noam Chomsky and the Media* (New York: Black Rose Books, 1995).

41 Noam Chomsky, "Noam Chomsky: The Five Filters of the Mass

Media," Public Reading Rooms, June 13, 2018, https://prruk.org/noam
-chomsky-the-five-filters-of-the-mass-media-machine/.

42 Wallace, "Host."

43 WebFX, "The 6 Companies That Own (Almost) All Media [Info-
graphic]," *WebFX*, July 7, 2015, https://www.webfx.com/data/the-6
-companies-that-own-almost-all-media/.

44 "Clear Channel Communications," *SourceWatch*, accessed April
15, 2019, https://www.sourcewatch.org/index.php/Clear_Channel
_Communications.

45 "Sinclair Broadcast Group," SourceWatch, accessed April 15, 2019,
https://www.sourcewatch.org/index.php/Sinclair_Broadcast_Group.

46 "Telecommunications Act of 1996," Federal Communications Commission, December 30, 2014, https://www.fcc.gov/general/telecom
munications-act-1996.

47 Ibid.

48 Jacey Fortin and Jonah Engel Bromwich, "Sinclair Made Dozens of
Local News Anchors Recite the Same Script," *The New York Times,*
April 2, 2018, https://www.nytimes.com/2018/04/02/business/media
/sinclair-news-anchors-script.html.

49 Rebecca Savransky, "Dan Rather Rips Sinclair over Media Bias Promo:
It's Not Journalism, It's Propaganda," *The Hill*, April 3, 2018, https://
thehill.com/homenews/media/381409-dan-rather-rips-sinclair-over
-media-bias-promos-its-not-journalism-its.

50 Ibid.

51 Michael Farrell, "Tribune Media Shareholders Approve Nexstar
Deal," *Broadcasting & Cable,* March 12, 2019, https://www.broad
castingcable.com/news/tribune-media-shareholders-approve-nexstar
-deal.

52 Alexis C. Madrigal, "When Did TV Watching Peak?" *Atlantic,* May
30, 2018, https://www.theatlantic.com/technology/archive/2018/05
/when-did-tv-watching-peak/561464/.

53 Frederick Clarkson, "Behind the Times." *FAIR*, August 1, 1987.
https://fair.org/extra/behind-the-times/.

54 Alex Shephard, "Fox News Is Officially Trump TV," *The New Republic,* November 6, 2018, https://newrepublic.com/minutes/152050/fox
-news-officially-trump-tv.

55 "Fox News Drops 'Fair and Balanced' Slogan Without Announcement,"

BBC News, June 15, 2017, https://www.bbc.com/news/world-us
-canada-40289497.

56 Alex Shephard, "Fox News Is Officially Trump TV," *The New Republic*, November 6, 2018, https://newrepublic.com/minutes/152050
/fox-news-officially-trump-tv.

57 Mayer, "The Making of the Fox News White House."

58 Dorothy Wickenden, "Jane Mayer on the Revolving Door Between Fox News and the White House," *The New Yorker*, March 8, 2019, https://www.newyorker.com/podcast/political-scene/jane-mayer-on
-the-revolving-door-between-fox-news-and-the-white-house.

59 Jeet Heer, "The Breitbartization of Fox News," *The New Republic*, March 22, 2018, https://newrepublic.com/article/147605/breitbarti
zation-fox-news.

CHAPTER SEVEN: The Influencers

1 Tom McCarthy, "Trump's Cabinet Picks: Here Are All of the Appointments So Far," *The Guardian,* January 3, 2017, https://www.the
guardian.com/us-news/2016/dec/09/donald-trump-administration
-cabinet-picks-so-far.

2 William S. Lind, "The Changing Face of War: Into the Fourth Generation," *Lind*, accessed April 19, 2019, https://globalguerrillas.typepad
.com/lind/the-changing-face-of-war-into-the-fourth-generation.html.

3 James Scaminaci III, "Battle Without Bullets: The Christian Right and Fourth Generation Warfare," *The Public Eye*, summer 2017, https://
www.politicalresearch.org/2017/08/16/battle-without-bullets-the
-christian-right-and-fourth-generation-warfare.

4 Frederick Clarkson, "A Manual to Restore a Christian Nation That Never Was," *The Public Eye*, winter 2018, https://www.politicalre
search.org/2018/01/19/a-manual-to-restore-a-christian-nation-that
-never-was/.

5 Jon Wiener, "Jane Mayer: Dark Money and Donald Trump," *The Nation,* February 22, 2017, https://www.thenation.com/article/jane
-mayer-dark-money-and-donald-trump/.

6 Jane Mayer, "How Russia Helped Swing the Election for Trump," *The New Yorker,* September 24, 2018, https://www.newyorker.com/maga
zine/2018/10/01/how-russia-helped-to-swing-the-election-for-trump.

7 Ibid.

8 Tim Hains, "Malcolm Nance: Russians 'Hacked the Mindset of the American People,' Could Throw 2018 Midterms Into Doubt," *Real-Clear Politics*, accessed April 20, 2019, https://www.realclearpolitics .com/video/2018/02/07/malcolm_nance_russians_hacked_the_mind set_of_the_american_people.html.

9 Will Bunch, "This Prominent Penn Prof Didn't Believe Russia Got Trump Elected. Here's What Changed Her Mind," *The Philadelphia Inquirer,* October 9, 2018, https://www.philly.com/philly/columnists /will_bunch/trump-won-2016-election-russian-hacking-kathleen -hall-jamieson-book-20181009.html.

10 Kathleen Hall Jamieson, *Cyberwar: How Russian Hackers and Trolls Helped Elect a President: What We Don't, Can't, and Do Know* (New York: Oxford University Press, 2018).

11 Jane Mayer, "How Russia Helped Swing the Election for Trump."

12 Martin Matishak, Andrew Restuccia, Louis Nelson, and Eric Geller, "What We Know About Russia's Election Hacking," *Politico Magazine,* July 19, 2018, https://www.politico.com/story/2018/07/18/russia -election-hacking-trump-putin-698087.

13 Julia Manchester, "Author: Clinton's Loss in Wisconsin Emblematic of Dem Party's 'Abandonment' of Working Class," *The Hill,* July 27, 2018, https://thehill.com/hilltv/rising/399167-author-clintons -loss-in-wisconsin-emblematic-of-dem-partys-abandonment-of.

14 Gabriel Debenedetti, Glenn Thrush, Kyle Cheney, and Seung Min Kim, "How Clinton Lost Michigan—and Blew the Election," *Politico Magazine,* December 14, 2016, https://www.politico.com/story/2016 /12/michigan-hillary-clinton-trump-232547.

15 Noah Bookbinder, "Mueller's Damning Report," *The New York Times,* April 18, 2019, https://www.nytimes.com/2019/04/18/opinion /mueller-report-trump.html.

16 Rachel Frazin, "Fox's Napolitano: Mueller Report 'Might Be Enough to Prosecute' Trump," *The Hill,* April 19, 2019, https://thehill.com /homenews/media/439770-foxs-napolitano-mueller-report-might-be -enough-to-prosecute-trump.

17 DOJ Alumni. "Statement by Former Federal Prosecutors." *Medium,* May 6, 2019. https://medium.com/@dojalumni/statement-by-for mer-federal-prosecutors-8ab7691c2aa1.

18 Andrew Prokop, "All of Robert Mueller's Indictments and Plea Deals in the Russia Investigation," *Vox*, March 22, 2019, https://www.vox.com/policy-and-politics/2018/2/20/17031772/mueller-indictments-grand-jury.

19 Luke Harding et al., "The Hidden History of Trump's First Trip to Moscow," *Politico Magazine*, November 19, 2017, http://www.politico.com/magazine/story/2017/11/19/trump-first-moscow-trip-215842.

20 Ilan Ben-Meir, "That Time Trump Spent Nearly $100,000 on an Ad Criticizing U.S. Foreign Policy in 1987," *BuzzFeed News*, January 12, 2019, https://www.buzzfeednews.com/article/ilanbenmeir/that-time-trump-spent-nearly-100000-on-an-ad-criticizing-us#.xvmvrrMvE.

21 Michael Kruse et al., "The True Story of Donald Trump's First Campaign Speech—in 1987," *Politico Magazine*, February 5, 2016, https://www.politico.com/magazine/story/2016/02/donald-trump-first-campaign-speech-new-hampshire-1987-213595.

22 Michael Hirsh, "How Russian Money Helped Save Trump's Business," *Foreign Policy*, December 21, 2018, https://foreignpolicy.com/2018/12/21/how-russian-money-helped-save-trumps-business/.

23 Ibid.

24 David Frum, "The Crisis Facing America," *The Atlantic*, September 4, 2018, https://www.theatlantic.com/ideas/archive/2018/07/trump-putin/565310/.

25 Commonwealth Club, "Malcolm Nance: How Russia Is Destroying Democracy," YouTube, July 11, 2018, https://www.youtube.com/watch?v=QnefEDB8ig4.

26 Sophie Tatum, "Trump Defends Putin: 'You Think Our Country's So Innocent?'" CNN, February 6, 2017, https://www.cnn.com/2017/02/04/politics/donald-trump-vladimir-putin/index.html.

27 Zack Beauchamp, "Trump's Republican Party, Explained in One Photo," *Vox*, August 6, 2018, https://www.vox.com/policy-and-politics/2018/8/6/17656996/trump-republican-party-russia-rather-democrat-ohio.

28 Tara Isabella Burton, "The Biblical Story the Christian Right Uses to Defend Trump," Vox, March 5, 2018, https://www.vox.com/identities/2018/3/5/16796892/trump-cyrus-christian-right-bible-cbn-evangelical-propaganda.

29   Hemant Mehta, "'My Pillow' Guy at CPAC: Donald Trump Is the Best Because He 'Was Chosen by God,'" Friendly Atheist, accessed April 20, 2019, https://friendlyatheist.patheos.com/2019/02/28/my-pillow -guy-at-cpac-donald-trump-is-the-best-because-he-was-chosen-by-god/.

30   Kate Sullivan, "Sarah Sanders: God 'Wanted Donald Trump to Become President,'" CNN, January 31, 2019, https://www.cnn.com /2019/01/30/politics/sarah-sanders-god-trump/index.html.

31   National Council of Churches, accessed April 20, 2019, https://na tionalcouncilofchurches.us/.

32   Bill Berkowitz, "Christian Dominionists Meet at Trump's Washington Hotel to Answer the 'Divine Call to War,'" Truthout, March 9, 2018, https://truthout.org/articles/christian-dominionists-meet-at-trump-s -washington-hotel-to-answer-the-divine-call-to-war/.

33   Frederick Clarkson, "Dominionism Rising: A Theocratic Movement Hiding in Plain Sight," The Public Eye, summer 2016, https:// www.politicalresearch.org/2016/08/18/dominionism-rising-a-theo cratic-movement-hiding-in-plain-sight/.

34   Tara Isabella Burton, "How the National Prayer Breakfast Offers Foreign Lobbyists a Chance to 'Pay to Play,'" Vox, July 30, 2018, https://www .vox.com/2018/7/18/17586516/jeff-sharlet-maria-butina-national -prayer-breakfast-the-family.

35   Heather Timmons, "The Three Ultra-Rich Families Battling for Control of the Republican Party," Quartz, November 16, 2018, https:// qz.com/1085077/mercers-vs-kochs-vs-adelsons-the-three-ultra-rich -families-battling-for-control-of-the-republican-party/.

36   Kenneth P. Vogel and Elizabeth Dias, "At Prayer Breakfast, Guests Seek Access to a Different Higher Power," The New York Times, July 27, 2018, https://www.nytimes.com/2018/07/27/us/politics/national -prayer-breakfast.html.

37   "The History of the National Prayer Breakfast," Smithsonian Institution, accessed April 20, 2019, https://www.smithsonianmag.com/history /national-prayer-breakfast-what-does-its-history-reveal-180962017/.

38   Jeff Sharlet et al., "Jesus plus Nothing," Harper's Magazine, March 1, 2003, https://harpers.org/archive/2003/03/jesus-plus-nothing/.

39   Editorial Staff, "DC's 'Invisible Army' for Christ," July 23, 2009, The Week, https://theweek.com/articles/503433/dcs-invisible-army-christ.

40   Jeff Sharlet and Kathryn Joyce, "Hillary's Prayer: Hillary Clinton

and Politics," *Mother Jones*, September 1, 2007. https://www.mother
jones.com/politics/2007/09/hillarys-prayer-hillary-clintons-religion
-and-politics/.

41 Sharlet et al., "Jesus plus Nothing."

42 Ibid.

43 "The Secret Political Reach of 'The Family,'" NPR, November 24,
2009, https://www.npr.org/templates/transcript/transcript.php?story
Id=120746516.

44 "The 10 Best Members of Congress: Text Only Version," *Esquire*,
October 11, 2017, https://www.esquire.com/news-politics/a5110
/10-best-members-congress-text/.

45 Jonathan Mahler and Dirk Johnson, "Mike Pence's Journey: Catholic
Democrat to Evangelical Republican," *The New York Times*, January 20, 2018, https://www.nytimes.com/2016/07/21/us/politics/mike
-pence-religion.html.

46 Tara Isabella Burton, "How the National Prayer Breakfast Offers Foreign Lobbyists a Chance to 'Pay to Play,'" *Vox*, July 30, 2018.

47 "At Trump's Hotel, Spiritual Warriors Pray for President Trump," Religion News Service, March 6, 2019, https://religionnews.com/2018
/12/10/at-trumps-hotel-spiritual-warriors-pray-for-the-president-in
-his-darkest-hour/.

48 Joseph Mattera, "Donald Trump Makes Big Promises to Pastors,"
Charisma News, accessed April 21, 2019, https://www.charismanews
.com/opinion/the-pulse/57974-donald-trump-makes-big-promises
-to-pastors.

49 Frederick Clarkson, "'Project Blitz' Seeks to Do for Christian Nationalism What ALEC Does for Big Business," Religion Dispatches,
June 7, 2018, http://religiondispatches.org/project-blitz-seeks-to-do
-for-christian-nationalism-what-alec-does-for-big-business/.

50 Dutch Sheets Ministries website, accessed April 15, 2019, http://
Dutchsheets.org.

51 Capitol Ministries website, About page, accessed April 2, 2019, http://
Capmin.org/about.

52 Owen Amos, "Inside the White House Bible Study Group," *BBC
News*, April 8, 2018, https://www.bbc.com/news/world-us-canada
-43534724.

53 Ibid.

54 Steven Hassan, "Christian Nationalism, Dominionism, the New Apostolic Reformation; A Discussion with Dr. André Gagné," Freedom of Mind Resource Center, March 14, 2019, https://freedomofmind.com /christian-nationalism-dominionism-the-new-apostolic-reformation -a-discussion-with-dr-andre-gagne/.

55 Katherine Stewart, "The Museum of the Bible Is a Safe Space for Christian Nationalists," *The New York Times*, January 6, 2018, https://www.nytimes.com/2018/01/06/opinion/sunday/the-museum -of-the-bible-is-a-safe-space-for-christian-nationalists.html.

56 Nina Burleigh, "Does God Believe in Trump? White Evangelicals Are Sticking with Their 'Prince of Lies,'" *Newsweek*, October 6, 2017, https://www.newsweek.com/2017/10/13/donald-trump-white-evan gelicals-support-god-677587.html.

57 "Capitol Ministries Responds to False and Misleading Newsweek Story," Capitol Ministries, accessed April 21, 2019, https://capmin .org/capitol-ministries-responds-to-newsweek/.

58 Bill Ainsworth, "Bible Study Leader Stirs Controversy," *The San Diego Union-Tribune*, accessed April 21, 2019, http://legacy.sandiegounion tribune.com/uniontrib/20040609/news_1n9bible.html.

59 Shane Goldmacher, "Ministering to the Capitol," *Sacramento News & Review*, June 30, 2005, https://www.newsreview.com/sacramento /ministering-to-the-capitol/content?oid=36004.

60 Robert George, Timothy George, and Chuck Colson. Manhattan Declaration, November 20, 2009, https://www.manhattandeclaration .org/.

61 Frederick Clarkson, "Christian Right Seeks Renewal in Deepening Catholic-Protestant Alliance," *The Public Eye*, Summer 2013, https:// www.politicalresearch.org/2013/07/23/christian-right-seeks-renewal -in-deepening-catholic-protestant-alliance/.

62 "Conservative Heavyweight: The Remarkable Mind of Professor Robert P. George." *Crisis Magazine*, October 4, 2013, https://www .crisismagazine.com/2003/conservative-heavyweight-the-remarkable -mind-of-professor-robert-p-george.

63 Max Blumenthal, "A Hoax Exposed at Princeton." *The Nation*, June 29, 2015. https://www.thenation.com/article/hoax-exposed-princeton/.

64 Christopher Murphy, Hannah Wang, Siyang Liu, Ivy Truong, and Benjamin Ball, "Spotted History Aside, Opus Dei Forges Close Campus

Links," *The Princetonian*, Accessed May 28, 2019, http://www.daily
princetonian.com/article/2005/03/spotted-history-aside-opus-dei
-forges-close-campus-links.

65 Robert A. Hutchison, *Their Kingdom Come* (London: Corgi, 2012).

66 ODAN Opus Dei Awareness Network, accessed May 28, 2019.
https://odan.org/.

67 Frank Cocozzelli, "The Catholic Right, Part Two: An Introduction to
the Role of Opus Dei." *Talk2Action* (blog), accessed May 28, 2019,
http://www.talk2action.org/story/2006/5/16/201710/016.

68 "The Operation of Divine Grace on Hadley Arkes . . . and Friends."
Mirror of Justice, accessed May 29, 2019, https://mirrorofjustice
.blogs.com/mirrorofjustice/2010/04/the-operation-of-divine-grace
-on-hadley-arkes.html.

69 Michelle Boorstein, "Opus Dei Paid $977,000 to Settle Sexual Mis-
conduct Claim Against Prominent Catholic Priest." *The Washington
Post,* January 7, 2019, https://www.washingtonpost.com/religion
/2019/01/08/opus-dei-paid-settle-sexual-misconduct-claim-against
-prominent-catholic-priest/?utm_term=.99fc4f258d13.

70 http://mgrfoundationinfo.s5.yourdomain.com.ua/OpusDeiInUS
Government1.html.

71 Joe Heim, " 'Quite a Shock': The Priest Was a D.C. Luminary. Then
He Had a Disturbing Fall from Grace," *The Washington Post,* January
14, 2019, https://www.washingtonpost.com/local/quite-a-shock-the
-priest-was-a-dc-luminary-then-he-had-a-disturbing-fall-from-grace
/2019/01/14/99b48700-1453-11e9-b6ad-9cfd62dbb0a8_story.html
?noredirect=on&utm_term=.959ff5c49cf7.

72 Staff and Board of Directors, Catholic Information Center, accessed May 28, 2019, https://www.cicdc.org/about/staff-and-board-of
-directors/.

73 Robert O'Harrow Jr. and Shawn Boburg, "A Conservative Activist's
Behind-the-Scenes Campaign to Remake the Nation's Courts." *The
Washington Post,* May 21, 2019, https://www.washingtonpost.com
/graphics/2019/investigations/leonard-leo-federalists-society-courts/.

74 Jon Swaine, "The Anti-Abortion Conservative Quietly Guiding
Trump's Supreme Court Pick." *The Guardian*, July 6, 2018, https://
www.theguardian.com/law/2018/jul/06/leonard-leo-supreme-court
-replacement-trump-justice-nomination-abortion.

75 Heim, "'Quite a Shock': The Priest Was a D.C. Luminary. Then He Had a Disturbing Fall from Grace."

76 Robert O'Harrow Jr. and Shawn Boburg, "A Conservative Activist's behind-the-Scenes Campaign to Remake the Nation's Courts."

77 Jen Kirby, "Pat Cipollone Is Trump's New White House Counsel," *Vox*, October 18, 2018, https://www.vox.com/2018/10/17/17984010 /pat-cipollone-white-house-counsel-trump-don-mcgahn.

78 United States Committee on the Judiciary Questionnaire for the Non-Judicial Nominees: William Pelham Barr, https://www.judi ciary.senate.gov/imo/media/doc/William%20Barr%20Senate%20 Questionnaire%20(PUBLIC).pdf.

79 Mark Binelli, "Pope Francis: The Times They Are A-Changin'." *Rolling Stone,* June 25, 2018, https://www.rollingstone.com/culture /culture-news/pope-francis-the-times-they-are-a-changin-49434/#ix zz2rq33Aqkc.

80 Frank Cocozzelli, "Did Opus Dei Teach A.G. Barr to 'Put Away His Scruples'?" *Daily Kos*, accessed May 28, 2019, https://www.dailykos .com/story/2019/5/3/1855095/-Did-Opus-Dei-Teach-A-G-Barr-to -Puts-Away-His-Scruples.

81 Rob Boston, "William Barr Wants To Bring 'God's Law' To America." Americans United for Separation of Church and State, accessed May 28, 2019, https://www.au.org/blogs/wall-of-separation/william-barr -wants-to-bring-gods-law-to-america.

82 Shaya Tayefe Mohajer, "It Is Time to Stop Using the Term 'Alt Right,'" *Columbia Journalism Review,* accessed April 21, 2019, https://www .cjr.org/criticism/alt-right-trump-charlottesville.php.

83 Katherine Stewart, "The Museum of the Bible Is a Safe Space for Christian Nationalists," *The New York Times*, January 6, 2018.

84 "Alt-Right," *Southern Poverty Law Center*, accessed May 27, 2019. https://www.splcenter.org/fighting-hate/extremist-files/ideology/alt -right.

85 Ben Chapman, "Who Exactly Is the Alt-Right? As Told by the Alt-Right," *Medium*, July 3, 2018, https://medium.com/@Ben_Chapman /who-exactly-is-the-alt-right-as-told-by-the-alt-right-3f357e03ab41.

86 "Hate Groups Reach Record High," *Southern Poverty Law Center*, accessed April 21, 2019, https://www.splcenter.org/news/2019/02/19 /hate-groups-reach-record-high.

87 Patrick Ryan, "Steve Bannon Says He Hated 'Every Second' in Trump's White House," *The Sydney Morning Herald,* January 31, 2019, https://www.smh.com.au/world/north-america/steve-bannon -says-he-hated-every-second-in-trump-s-white-house-20190131-p50 uob.html.

88 Ben Mathis-Lilley, "Trump Has Retweeted at Least Four White Nationalist Accounts That Were Later Suspended," *Slate,* March 18, 2019, https://slate.com/news-and-politics/2019/03/trump-white-nationalist -accounts-suspended-retweets.html.

89 David Leonhardt, "It Isn't Complicated: Trump Encourages Violence," *The New York Times,* March 17, 2019, https://www.nytimes .com/2019/03/17/opinion/trump-violence.html.

90 Kirk Siegler, "A 'Mainstreaming Of Bigotry' as White Extremism Reveals Its Global Reach." NPR, March 16, 2019, https://www.npr .org/2019/03/16/704125736/a-mainstreaming-of-bigotry-as-white -extremism-reveals-its-global-reach.

91 Spencer Ackerman, "How Russia Is Exploiting American White Supremacy," *The Daily Beast,* October 9, 2018, https://www.thedaily beast.com/how-russia-exploits-american-white-supremacy-over-and over-again.

92 Jonathan Chait, "Donald Trump's Presidency Is the Libertarian Moment," *Intelligencer,* January 29, 2018, http://nymag.com/in telligencer/2018/01/donald-trumps-presidency-is-the-libertarian -moment.html.

93 James Scaminaci III, "Battle Without Bullets: The Christian Right and Fourth Generation Warfare," *The Public Eye,* Summer 2017, http:// www.politicalresearch.org/2017/08/16/battle-without-bullets-the -christian-right-and-fourth-generation-warfare/.

94 Frederick Clarkson, *Eternal Hostility: The Struggle Between Theocracy and Democracy* (Monroe, ME: Common Courage Press, 1997), pp. 45–75.

95 Ibid.

CHAPTER EIGHT: Trump's Followers

1 Jill Colvin, "Trump Has Held More than 2 Dozen Rallies as He Kicks into High Gear Ahead of the High-Stakes Midterms," *Business Insider,*

October 14, 2018, https://www.businessinsider.com/trump-rallies-increase-ahead-of-midterms-2018-10.

2 Chris Sikich, Holly V. Hays, and Kaitlin Lange, "Here's What Donald Trump Said at His Monday Night Rally in Fort Wayne in Support of Mike Braun," *The Indianapolis Star,* November 6, 2018, https://www.indystar.com/story/news/politics/2018/11/05/heres-what-donald-trump-said-his-monday-night-rally-fort-wayne/1889408002/.

3 Colvin, "Trump Has Held More than 2 Dozen Rallies."

4 Ibid.

5 "Presidential Election Results: Donald J. Trump Wins," *The New York Times,* accessed April 20, 2019, https://www.nytimes.com/elections/2016/results/president.

6 "Trump Presidential Campaign Ad," C-SPAN, accessed April 20, 2019, https://www.c-span.org/video/?418167-101%2Ftrump-presidential-campaignad&start=16.

7 Omarosa Manigault Newman, personal interview with Steve Hassan, February 1, 2019.

8 David Cay Johnston, personal interview with Steve Hassan, April 4, 2019.

9 Paige Williams, "Sarah Huckabee Sanders, Trump's Battering Ram," *The New Yorker,* September 18, 2018, https://www.newyorker.com/magazine/2018/09/24/sarah-huckabee-sanders-trumps-battering-ram.

10 Jennifer Rubin, "Why Did Hope Hicks Resign?" chicagotribune.com, March 1, 2018, https://www.chicagotribune.com/news/opinion/commentary/ct-hope-hicks-resigns-trump-20180228-story.html.

11 Erik Wemple, "Hope Hicks Lands Executive Job at Fox. Of Course," *The Washington Post,* October 8, 2018, https://www.washingtonpost.com/blogs/erik-wemple/wp/2018/10/08/hope-hicks-lands-executive-job-at-fox-of-course/?utm_term=.81040d944ad8.

12 Shane Savitsky, "7 Takeaways from the Mueller Report," *Axios*, April 18, 2019, https://www.axios.com/mueller-report-takeaways-ee6cfae3-37e3-429e-b3c5-fcae8994b09d.html.

13 Emily Ekins, "The Liberalism of the Religious Right," *The New York Times,* September 20, 2018, https://www.nytimes.com/2018/09/19/opinion/liberalism-religious-right.html.

14 Ibid.

15 Philip Bump, "Nearly Half of Republicans Think God Wanted

Trump to Be President." *The Washington Post*, February 14, 2019, https://www.washingtonpost.com/politics/2019/02/14/nearly-half-republicans-think-god-wanted-trump-be-president/?utm_term=.531d840e98f2.

16 John Weaver, *The New Apostolic Reformation: History of a Modern Charismatic Movement* (Jefferson, NC: McFarland, 2016).

17 John Weaver, personal interview with Steven Hassan, March 23, 2019.

18 John Weaver, personal interview with Steven Hassan, February 2019.

19 Rachel Tabachnick, "Spiritual Warriors with an Antigay Mission: The New Apostolic Reformation," *The Public Eye*, spring 2013, https://www.politicalresearch.org/2013/03/22/spiritual-warriors-with-an-antigay-mission/.

20 Tara Isabella Burton, "An Evangelical University Is Helping Make a Film That Implies God Chose Trump," Vox, May 30, 2018, https://www.vox.com/2018/5/30/17405720/liberty-evangelical-movie-trump-prophecy.

21 Joe Heim, "Jerry Falwell, Jr. Can't Imagine Trump 'Doing Anything That's Not Good for the Country,'" *The Greenville News*, January 1, 2019, https://www.greenvilleonline.com/story/news/2019/01/01/jerry-falwell-jr-cant-imagine-president-donald-trump-doing-anything-thats-not-good-country/2457767002/.

22 Mark Taylor, *The Trump Prophecies: The Astonishing True Story of the Man Who Saw Tomorrow . . . and What He Says Is Coming Next* (Crane, MO: Defender, 2017).

23 U.S. Department of Education's National Center for Education Statistics. "1.5 Million Homeschooled Students in the United States in 2007," U.S. Department of Education NCES 2009–030, December 2008, https://nces.ed.gov/pubs2009/2009030.pdf.

24 Heidi Ewing and Rachel Grady, *Jesus Camp*, United States: Magnolia Pictures, 2006.

25 Ibid.

26 J. D. Vance, *Hillbilly Elegy: A Memoir of a Family and Culture in Crisis* (New York: HarperCollins, 2016).

27 "FACT CHECK: Did Donald Trump Say Not Paying Taxes 'Makes Me Smart'?" *Snopes.com*, http://www.snopes.com/fact-check/trump-taxes-smart/.

28 Emma Newburger. "Secretive Cabals, Fear of Immigrants and the Tea
    Party: How the Financial Crisis Led to the Rise of Donald Trump,"
    CNBC, September 11, 2018, https://www.cnbc.com/2018/09/10
    /how-the-financial-crisis-led-to-the-rise-of-donald-trump.html.

29 Mark Leibovich, "How Lindsey Graham Went from Trump Skeptic
    to Trump Sidekick," *The New York Times,* February 25, 2019, https://
    www.nytimes.com/2019/02/25/magazine/lindsey-graham-what-hap
    pened-trump.html.

30 Lincoln Mitchell, "Commentary: Why a Republican Won't Beat
    Trump in 2020," Reuters, January 14, 2019, https://www.reuters
    .com/article/us-mitchell-primary-commentary/commentary-why-a
    -republican-wont-beat-trump-in-2020-idUSKCN1P81HN.

31 Brett Samuels, "Gap between Republican, Democratic Approval of Trump
    Sets Record," *The Hill,* January 16, 2019, https://thehill.com/blogs
    /blog-briefing-room/425564-gap-between-republican-democratic
    -approval-of-trump-sets-record.

32 Russell J. Dalton, "Party Identification and Its Implications," *Oxford
    Research Encyclopedia of Politics,* May 16, 2017, http://oxfordre.com
    /politics/view/10.1093/acrefore/9780190228637.001.0001/acrefore
    -9780190228637-e-72.

33 Alexander Burns and Jonathan Martin, "Michael Cohen's Testimony
    Opens New Phase of Political Turbulence for Trump," *The New York
    Times,* March 1, 2019, https://www.nytimes.com/2019/03/01/us/politics
    /michael-cohen-trump-reelection.html?smid=nytcore-ios-share.

34 Moira Donegan, "Half of White Women Continue to Vote Republican.
    What's Wrong with Them?" *The Guardian,* November 9, 2018. https://
    www.theguardian.com/commentisfree/2018/nov/09/white-women
    -vote-republican-why.

35 Ibid.

36 Footsteps, accessed May 28, 2019, https://www.footstepsorg.org/.

37 Ada Rapoport-Albert, "Hasidism," *Jewish Women's Archive*, accessed
    May 28, 2019, https://jwa.org/encyclopedia/article/hasidism.

38 "The Rebbe: A Brief Biography," Chabad.org, December 23, 2004,
    https://www.chabad.org/therebbe/article_cdo/aid/244372/jewish
    /The-Rebbe-A-Brief-Biography.htm.

39 Jim Yardley, "Messiah Fervor for Late Rabbi Divides Many Lubavitch-
    ers," *New York Times,* June 29, 1998, https://www.nytimes.com

/1998/06/29/nyregion/messiah-fervor-for-late-rabbi-divides-many
-lubavitchers.html.

40 Allison Kaplan Sommer, Richard C. Schneider, Elon Gilad, et al.
"WATCH: Ivanka Trump, Jared Kushner Visit Lubavitcher Rebbe's
Grave to Pray for Election Victory," Haaretz, April 24, 2018, https://
www.haaretz.com/world-news/watch-ivanka-jared-pray-for-victory
-at-chabad-rebbe-s-grave-1.5457632.

41 Robert Philpot Toi, Matthew Lee, Susannah George, Sam Sokol,
Raoul Wootliff, Jacob Magid, et al. "'Putin's Rabbi' Said to Have
Secretly Visited Iran," The Times of Israel, accessed May 28, 2019,
https://www.timesofisrael.com/putins-rabbi-said-to-have-secretly
-visited-iran/.

42 "Vital Statistics," Latest Population Statistics for Israel, accessed May 27,
2019, https://www.jewishvirtuallibrary.org/latest-population-statistics
-for-israel.

43 Jay Michaelson, "Why Is Chabad Helping Christian Extremists?" The
Forward, October 26, 2015, https://forward.com/opinion/323267
/why-is-chabad-helping-christian-extremists/.

44 Michael D'Antonio and Peter Eisner, The Shadow President: The
Truth About Mike Pence (New York: Thomas Dunne Books, 2018).

45 Amit Gvaryahu, "Lucky the Jews Didn't Understand What Mike Pence
Was Really Saying," Haaretz, January 27, 2018, https://www.haaretz
.com/opinion/lucky-the-jews-didn-t-get-what-pence-was-really
-saying-1.5764424.

46 Weiyi Cai and Simone Landon, "Attacks by White Extremists Are
Growing. So Are Their Connections," The New York Times, April 3,
2019, https://www.nytimes.com/interactive/2019/04/03/world/white
-extremist-terrorism-christchurch.html.

47 "Incidents and Offenses," FBI, November 1, 2018, https://ucr.fbi.gov
/hate-crime/2017/topic-pages/incidents-and-offenses.

48 Steven Hassan, "Former Leader of White Supremacy Group and
Docuseries Exposing Hate Needs to Be Aired!" Freedom of Mind
Resource Center, December 16, 2018, https://freedomofmind.com
/former-leader-of-white-supremacy-group-and-docuseries-exposing
-hate-needs-to-be-aired/.

49 Frederick Clarkson, "The Eliminationists: How Hate Talk Radicalized the American Right," Religion Dispatches, October 20, 2009,

religiondispatches.org/ithe-eliminationists-how-hate-talk-radicalized
-the-american-righti/.

50   Arno Michaelis, personal interview with Steven Hassan, January 19,
     2019.

51   Brandy Zadrozney and Ben Collins, "Who Is Behind the Qanon Con-
     spiracy? We've Traced It to Three People," NBC News, accessed April
     20, 2019, https://www.nbcnews.com/tech/tech-news/how-three-con
     spiracy-theorists-took-q-sparked-qanon-n900531.

52   Henry Brean, "Suspect in Hoover Dam Standoff Writes Trump, Cites
     Conspiracy in Letters," *The Las Vegas Review-Journal,* July 17, 2018,
     https://www.reviewjournal.com/crime/courts/suspect-in-hoover-dam
     -standoff-writes-trump-cites-conspiracy-in-letters/.

53   Anne Claire Stapleton, "Man Who Blocked Traffic on Hoover Dam
     Bridge Wanted Release of Government Report," CNN, June 17,
     2018, https://www.cnn.com/2018/06/15/us/hoover-dam/index.html.

54   Scott Adams, "The Truth About QAnon," https://www.youtube.com
     /watch?v=kn_xxZrElow.

55   Ben Collins, "On Amazon, a Qanon Conspiracy Book Climbs the
     Charts—with an Algorithmic Push," NBC News, accessed April 20,
     2019, http://www.nbcnews.com/tech/tech-news/amazon-qanon-con
     spiracy-book-climbs-charts-algorithmic-push-n979181.

56   "QAnon Conspiracy Theorists Increase Their Presence at Trump
     Rallies," MSNBC, http://www.msnbc.com/the-last-word/watch/qanon
     -conspiracy-theorists-increase-their-presence-at-trump-rallies-14682
     33283703.

57   Christopher Ingraham, "There Are More Guns than People in the
     United States, According to a New Study of Global Firearm Own-
     ership," *The Washington Post,* June 19, 2018, https://www.wash
     ingtonpost.com/news/wonk/wp/2018/06/19/there-are-more-guns
     -than-people-in-the-united-states-according-to-a-new-study-of-global
     -firearm-ownership/?utm_term=.1477b0b30dcb.

58   Dave Gilson et al., "The NRA Says It Has 5 Million Members.
     Its Magazines Tell Another Story," *Mother Jones,* June 13, 2018,
     https://www.motherjones.com/politics/2018/03/nra-membership
     -magazine-numbers-1/.

59   NRA TV website, http://www.nratv.com.

60   Max Greenwood, "Poll: 82 Percent Support a Ban on Bump Stocks,"

The Hill, October 13, 2017, https://thehill.com/blogs/blog-briefing
-room/news/355376-poll-82-support-a-ban-on-bump-stocks.

61 Donald Trump, *The America We Deserve* (Los Angeles: Renaissance
Books, 2000), p. 102.

62 Anthony Zurcher, "How Trump Turned Against Gun Control," BBC
News, October 2, 2017, https://www.bbc.com/news/world-us-canada
-41478293.

63 Ed Pilkington, "Feel the Love, Feel the Hate—My Week in the Caul-
dron of Trump's Wild Rallies," *The Guardian,* November 1, 2018,
https://www.theguardian.com/us-news/2018/nov/01/trump-rallies
-america-midterms-white-house.

CHAPTER NINE: How to Undo Mind Control

1 Mark Mazzetti and Maggie Haberman. "Trump vs. Cohen: The
Breakup of a New York Relationship," *The New York Times,* February
27, 2019, https://www.nytimes.com/2019/02/27/us/politics/trump
-cohen-history.html.

2 Peter Waldman, Lizette Chapman, and Jordan Robertson, "Peter
Thiel's Data-Mining Company Is Using War on Terror Tools to Track
American Citizens. The Scary Thing? Palantir Is Desperate for New
Customers," *Bloomberg.com*, accessed April 21, 2019, https://www
.bloomberg.com/features/2018-palantir-peter-thiel/.

3 Jane Mayer, "Donald Trump's Ghostwriter Tells All," *The New Yorker,*
July 31, 2017, https://www.newyorker.com/magazine/2016/07/25
/donald-trumps-ghostwriter-tells-all.

4 David Weissman, "I Used to Be a Trump Troll—Until Sarah Silverman
Engaged with Me," *The Forward,* June 5, 2018, https://forward.com
/scribe/402478/i-was-a-trump-troll/.

5 David Brooks, "Cory Booker Finds His Moment," *The New York
Times*, March 18, 2019, https://www.nytimes.com/2019/03/18/opinion
/cory-booker-2020.html.

6 Eleanor Roosevelt, *You Learn by Living: Eleven Keys for a More Fulfilling Life* (New York: Harper & Row, 1960).

7 Weissman, "I Used to Be a Trump Troll."

8 Ibid.

9 Ibid.

10 David Weissman, "Why I Left Team MAGA," *The Times of Israel,* accessed April 21, 2019, https://blogs.timesofisrael.com/why-i-left-team
-maga/.

11 Scott Huver, "Sarah Silverman on Hollywood Harassment, Jewish Representation On Screen," *The Hollywood Reporter*, April 20, 2019, https://www.hollywoodreporter.com/live-feed/sarah-silverman
-talks-hollywood-harassment-at-vulture-fest-1060203.

12 Rod Dubrow-Marshall and Linda Dubrow-Marshall, "How to Talk Someone Out of a Damaging Cult," *The Conversation*, March 28, 2019. theconversation.com/how-to-talk-someone-out-of-a-damaging
-cult-68930.

13 "Leah Remini on Scientology: 'No One Is Going to Tell Me How I Need to Think,'" *People Magazine*, http://www.people.com/celebrity
/leah-remini-on-scientology-no-one-is-going-to-tell-me-how-i-need
-to-think/.

14 Steven Hassan, *Freedom of Mind: Helping Loved Ones Leave Controlling People, Cults, and Beliefs* (Newton, MA: Freedom of Mind Press, 2012), chapter 10.

CHAPTER TEN: The Future

1 Terrence McCoy, "'I Don't Know How You Got This Way,'" *The Washington Post*, February 23, 2018, http://www.washingtonpost
.com/news/local/wp/2018/02/23/feature/i-dont-know-how-you
-got-this-way-a-young-neo-nazi-reveals-himself-to-his-family/?utm
_term=.792ec421c036.

2 Persuasive Technology Lab, "What Is Captology?" *Persuasive Tech*, accessed April 21, 2019, https://captology.stanford.edu/about/what
-is-captology.html.

3 K.N.C. and A.L., "On Tyranny, Populism—and How Best to Respond Today," *The Economist,* July 30, 2018, https://www.economist.com
/open-future/2018/07/30/on-tyranny-populism-and-how-best-to-re
spond-today.

4 Carlin Romano, "Here There Is a Why: Primo Levi, Humanist," *The Chronicle of Higher Education,* May 22, 2011, https://www.chronicle
.com/article/Here-There-Is-a-Why-Primo/127574.

5 Timothy Snyder, *On Tyranny: Twenty Lessons from the Twentieth Century* (New York: Tim Duggan Books, 2017).

6 Paul Krugman, "The G.O.P. Goes Full Authoritarian," *The New York Times,* December 10, 2018, https://www.nytimes.com/2018/12/10/opinion/trump-gop-authoritarian-states-power-grab.html.

7 World Mental Health Coalition website, https://dangerouscase.org/.

8 Alan Scheflin, "Supporting Human Rights," ICSA, accessed April 21, 2019, https://www.icsahome.com/articles/supporting-human-rights.

9 Patrick Evans, "Will Germany's New Law Kill Free Speech Online?" BBC News, September 18, 2017, https://www.bbc.com/news/blogs-trending-41042266.

10 Cecilia Kang and Sheera Frenkel, "Facebook Says Cambridge Analytica Harvested Data of Up to 87 Million Users," *The New York Times,* April 4, 2018, https://www.nytimes.com/2018/04/04/technology/mark-zuckerberg-testify-congress.html.

11 David Taylor, "'In God We Trust'—the Bills Christian Nationalists Hope Will 'Protect Religious Freedom,'" *The Guardian,* January 14, 2019, https://www.theguardian.com/us-news/2019/jan/14/christian-nationalists-bills-religious-freedom-project-blitz.

12 "Project Blitz," Americans United for Separation of Church and State, accessed April 21, 2019, https://www.au.org/tags/project-blitz.

13 "Monitoring Project Blitz & Christian Nationalists," BlitzWatch, accessed April 21, 2019, https://www.blitzwatch.org/.

14 John F. Harris et al., "Trump May Not Be Crazy, but the Rest of Us Are Getting There Fast," *Politico Magazine,* October 12, 2018, https://www.politico.com/magazine/story/2018/10/12/donald-trump-anxiety-disorder-pscyhologists-221305.

15 Rebecca Muller, "'Trump Anxiety Disorder' Is Real and on the Rise, Therapists Say," *Thrive Global*, July 30, 2018, https://thriveglobal.com/stories/trump-anxiety-disorder/.

16 American Psychological Association, accessed April 21, 2019, https://www.apa.org/news/press/releases/2017/11/lowest-point.

17 "Worldwide Round-Up of Journalists Killed, Detained, Held Hostage, or Missing in 2018," Reporters Without Borders for Freedom of Information, https://rsf.org/sites/default/files/worldwilde_round-up.pdf.

18 The Fund for Investigative Journalism, accessed May 28, 2019, http://
fij.org/.

19 About Us page, *ProPublica*, accessed May 28, 2019, https://www
.propublica.org/about/.

20 "United States Population 2019," accessed April 21, 2019, http://
worldpopulationreview.com/countries/united-states-population/.

21 Kevin Roose, "YouTube Unleashed a Conspiracy Theory Boom. Can
It Be Contained?" *The New York Times,* February 19, 2019, https://
www.nytimes.com/2019/02/19/technology/youtube-conspiracy-stars
.html?action=click&module=Well&pgtype=Homepage&section=
Technology.

22 Sheera Frenkel, "Facebook to Remove Misinformation That Leads to
Violence," *The New York Times,* July 18, 2018, https://www.nytimes
.com/2018/07/18/technology/facebook-to-remove-misinformation
-that-leads-to-violence.html?module=inline.

23 "Standing Against Hate," Facebook Newsroom, accessed April 21,
2019, https://newsroom.fb.com/news/2019/03/standing-against-hate/.

24 "Heroic Imagination Project," accessed April 21, 2019, https://www
.heroicimagination.org/.

25 Baker, Peter. "What We Know So Far from the Mueller Report," *The
New York Times,* April 18, 2019, https://www.nytimes.com/2019/04
/18/us/politics/mueller-report-released-live.html.

26 Tony Schwartz, Twitter post, May 5, 2019, 4: 37 P.M., https://twitter
.com/tonyschwartz/status/1125182878952898561.

27 "The Dangerous Case of Donald Trump," C-SPAN, accessed April 21,
2019, https://www.c-span.org/video/?458919-1%2Fthe-dangerous
-case-donald-trump.

28 Ibid.

INDEX

Page number in *italics* refer to illustrations.